What to Study

101 Fields in a Flash

By Eric Freedman and Edward Hoffman

Simon & Schuster

Kaplan Books
Published by Kaplan Educational Centers and Simon & Schuster
1230 Avenue of the Americas
New York, NY 10020
Copyright © 1997, by Kaplan Educational Centers

For bulk sales to schools, colleges, and universities, please contact Renee Nemire, Simon & Schuster Markets, 1633 Broadway, 8th Floor, New York, NY 10019.

Project Editor: Doreen Beauregard
Cover Design: Suzanne Noli
Interior Design: Michael Syrquin
Production Editor: Maude Spekes
Assistant Managing Editor: Brent Gallenberger
Managing Editor: Kiernan McGuire
Executive Editor: Del Franz

Special thanks to Linda Volpano

Manufactured in the United States of America
Published simultaneously in Canada

September 1997
10 9 8 7 6 5 4 3 2 1

Library of Congress Cataloging-in-Publication Data
Freedman, Eric.
    What to study: 101 fields in a flash / Eric Freedman and Edward Hoffman.
      p.   cm.
    Includes bibliographical references.
    ISBN 0-684-84388-9
    1. College majors—United States.   I. Hoffman, Edward.   II. Title.
LB2361.5.F74 1997
378.1'99--dc21   97-21904
                                                 CIP

ISBN 0-684-84388-9

Contents

About the Authors

Eric Freedman, J.D., is a Pulitzer Prize–winning newspaper reporter who teaches journalism at Michigan State University in East Lansing. His articles have appeared in more than 125 U.S. and foreign newspapers and magazines. He is the author of four other books, including *Great Lakes, Great National Forests* and *Michigan Free*. He graduated from Cornell University and New York University Law School.

Edward Hoffman, Ph.D., is a licensed clinical psychologist in the New York City area and former college professor. He is the author of ten books, including *The Drive for Self: Alfred Adler and the Founding of Individual Psychology*, which won the 1996 Gradiva Award from the National Association for the Advancement of Psychoanalysis. He received his B.A. from Cornell University and his graduate degrees from the University of Michigan.

Dedications

To Mary Ann, Ian, and Cara, who have explored learning with me.

—*Eric Freedman*

To Laurel and our children, Aaron and Jeremy, all partners in the adventure of learning.

—*Edward Hoffman*

A Special Note for

International Students

About a quarter of a million international students pursued advanced academic degrees at the master's or Ph.D. level at U.S. universities during the 1995–96 academic year, according to the Institute of International Education's *Open Doors* report. This trend of pursuing higher education in the United States, particularly at the graduate level, is expected to continue well into the next century. Business, management, engineering, and the physical and life sciences are particularly popular majors for students coming to the United States from other countries. Along with these academic options, international students are also taking advantage of opportunities for research grants, teaching assistantships, and practical training or work experience in U.S. graduate departments.

If you are not from the United States, but are considering attending a graduate program at a U.S. university, here's what you'll need to get started.

- If English is not your first language, start there. You'll probably need to take the Test of English as a Foreign Language (TOEFL) or show some other evidence that you are proficient in English. Graduate programs will vary on what is an acceptable TOEFL score. For degrees in business, journalism, management, or the humanities, a minimum TOEFL score of 600 is expected. For the hard sciences and computer technology, a TOEFL score between 500 and 550 may be acceptable.
- You may also need to take the Graduate Record Exam (GRE).
- Since admission to many graduate programs is quite competitive, you may also want to select three or four programs and complete applications for each school.
- Selecting the correct graduate school is very different from selecting a suitable undergraduate institution. You should especially look at the qualifications and interests of the faculty members teaching and/or doing research in your chosen field. Look for professors who share your specialty.
- You need to begin the application process at least a year in advance. Be aware that many programs will have September start dates only. Find out application deadlines and plan accordingly.

- Finally, you will need to obtain an I-20 Certificate of Eligibility in order to obtain an F-1 Student Visa to study in the United States.

For details about the admissions requirements, curriculum, and other vital information on top graduate schools in a variety of popular fields, see Kaplan's guide to United States graduate programs, *Getting into Graduate School.*

Access America™

Kaplan's Access America program offers international students English language training for academic and professional purposes, university and graduate college admissions counseling, advice on obtaining internships while studying, and programs for acquiring professional certification.

Whether you want to work and study in the United States or in your home country, Access America's unique approach to understanding the American system can assist you. The guidelines in this book will help you find an internship that will give you the kind of experience you need to find the right job when you finish your educaton. For more information on job hunting once you complete your degree, see *Access America's Guide to Studying in the U.S.A.*

Here's a brief description of some of the programs available at Kaplan centers through Access America:

The TOEFL Plus Program

At the heart of the Access America program is the intensive TOEFL Plus Academic English program. This comprehensive English course prepares students to achieve a high level of proficiency in English in order to complete an academic degree successfully. The TOEFL Plus course combines personalized instruction with guided self-study to help students gain this proficiency in a short period of time. Certificates of Achievement in English are awarded to certify each student's level of proficiency.

Graduate School/GRE Preparation

If your goal is to enter a master's or Ph.D. program in the United States, Kaplan will help you prepare for the GRE, while helping you understand how to choose a graduate degree program in your field.

Preparation for Other Entrance Exams

If you are interested in attending business school, medical school, or law school in the United States, you will probably have to take a standardized entrance exam. Admission to these programs is very competitive, and exam scores are an important criteria.

Applying to Access America

To get more information, or to apply for admission to any of Kaplan's programs for international students or professionals, you can write to us at:

Kaplan Educational Centers, International Admissions Department
888 Seventh Avenue, New York, NY 10106

Or call us at 1-800-522-7770 from within the United States, or at 01-212-262-4980 outside the United States. Our fax number is 01-212-957-1654. Our E-mail address is world@kaplan.com. You can also get more information or even apply through the Internet at http://www.kaplan.com/intl.

Part One

Choices

Chapter 1

Welcome to the Smorgasbord

College is an opportunity to experiment, to boldly explore a smorgasbord of academic offerings—some as paths to potential careers, some as intellectual challenges, some as vehicles of cultural enrichment, some for a change of pace, and some just for fun.

Whether you live at home and commute to a nearby college or move thousands of miles away, whether you attend a small college or a huge university, higher education is very different from high school. There are so many more course options to consider, even in a small college. There are lifestyle decisions. Should you live in a dorm or live at home? Fraternity or sorority? Apartment, house, or co-op? There are work decisions. Should you take a part-time job? Work on campus or off campus? There are extracurricular activities galore, from intercollegiate and intramural athletics to cultural groups, ethnic and religious organizations, campus publications and broadcast stations, charitable groups, and recreational clubs.

Choice is the keystone of college life. You must weigh alternatives, make decisions, and be flexible enough to change your mind, maybe several times.

That's especially true in picking an academic direction. There are many fields of study that are very unfamiliar to you. But what's new and strange could prove to be ideal for you—if you find it. Did your high school expose students to linguistics, for instance, or petroleum engineering, child development, or social work? Unlikely. What did you learn in high school about accounting, landscape architecture, or telecommunications? Not much, if anything. Do you know what's involved in occupational therapy or public relations? In urban planning or civil engineering? In animal science or biochemistry? Probably not.

An associate director of a speech communication association observes, "Outside of broadcasting and journalism, most students come to a university knowing little or nothing about communication processes. They take an introductory course where that material is covered and, in some cases, make a decision to major in communication. Outside broadcasting and journalism, most communication departments obtain most of their majors by transfer from 'undecided' or other majors; few students opt for a communication major when they enter college."

Even the topics you *did* study in high school may bear little resemblance to your college's version of these topics. You know your own neighborhood—things are familiar, well studied, and well defined—but there are still rocks unturned, mysteries undiscovered. Think about your tenth- and eleventh-grade English classes that surveyed American and British literature. In college, you can go many steps beyond that, and study Middle English literature, twentieth-century English poetry, Canadian literature, Shakespearean literature, Russian literature, Jewish American literature, screenwriting, the work of Chaucer, or American women writers—to name a few.

What happens if one of those classes clicks, say an introduction to Russian literature? You could go further—nineteenth-century Russian prose, the work of Tolstoy, Gogol, or Chekhov, Russian drama, Russian culture, civilization, and folklore, and more.

Venture forth and explore. Push the envelope.

"If I were introducing you to vanilla ice cream for the first time to see if you like it or don't like it, how would I do it?" asks L. Patrick Scheetz, director of the Collegiate Employment Research Institute at Michigan State University. "The best way is through a taste test."

Investigate Related Fields

You're not locked into a rigid major, and every major requires you to take courses in related disciplines. You might love history, but how can you understand history without studying economics, anthropology, and political science?

A biochemist's work needs an understanding of chemistry, physics, mathematics, and computer science. Foresters need a basic scientific foundation in biology, physics, chemistry, and ecology. How can a mathematician or civil engineer function today without a mastery of computers? Philosophers can't ignore religious studies, nor can labor relations specialists ignore psychology.

When you evaluate potential majors, check out which courses in other departments are mandatory. If those requirements turn you off completely, maybe you should consider another major.

Does It Fit?

Selecting a major is an important decision but not an irreversible one. Many students (in some schools, the majority) change their intended majors at least once while they're in college. Many will choose graduate or professional schools in disciplines different from those of their undergraduate studies. And most people will change jobs and even careers at least once before retirement.

Of course, the prospects of a decent-paying job after graduation frequently factor into the choice of majors, but the bottom line shouldn't be solely financial, advises Michigan State's Scheetz. "You can force students to be ducks out of water, but they don't fit. Students should pick majors because that's where their heart is and that's what matches their skills."

Using Career-Planning Inventories

Many students find it helpful to use one or more of the growing number of standardized career-planning instruments now available. With the assistance of your college's career-guidance advisor, you can focus much more accurately on your interests and abilities. As a career advisor at a New York university observes, "No matter how much useful advice a student gets from other people, including faculty, these interest inventories can make a huge difference. There are some wonderful standardized tests out there."

Two of the most widely used tests are the Strong Interest Inventory (SII) and the Self-Directed Search (SDS). The "granddaddy" of all vocational interest surveys, the SII has been revised several times since its inception more than 60 years ago. Originally known as the Strong-Campbell Vocational Interest Test and designed by Edward Strong and David Campbell, its value has been affirmed by hundreds of research studies. Today, the SII comprises 317 items. It takes about 30 minutes to complete by pencil and is scored by computer. The SII's two main components are its Basic Interest Scales and General Occupational Scales. Through these scales, countless people have learned about their general interests, and about specific activities and occupations that match these interests. In addition, they've been able to compare their personal interests to those of people already employed in a wide variety of occupations.

For example, are you unsure whether to become a physical therapist or a social worker? The SII not only can identify whether your interests are compatible with these two fields, but it can also reveal to what extent practicing physical therapists and social workers share your particular range of interests. Such information is valuable to those planning a career, or changing careers.

The Self-Directed Search is a simple, self-administered test that can be completed in less than 30 minutes. It was developed over a 30-year period by Professor John Holland of Johns Hopkins University. SDS is based on Holland's well-supported theory that people can be loosely grouped into six personality types—Realistic, Investigative, Artistic, Social, Enterprising, and Conventional—and that each type is suited to certain kinds of careers or fields. For example, the theory suggests that Investigative types will do best in scientific, research-oriented work like biology, chemistry, and geology. Artistic types will be most productive in fields such as graphic design, music, and theater, while Social types will find success in secondary education, psychology, and social work.

SDS also classifies 1,334 occupations according to the specific personality type, or blend of types. Say you're primarily an Investigative type with both Social and Enterprising characteristics. Then a career in psychology or optometry would be a good match. However, if you're mainly an Artistic type with both Enterprising and Realistic qualities, then working in art, graphic design, or dance might be a good fit.

Regardless of which test you might take, always use your own judgment and the guidance of others—including your college advisors—in addition to the results. At best, these are terrific tools that can give detailed information about your unique mix of interests. But it's ultimately up to you to apply the information meaningfully in planning a college major and subsequent career.

Multidisciplinary Studies

We live in a complex, intertwined world in which careers and fields of study often mesh. An environmental scientist, for example, must know about resource economics as well as biology, population geography, forestry, public policy development, and oceanography.

As a result, many colleges allow students to major in a multiple-discipline field that erases some traditional borders between areas of study and open up new arenas to explore. Here's how John Stephens, executive director of the American Studies Association, explains the goal of his field: "American Studies scholars are critically examining the myths and realities of U.S. society and seeking answers to complex questions about U.S. history and culture that cannot be adequately addressed within established disciplinary boundaries." (John Stephens, "American Studies in the United States," *U.S. Society and Values* [electronic journal of the U.S. Information Agency], October 1996.)

If you're interested in African American studies as a major, that umbrella includes course options in sociology, music, urban studies, theater, and economics. If you're interested in women's studies as a major, try thematically related courses in English, psychology, sociology, and political science.

Some colleges have restructured even more broadly to reflect a multidisciplinary approach to their entire teaching and learning curriculum. Hampshire College in Massachusetts is one of them. As explained in Hampshire's 1996–97 catalog, "Hampshire has replaced single-subject departments with four comprehensive schools: Cognitive Science and Cultural Studies, Humanities and Arts, Natural Science, and Social Science. This flexible structure permits a great richness and variety of academic activity."

Course Titles and Availability

This book covers 101 fields of study, but no university in the United States offers every one of them. Some colleges provide a broad array of majors and minors, while others have a narrower focus—sciences and engineering, perhaps, or the performing arts, or religion.

If your college doesn't have a dance department, journalism department, or horticulture department but one of those fields strikes your fancy, look at related departments. Departments of theater and drama or physical education and exercise science may offer dance classes, while you may find journalism classes in the English department and horticulture classes in the biology or botany departments.

Remember that not all schools use the same name for a field of study. The term *political science* at most colleges is synonymous with *government* in others; one school's speech science and audiology department is another school's communicative disorders department.

When you're picking courses, those with the words *introduction, fundamentals,* or *survey* in the title are usually entry-level overviews. Also, those with lower course numbers are less advanced than those with higher numbers, though the specific numbering system varies from college to college.

It's impossible to list every major offered by every undergraduate institution in the United States. The 101 we detail here cover most bases and represent a cross section of what you'll find. We don't list fields that require an advanced degree, such as law, medicine, dentistry, or veterinary science. However, in some fields mentioned (including psychology, social work, and architecture), career opportunities—usually at higher salaries—improve greatly for those with advanced degrees.

Be aware that financial pressures and insufficient enrollment induce colleges to eliminate courses and, sometimes, entire majors. That might mean that a survey course in philosophy or principles of chemistry will remain available, but upper-level courses such as "British Empiricism" or "Atomic and Molecular Structure" are eliminated. It could mean the disappearance of an entire curriculum, such as nursing.

As an official of the State Higher Education Executive Officers Association puts it, "Higher education has become a market-responsive enterprise. And the market is saying in the traditional arts and science fields, the jobs aren't there. There's an increasing vocational and professional orientation to collegiate curriculum. But the reality is that students vote with their feet" (Tovia Smith, "Colleges Dropping Unpopular Majors," National Public Radio *Morning Edition,* Feb. 3, 1997). So you should inquire closely about potential plans to drop or combine departments. If that happens at your school, consider transfer and cross-enrollment options.

General Education Requirements

Most colleges require students to take a minimum number of courses in general areas of studies. Those requirements go by different names, including *core curriculum, general education requirements,* and *distribution requirements*. The purpose of these required courses is to help prepare you for the outside world. The aim is to expand your undergraduate experience beyond your major and to teach you skills that let you synthesize your experience into a better understanding of yourself and the world.

Colleges typically make you take one or more courses in math, in social and behavioral sciences, in writing or literature, in natural sciences, and in the humanities. Many schools require course work—perhaps a proficiency test—in a foreign language as well. An increasing number of schools mandate coursework in cultural and gender diversity, because we live in a diverse world. Political, social, and religious barriers are coming down. Our own American society is increasingly ethnically and racially mixed. We interact more with people from other nations and other cultures. Women—in the United States and elsewhere—are gaining a larger, fairer share of economic, political, occupational, and social power. You're a player in these changing arenas, so you should learn about groups long excluded from traditional academic studies and should strive to understand diverse cultures that are dealing with similar problems.

True, many students view general education requirements as a burden. After all, if you don't plan to work in the sciences, why be forced to take chemistry, astronomy, or physics? Some students postpone those courses until their final semester, perhaps in a misguided belief that their colleges will let them graduate without taking the courses. Procrastinate too long and you'll still be in school the summer *after* your scheduled graduation, sweating to finish that math or language or lab science course.

Like them or not, there are solid reasons for the requirements. Here's how the University of Colorado's catalog explains two of them:

- "Quantitative Reasoning and Mathematic Skills," which includes economics, math, geology, and physics courses: "Liberally educated people should be able to think at a certain level of abstraction and to manipulate symbols. Students completing this requirement should be able to construct a logical argument based on the rules of inference; analyze, present, and interpret numerical data; estimate orders of magnitude as well as obtain exact results; and apply mathematical methods to solve problems in their university work and in their daily lives."

- "Historical Context," which includes courses in history, classics, religious studies, economics, and philosophy: "Students study historical problems or issues and develop an understanding of earlier ideas, institutions, and cultures. Courses explore the times and circumstances in which social, intellectual, artistic, or other developments occurred. Among the educational aims are to contribute historical perspectives that help clarify issues that arise today or will arise tomorrow; to arouse the curiosity of students concerning historical conditions that may be relevant to other courses; and to expand the imagination by generating an awareness of the diverse ways in which our common humanity expressed itself."

Collectively, mandatory courses help develop college-level competence in written and verbal communication, reading comprehension, and quantitative reasoning—regardless of your career goals and major. They also teach you to examine and solve problems and to develop research and library skills. In addition, as Central Michigan University's 1996–97 catalog puts it, the requirements encourage such intellectual concerns as "the logic and substance of science, an understanding of American society and culture, a cross-cultural perspective through the study of diverse cultures, an awareness of human nature from differing theoretical points of view, and the fine arts."

Even if you bristle at the idea of having to study a particular topic, view it as an opportunity to experiment. Be bold. After four years of French in high school, it's understandable if you don't want more in college. So try Japanese, Bulgarian, or Swahili for a year. Instead of a survey course on art history or music appreciation to meet a humanities requirement, "Beginning Drawing," "Music of Bach and Handel," or "Acting Fundamentals" may have more appeal. For a requirement in contemporary issues, you could take a basic geography, history, or political science course—but your college might also accept "World Urbanization," "International Perspectives on Adolescent Parenthood and Sexuality," or "Prehistory of Environment and Culture." As for a requirement in natural science, you may be permitted to bypass introductory biology or geology and take "Terrain Analysis" in landscape architecture, "Principles of Animal Systems Physiology" in animal science, or "Science of Food" in nutrition and food science.

The president of a Florida zoo and alligator farm and a former orca trainer at Sea World knows all about the potential spin-off from required courses. He grew up 500 miles from salt water and came to Southwest Texas State University to study accounting. There he faced a required science course. "By the end of my second semester, I was much more interested in zoology than business, not to mention more academically successful. I buried my head in biology and never looked back." He focused on marine biology, chemistry, and—although he "knew zilch about marine life" before getting to college—a career in marine mammology.

The Courses That Changed Their Lives

Can a single course—a single experiment—change your life? Yes indeed.

The sister of CNN foreign correspondent Christiane Amanpour enrolled in a journalism class in London, only to find after a couple of months that she didn't want to continue the class. Christiane went along with her to try to get a refund. The school wouldn't refund the money, but it did allow Christiane to take the rest of the class in her sister's place. That class set Christiane on her way. She then came to the United States and studied journalism at the University of Rhode Island.

Rachel Carson, author of the landmark environmental best-seller *Silent Spring*, planned to major in English at Chatham College in Pittsburgh. The college's communications director, Sharon Iacobucci, recounts what happened: "As part of her general education requirements, she had to take a biology class. This course fascinated her. She changed her major to biology and became one of the world's leading environmentalists. *Silent Spring* was the result of the marriage of her love for the written word and her new-found affinity for science and research."

A news writer at the University of Chicago took her life-changing course in her first semester at the University of Kansas, where she planned to study psychology to prepare for medical school, then psychiatric practice. She had a hole to fill in her schedule, so she signed up for "Introduction to Mass Communications" at her advisor's suggestion. "I took it and fell in love. Since then, I've been a practicing reporter and city editor and now am in academic public relations." Before that course, she admits, "I never even read newspapers very well. And I think I would have been a horrible shrink, now that I know myself better."

Sheldon Tapley, who came to Iowa's Grinnell College as a pre-med student seeking a chemistry major, took a beginning art course with a professor who "was almost evangelical in teaching drawing. He didn't try to pressure me in any way to become an artist, but my trajectory was completely deflected when I walked into his class." Medical school was out. Now, Tapley teaches art at Centre College in Kentucky.

Melissa Swetland, who arrived at the University of Mississippi aiming for law school, took her life-changing course at the end of her undergraduate years. After three years, she took an accounting course "on a whim" and it sent her off in a totally new direction. She finished her political science degree since she was almost done, then added an accounting degree and a master's degree in tax. The result: a job with an international accounting and consulting firm.

In some instances, a course or two can unexpectedly provide focus and direction. Sarah Adams was majoring in biological anthropology at Swarthmore College in Pennsylvania when she took two decisive courses, one in statistics and the other about AIDS in literature and film. They led her to epidemiology and a job as coordinator of the hepatitis-prevention program in the Maryland State Health Department.

Be Flexible

Philosopher-educator John Dewey put it this way: "Education is not preparation for life. Education is life itself."

Never forget that learning should be an adventure, filled with challenges, memorable experiences, and enrichment—and some inevitable frustrations. Don't lock yourself into a rigid plan that fails to reflect what *you* want to learn, what *you* do well, and what *you* feel comfortable with.

Be willing to experiment, to take risks, and to explore new fields of knowledge. Remember that interests should evolve and change as you mature. The process is natural and exciting, so don't ignore these opportunities. They may shape the course of your entire professional life.

Key Definitions

You should understand the following terms as you read this book, review college catalogs, select courses, and decide on the fields of study that intrigue you.

Cognate: A course related to your major but offered by a different department. A business administration major may choose accounting or economics as a cognate.

Credit load: The total number of credits a student carries for the term or semester. Most colleges require 12 or more credits at once for full-time status.

Double major: Meeting the full requirements for a major in two related or unrelated fields, such as political science and international relations, or mathematics and art history.

Emphasis: An area of concentration within a major or minor. A dance major may have an emphasis in ballet or tap.

Independent study: An individualized, self-designed course supervised by a faculty member.

Internship: Supervised work related to your field of study and done for a business, government agency, organization, or professor. An advertising or public relations major might intern in a public relations firm to gain experience and sometimes receive pay or college credit.

Major: A concentration of related courses in a field of study. Each college determines the number of credits you need to graduate with that major.

Minor: Also a concentration of related courses, with fewer credits required than for a major. A minor may be related or unrelated to your major. An occupational therapy major could minor in psychology or music.

Prerequisite: A requirement to get into a course. You might need to take a class in physical geology to qualify for a class in mineralogy, which you might then need to get into a class in optical mineralogy.

Seminar: A small class with an emphasis on group discussions rather than the professor's lecture.

Chapter 2

Decisions, Decisions

To make the most of college explorations, don't expect all your learning—or even the most important part of it—to come through standard, structured courses in the classroom on your own campus. Learning opportunities are far wider than that, from independent study and study abroad to assistantships and volunteer work. As a result you'll need to make realistic decisions about how and where to spend your time, to reassess your goals repeatedly, and to determine how those opportunities can supplement or fit into the traditional curriculum. By pursuing these alternatives, the knowledge you'll gain, the people you'll meet, and the experiences you'll encounter can enrich your education and your life.

Career Planning Strategies

Selection of majors, minors, and career directions shouldn't be haphazard, although you should remain flexible to adapt to changes in your interests, course offerings, the job market, graduate school opportunities, and the economy.

Wise choices that fit your personality and talents take academic preparation and career planning throughout student life. To assist in that process, here are some year-by-year guideposts compiled by Career Services and Placement at Michigan State University.

In High School

- Consult with school counselors, teachers, and parents about career interests.
- Take prerequisite courses for admission to your preferred academic program.

- Explore career options. Consider associated work environments, career paths, and lifestyles.

- Decide as much as possible on your academic direction with the aim of choosing a major, but remember that it's all right to be uncertain. Take one step at a time toward achieving your goals. Don't allow yourself to be pressured into making premature career choices.

First Year of College

- Visit your advisor and meet with the academic advisors in all departments that interest you.

- Review your precollege testing results with an advisor, as they may affect your academic and career choices.

- Aptitude tests and vocational interest surveys may provide clues to your academic goals (see the discussion of such tests in the first chapter of this book).

- Attend career fairs and programs sponsored by colleges and student organizations to increase your knowledge of the full range of jobs that people perform.

- Talk about your interests with parents, friends, professors, and people already employed in related jobs.

- Volunteer for work experiences related to your career interests.

- Pursue part-time and summer employment opportunities to gain work experience and learn more about your work preferences.

Second Year of College

- Continue to meet with your academic advisor every semester.

- Outline a plan for course work that will satisfy your degree requirements.

- Talk with faculty members in your areas of academic interest. Invite faculty members to student group meetings. Talk with other students in your chosen major.

- Select courses to complement and supplement those required for your academic program. Match these electives to your assessed abilities, needs, values, and interests.

- Consider special academic options such as overseas studies, thematic programs, or specializations related to personal career goals. Augment your major with foreign language competency to prepare yourself for a global society.

- If you can't meet the admission requirements of your preferred major, immediately explore other options. Keep a positive attitude.

Third Year of College

- Ask faculty about career prospects in your chosen area. Develop associations with faculty who could become your academic mentors.

- Continue to explore electives that will expand your knowledge of other cultures.

- Attend conferences, seminars, and association meetings targeted to professionals in your academic area. Become an active member of organizations related to your major.

- Increase your work experiences, skills, and aptitudes for careers by finding professionally related part-time work or summer employment.

- Find a career-related internship or volunteer work.

- List your tentative decisions about work preferences, values, interests, and skills. What entry-level positions and career options link with your aptitudes, interests, and values?

- Research work environments and job responsibilities of related career areas. Read and study appropriate materials on career options.

- Attend career fairs for summer employment and internship opportunities.

Fourth Year of College

- Assist a faculty member with an academic project. Develop a special project for independent study that will enhance your knowledge and information and will be attractive to prospective employers or graduate and professional schools.

- Continue association with mentors and faculty in your academic areas.

- Become a tutor or teaching assistant.

- Attend career fairs. Check job listings and pursue job opportunities.

- Develop lists of possible contacts for job opportunities or professional schools. Use your network contacts.

- Finalize plans for an entry-level position that meets your career objectives. Refine and revise your career plans if necessary.

Alternative Strategies

Perhaps your school doesn't offer a field of study or a specific course that you would like to try. Don't give up. There are ways to get what you want.

Independent Study

Think of independent study as a design-your-own course or curriculum, a customized, one-of-a-kind exploration of a particular subject. It could cover something not included in your school's curriculum. For example, an art history major might want to study the history of photography, although his or her school doesn't offer such a course. Or independent study could be an in-depth look at a topic that a broader, more basic course only touches on. For example, an English or American studies major who took a survey course on children's literature might want to look in detail at the literary and societal elements of Horatio Alger's novels.

Follow your college's rules on independent study. Those rules typically spell out the faculty and administrative approval process, determine how many credits an independent study is worth, and cap the total number of independent study credits you can apply toward graduation. Find a sponsoring faculty member who will help you design the contents and workload requirements of your independent study. This should be someone whose work, teaching style, or research you admire. Because an independent study, by definition, does not come with a standard syllabus, the advisor should help compile a list of readings, evaluate proposed research and paper topics, provide guidelines for lab experimentation, and, when appropriate, prepare and grade exams.

Transfer Credits

You may decide to take a course at a different college because that course isn't available at your own school. Make sure ahead of time that your school will accept those credits toward the number you need for graduation. Ask ahead of time if the class can be used to meet general education, major, or minor requirements.

One way to benefit from this strategy is to take community college courses, then transfer the credits to your own school. There are several reasons this strategy makes sense. It might be easier to get into some courses at a community college, especially popular introductory or prerequisite courses that frequently close out at your school. Or the community college might offer a course that's unavailable at your school. Other common benefits include smaller class size, more convenient scheduling, and lower tuition. Many community colleges have cross-enrollment agreements with nearby colleges, making it simple to arrange for credit transfers.

Consortiums

Don't ignore the possibility of cross-registering for courses at other colleges that have cooperative arrangements with your school. One example of such a cooperative arrangement is Five Colleges Consortium in central Massachusetts, in which students from Amherst College, Hampshire College, University of Massachusetts, Smith College, and Mount Holyoke College can take courses at and use the academic facilities of all five colleges. Other examples include Associated Colleges of the Twin Cities in Minnesota (Augsburg College, Macalester College, Hamline University, College of St. Catherine, and University of St. Thomas); the Central Pennsylvania Consortium (Dickinson College, Franklin and Marshall College, and Gettysburg College); and Claremont Colleges in California (Claremont McKenna College, Harvey Mudd College, Pitzer College, Pomona College, Scripps College, and Claremont University Center.)

Sometimes, the alliances encompass two-year and professional schools as well. The Colleges of Worcester Consortium in Massachusetts includes Quinsigamond Community College, University of Massachusetts Medical Center, and Tufts University School of Veterinary Medicine as well as institutions that grant bachelor's degrees: Anna Marie College,

Assumption College, Becker College, Worcester State College, Clark University, Worcester Polytechnic Institute, and College of the Holy Cross. Because consortiums are formal, structured arrangements, students register through their own schools, generally pay no extra tuition, and are assured the credits can be transferred.

In addition to formal consortiums, some pairs of colleges have bilateral cross-enrollment arrangements. Such an arrangement increases the availability of courses, especially for students at the smaller institutions, and ensures the credits will transfer.

Foreign Study

Increasingly, colleges encourage their students to study abroad. Academic leaders recognize how the economic, political, and cultural fate of the United States meshes with the fates of other nations, developed and developing. They know how technological, scientific, industrial, computer, communications, and transportation advances continue to link our nation with others. They see populations and opportunities expanding elsewhere, and they want their students prepared for those opportunities. They also see foreign nations as a pool from which to draw more students to U.S. colleges. That makes international education a hot trend, one you can take advantage of by broadening your horizons abroad. However, you'll find that some schools are more enthusiastic proponents of foreign study than others.

Beyond intellectual and cultural challenges, foreign study can dramatically impact your life. Consider the student who signed up for summer study in Africa through Nebraska Wesleyan University. As part of her course, "Development in Zimbabwe and South Africa," she performed service work in an orphanage in Zimbabwe. "My whole perspective on life changed because of that trip," she says. "When I came to Wesleyan, I wanted to work in a tall office building, be on the top floor, a vice president. Now I want to get down and dirty and do child development programs for at-risk kids."

There are a number of ways to tackle study abroad. You could do so through a single course in a foreign country during a summer or semester break—maybe reporting in London through Michigan State University, peace studies in Ireland through Pennsylvania's Beaver College, environmental studies in Nepal through the University of Wisconsin, or agricultural studies in Senegal through the University of Minnesota. Or you could try a full summer program at an overseas university, or spend a semester or a year overseas. In addition to doing course work in a substantive field, you could develop and hone language skills that might prove useful when you look for a job, apply to graduate school, or travel.

When Michigan State University professor Paulette Stenzel wanted her American business students to learn how trademark and copyright laws are enforced in Mexico, she sent them into the streets of Merida, the centuries-old capital of Yucatan, where they were enrolled for the semester at La Universidad Autonoma de Yucatan. They found Nike™ knock-offs selling for $5 and day care centers named "Disneyland." To gain perspective on job discrimination, they scoured the help-wanted ads in the local newspapers, where they read ads seeking only men or applicants of certain ages. They lived with local families, so when a civil jury in Los Angeles found O. J. Simpson liable for the murders of his ex-wife and her friend, Professor Stenzel assigned them to discuss the case with their hosts. "They came back with amazing insights about the justice system and racism."

Most foreign programs have prerequisites, and some maintain language requirements as well. Some overseas programs are targeted to particular majors, while others are wide open to students regardless of what field they're studying. It's vital to plan ahead and consult with your advisor to ensure a foreign program meets your academic needs.

Your college may have a formal relationship with one or more foreign universities. For example, Illinois State University has relationships with about 20 colleges in Australia, Austria, England, France, Germany, Italy, Russia, Japan, Spain, Wales, Sweden, and Scotland. The University of Colorado offers study-abroad programs in 45 locations on every continent except Antarctica. Iowa State University has ties to more than 100 institutions all over the world. To participate in such a program, stay registered in your own college. Credits earned abroad are treated the same as if earned on your home campus. In most cases, you can apply your financial aid—scholarships and loans—to the cost of the program. Many schools also offer special study-abroad scholarships.

You could also study abroad through another U.S. college or directly through a foreign institution. This further expands the possibilities because you're not limited by the formal programs your own school offers. Do your homework before enrolling. Consult your advisor well ahead of time to make sure that the credits will transfer and that appropriate courses will count toward your major, minor, or general education requirements. Get written approval in advance.

Take Graduate Courses

As a junior or senior, you may be permitted to take one or more graduate-level or professional-level courses. That way, a political science major considering a legal career could register for a first-year law school course such as "Constitutional Law" or "Torts." A statistics major might try a graduate course such as "Econometrics" or "Sample Surveys."

If that option is available, it can provide a taste of the substance and rigors encountered beyond the bachelor's degree. Also, there might be more personal interaction between faculty and students in postgraduate courses than in undergraduate courses.

Enriching Your Studies

What you learn in class is certainly important—but it's far from everything. In fact, no student should feel that his or her higher education is comprehensive based solely on what was absorbed from classes and course work. L. Patrick Scheetz, director of Michigan State's Collegiate Employment Research Institute, strongly emphasizes the importance of going beyond the classroom: "Employers tell us that those students who are making it in their fields have significant career-related experience and come in with fewer bumps and bruises than students who think they hold the world by the tail. They're tempered and more realistic in their expectations."

The following approaches will help you round out your education and better understand its relationship to your future.

Internships

Some majors require internships. Even if yours doesn't, an internship is a worthwhile experience that can pay off in job skills and contacts. The standards and goals should be set by your college or advisor, and there should be supervision and responsibility on the job—an internship is of little benefit if it involves only filing, answering phones, running errands, and doing gruntwork.

There are plenty of options for structuring an internship. It might be full-time or part-time, paid or unpaid, offer course credit or not, and take place during the school year or during summer break. No matter what the permutation, an internship can provide a leg up in job hunting and in winning admission to graduate school or professional school.

LaTonya Hardy did a semester-long internship with the Black Family Development Corporation in Detroit, a position she lined up through the Family and Child Ecology Program at Michigan State University. "I learned just about every aspect of how the organization worked. The internship gave me a chance to show my abilities," says LaTonya, who was hired by the company after she finished college. (Sharon Terlep, "Program Gives Students Boost into Job Market," *State News*, Jan. 14, 1997.)

After his graduation as a government major from Cornell University, Eric Freedman—one of the authors of this book—took a summer internship in Washington, D.C., with a member of the U.S. House of Representatives. When a full-time staff position opened late that summer, he was hired to handle constituent problems and answer mail. Within two months, he was promoted to legislative assistant analyzing and drafting bills, preparing press releases and newsletters, and preparing speeches and articles for publication. After a year, he enrolled in law school but remained on the congressional staff as a part-time press and legislative aide.

As a psychology major, Edward Hoffman—the other author of this book—did a summer internship at a state facility for the developmentally disabled in California. The program, cosponsored by the State University of California at Fullerton, proved a turning point in his life. While still an undergraduate, he wrote his first professional article for the journal *Mental Retardation* and discovered a love for psychology research and writing. His work also motivated him to take additional courses in child development at Cornell University.

And David Lanzoni started as a sociology major at Merrimack College in Massachusetts. The internship he served in a local court between his junior and senior years led to a complete turnabout in his career plans. He went on to graduate school in criminal justice with plans to become a probation officer.

An internship may also persuade you to look for a *different* career direction. That's because it's a chance to find out whether a career feels right or wrong for you.

Cooperative Education

Cooperative education alternates periods of classroom study with periods of paid employment in jobs connected with your academic, career, and personal interests. The goal is to provide skilled, meaningful jobs with salaries that reflect your college education, experience, and market standards.

Northeastern University in Boston is one of the pioneers in cooperative education. It describes the co-op approach as a way to link study and work, to encourage career exploration, to develop maturity, to create networks, and to help students earn money. "Seeing the connection between work and study sharpens a student's intellectual curiosity for a lifetime," as a university publication explains. "Co-op lets students evaluate their career decisions early in their college years. Educated in the classroom and the workplace, co-op students bring employers the latest in professional knowledge, a fresh perspective, maturity, and an unbounded enthusiasm" (Quotes in this section from "Your Leading Edge: Cooperative Education at Northeastern University," published by Northeastern University).

Linda Driebrek, an engineering manager for Barry Controls in Massachusetts, notes that three of her group's four full-time engineers first came to the company through Northeastern's program. "To see a 20-year-old co-op student and a 60-year-old engineer looking at a computer screen together is a wonderful blend. The older person serves as a mentor, and the younger person brings fresh insights and ideas to the project" (from "Your Leading Edge: Cooperative Education at Northeastern University").

Lou Gaglini, a recruitment director for the Big Six accounting firm of Deloitte & Touche, emphasizes that co-op students do real work. "Students don't stand around photocopying. We want them out in the field helping our regular staff with audits or working with clients on tax returns, both corporate and personal" (from "Your Leading Edge: Cooperative Education at Northeastern University").

Student Teaching

Student teaching is not limited to traditional elementary and secondary education majors; it's also available if you major in special education or early childhood education. Some colleges now call these programs "teaching internships" or "directed teaching," but the elements are the same. Whatever the name, student teaching is generally required to obtain state certification to teach.

Student teachers participate with a collaborating teacher in developing lesson plans, presenting lessons, grading assignments, conferring with parents, and advising students. They follow school district policies, attend faculty and parent-teacher meetings, and take part in in-service training programs offered by the school district.

Student teaching might demonstrate that you *don't* belong at the front of a classroom. It's better to discover that before graduation than after you hunt for and accept a full-time teaching job. A secondary math education major at the State University of New York College at Oneonta took a student teaching assignment, and found out right away that teaching wasn't for him. So he took a leave of absence for the rest of the semester and then returned to complete the requirements for a math major.

Research and Laboratory Assistantships

A research assistantship or laboratory assistantship is another way to gain experience under academic supervision. Many professors write books and articles, consult for government agencies and businesses, do laboratory research into new products and scientific processes, lecture off campus, and participate in national and international scholarly organizations. Those responsibilities might benefit from the help of an undergraduate.

As an assistant, you would get a behind-the-scenes look at how a professor operates while improving your research, writing, and technical skills and building your substantive knowledge of the field. This type of position is an asset when you look for a job or apply to graduate school. Some assistantships are paid through work-study programs or grants, so there's the potential for immediate financial reward as well. Also, you'll get a chance to better know a professor outside the formal restraints of the classroom.

What's involved? An assistant may research material in libraries and through the Internet and electronic databases, enter survey results and data into computers, monitor lab experiments, proofread manuscripts, and handle clerical chores.

As a chemical engineering major at Michigan State University, Jeremy VanAntwerp worked as a research assistant for a professor, doing experiments and mathematical modeling—"a pretty good mix really." The result was research experience, a publication, and strong letters of recommendation to support his successful application for a graduate program at the University of Illinois. "It definitely helped me get into grad school."

Most professors are glad to find motivated, enthusiastic students and to serve as mentors. Look for one whose reputation and research topics interest you, topics in which you want more expertise or knowledge.

How do you find a research or laboratory assistantship? Some colleges handle them through their financial aid or placement offices. But don't be too shy to knock on a professor's office door and express your interest in helping; at worst, you'll be politely turned down and, if that happens, knock on more doors.

Community Service

Only a handful of schools require community service to graduate, although many others—often those with a religious affiliation—strongly encourage their students to work in the local community. All students at Wittenberg University in Ohio have a 30-hour service requirement, with 27 hours of actual work and three hours of group reflection. "Social consciousness and cultural awareness are the keys to a better society. Doing my community service gave me a chance to interact with the community in a more personal environment," says student Katarina Saevig. Adds Melanie Nehls, another Wittenberg undergraduate, "It gives you a chance to do what you want to do in the future" (from "Service and Community," brochure published by Wittenberg University).

There are several benefits to community service, all of which can enrich your college experience and shape your career direction: You can:

- Apply what you learn in class to the real world. If early childhood education grabs you, volunteer in a local day care center or preschool. If art history's on your mind, volunteer as a docent (tour guide) at a community museum. If you're thinking of a future in criminal justice, many law enforcement agencies run cadet programs.

- Build your résumé and references. Service work—especially tied to your field of study—counts more with potential employers than a part-time job flipping burgers, mowing lawns, or selling perfume. It often carries more weight than your grade point average, too. If you do well, supervisors can provide valuable job references from the nonacademic world. Recruiters regard community service as one sign an applicant is well rounded.

- Parlay volunteer work into a job or graduate school. The organization with which you volunteer may keep you in mind if a paying position opens. And if you network, the staff can let you know about jobs, graduate study, and fellowship opportunities elsewhere.

- Discover new career directions. A pre-med student who volunteers in a hospital or clinic also gains exposure to an array of other fields, including nutrition, social work, medical technology, and physical therapy. Maybe one of them will click.

- Learn more about the community in which you're spending four or more years. People you meet through service work can make you feel part of a nonacademic world that includes children and families, local policy debates, jobs unrelated to the college, and municipal government political activities.

Those benefits proved tangible for two former Michigan State biology majors who parlayed unpaid community service into full-time jobs with the Nature Conservancy. Brian Palmer and Sara Ross each began by helping a staff ecologist at the Michigan chapter of the nonprofit environmental group pin and label insects for an ecology project. Palmer, initially an intern, was also asked to do data entry and discovered he had a knack for computers. He was hired as the organization's accounting assistant. Ross, who volunteered at the Nature Conservancy after being laid off from her job at a medical technology company, rose to become the administrative assistant for science programs.

Part Two

101 Fields

How to Use the Directory

To make this book easy to use, we break down each of the 101 fields of study into the following sections:

- What to Expect

- Trends

- What You Need to Succeed

- Related Fields

- Typical Basic Courses

- An Array of Electives

- On-Campus Opportunities

- Job Opportunities

- Reading to Explore

- To Learn More

What to Expect

It's often tough to find an objective, up-to-date description of a field of study. Our goal here is to provide a short but comprehensive overview of each major, giving you a sense of what you'll learn in your courses. This includes basic courses as well as higher-level courses that delve into specialties and advanced techniques. This information has been drawn from interviews with professors, professional and accreditation organizations, and other knowledgeable sources.

Trends

This section discusses academic and career trends in the field. True, it's difficult to forecast the future; how many far-sighted people predicted 25 years ago the medical and technological advances we now take for granted, or the medical and technological problems that confront us? But our aim here is to clue you in to what experts and authorities in the field believe the future may bring.

What You Need to Succeed

Let's face it, our personalities differ. Your personality affects how well you'll fit into certain fields, as a student and as an employee.

If you feel cramped and imprisoned working indoors, you might be better suited to forestry or fisheries and wildlife than to accounting or chemistry. If you feel uncomfortable with children, does it make sense to pursue family and child development or elementary education? If you can't concentrate on details, you probably wouldn't do well in mechanical engineering or architecture. But you might excel in philosophy or religious studies and theology, where creativity counts more heavily than meticulous attention to detail does. On the flip side, if you prefer concrete to abstract thinking, you probably wouldn't enjoy philosophy or religious studies and theology.

If technology makes you wary, your place may be in Romance languages or music history, although computers and other technological tools are used in those fields as well. Uncomfortable with strangers? Avoid nursing and optometry. Slow or unwilling to learn languages? Avoid international studies.

Related Fields

What other majors overlap with the one you're considering? For example, as a journalism major, you may also be want to take courses in advertising, public relations, and telecommunications. The biochemistry student could select complementary classes in biology, chemistry, chemical engineering, micro- and molecular biology, and physics. The aspiring landscape architect can benefit from classes in civil engineering, parks and recreation, forestry, and horticulture.

Typical Basic Courses

In this section, we list eight fairly standard or common courses you may encounter, usually in your first two years in the major. (Course names vary from school to school, even though the course content may not vary that much.) This section and the one that follows are based on our review of curricula at dozens of colleges—public and private, large and small, general studies and specialized, competitive and noncompetitive—from all regions of the United States.

An Array of Electives

Your college may offer 50 or more undergraduate courses in some majors, while choices are narrower in other departments or at other schools. This section samples the variety you may find, often on the junior and senior level. To add to your options, some colleges allow juniors and seniors to take graduate-level seminars.

On-Campus Opportunities

Where on campus can you put some of your classroom knowledge to practical use? How can you explore a field further, aside from course work? Be on the look-out for on-campus jobs and assistantships. Some of these are paying positions. Others are strictly volunteer work, or may be worth college credit. Look also for clubs, organizations, and honor societies related to your field of interest.

Job Opportunities

Here you'll find information on estimated supply of and demand for college graduates in each field of study. Our information is based on research conducted each year by the Career Services and Placement office at Michigan State University, U.S. Labor Department findings, and information from professional organizations and other experts. Factors in the analysis include employer requests for graduating students, the placement rates for recent graduates, and the experience of advisors and career counselors in placing graduating students and alumni. To find more details on job prospects, check with state or local affiliates of professional associations and the placement office at your own college.

Keep in mind that these are only broad indicators, not gospel. Just because there's a substantial surplus of seniors graduating with bachelor's degrees in linguistics doesn't mean you wouldn't be able to find a job in that field. Nor does a high demand for computer science graduates guarantee that everyone in that field will find a satisfactory job. There are many variables within some disciplines; consider education, for example. As this book goes to press, demand is high for teachers of chemistry, earth science, math, physics, and industrial arts. At the same time, there's a surplus of would-be teachers of biology, geography, government, Latin, physical education, and health education. Supply and demand in education are fluid, changing over time, and there are regional differences as well.

There are many unpredictable factors and variables that affect job prospects, including changes in the world, national, regional, and local economies; the way your college categorizes a major or field of study; established networks between your college and potential employers; your own work background, career-related experiences, and depth of study; and location of employment opportunities. And while job prospects are one factor you can weigh in selecting a major, they shouldn't be the sole factor.

Here are the five categories used in this book:

- *High demand / limited supply:* appear to be more positions than graduates.
- *Good demand / possible shortage:* a few more positions than graduates.
- *Near balance / supply equals demand:* about as many graduates as positions.
- *Adequate supply / some oversupply:* a few more graduates than positions.
- *Surplus / substantial oversupply:* many more graduates than positions.

Reading to Explore

One way to get a feel for a field is to read about it—and generally not through textbooks. Instead, try general nonfiction, biography, history, magazines, or even novels that offer insights into what it's like to study or work in a particular discipline. Our suggestions include some "classics" in their fields, but most are recent publications that reflect new developments, trends, and areas for exploration. Sampling some of these recommendations can dispel—or reinforce—your preconceptions and give you a better sense of whether you would like to pursue a field.

To Learn More

For each field of study, we list one or two national organizations that can provide more detailed information. Contact them to learn more about the field and about career directions and opportunities. Most of them have Internet sites, but the addresses (as well as the E-mail addresses) often change. If you have trouble connecting, call or fax the organization for the new address of its Internet site.

Accounting

Today, working in business and not knowing accounting terminology is like being in a foreign country and not knowing its language.
—*Roger H. Hermanson, James Don Edwards, and Michael W. Maher, accounting professors, in* Accounting Principles

What to Expect

Your foundation in this field will encompass several basic areas, including auditing, taxation, financial accounting, and managerial accounting. Introductory courses familiarize you with underlying principles and theories, while more advanced classes provide in-depth knowledge of technical areas and show you how to apply these concepts to real-life situations. You'll learn about financial reporting requirements and audit investigation techniques. Related business administration and finance courses help you understand the processes and institutions involved in marketing and producing goods and services, as well as the financing of businesses and operation of government agencies.

Courses should cover computer applications and software for auditing, tax preparation, financial analysis, and financial management. Studies in macroeconomics, microeconomics, business law, investments, and management will illuminate the relationships among accounting and other business and governmental disciplines. Professional ethics should be woven into the curriculum because clients rely on accountants' integrity, confidentiality, and personal honesty. Finally, your studies should place accounting into the regulatory and legal framework that government and the private sector use to protect the public interest.

Trends

Trends in accounting include its adaptability to innovations in business practices, such as risk management and development of complex financing arrangements, and increasingly sophisticated approaches to auditing. At the same time, globalization of businesses will require accountants to learn more about foreign finance, banking, and marketing. Computerized accounting information systems will become omnipresent. And accountants will play a growing role in the move toward total quality management, a philosophy of continuous improvement within a company, government agency, or nonprofit organization.

What You Need to Succeed

On one level, you need solid technical accounting and business knowledge, as well as an understanding of business systems, computers, spreadsheets, and accounting software. But technical mastery isn't enough. Problem-solving skills and a commitment to detail are vital, including the ability to analyze, compare, and interpret facts and figures. In many instances, your responsibilities will be those of a detective or forensic investigator, ferreting out improprieties, omissions, and mistakes. That means you'll need a willingness to take adversarial positions and to confront clients when wrongdoing is uncovered.

Creative thinking is important to devise innovative solutions to complex business problems that confront accountants every day. Also, this is a service profession—not merely number crunching—so you need strong interpersonal, verbal, and written communication skills. Audit work often involves travel and long hours. Finally, high ethical standards are mandatory because people rely on the information you provide to help them make financial and management decisions.

Related Fields

Business Administration
Economics
Finance and Banking
Statistics

Typical Basic Courses

Accounting Principles
Auditing
Business Information Systems
Business Systems Analysis
Cost and Managerial Accounting
Financial Reporting
Intermediate Accounting
Tax Principles

An Array of Electives

Advanced Income Tax
Auditing Theory
Comptrollership
Fund Accounting
Governmental and Nonprofit Accounting
Information Management
Internal Auditing
Tax Research

On-Campus Opportunities

Business, bursar, comptroller's, and financial aid offices

Job Opportunities

Good demand / Possible shortage

Reading to Explore

Den of Thieves, by James B. Stewart (Simon & Schuster)

Movie Money: Understanding Hollywood's (Creative) Accounting Practices, by Bill Daniels (Silman-James)

Schindler's List, by Thomas Keneally (Simon & Schuster)

Unbridled Power: Inside the Secret Culture of the IRS, by Shelley L. Davis (HarperBusiness)

Under the Green Eyeshade: Confessions of a Tax Accountant, by Noell Allen (Canyon View Institute)

To Learn More

American Institute of Certified Public
  Accountants
1211 Avenue of the Americas
New York, NY 10036
(212) 596-6200; fax (212) 596-6213
E-mail: jryan@aicpa.org
Internet site: http://www.aicpa.org

Advertising

Sanely applied advertising could remake the world.
—*Stuart Chase, economist and writer, in* Power of Words

What to Expect

You'll find glamour and gruntwork in advertising—along with elements of psychology, communications, art, government regulation, management, business administration, and social responsibility. Basic courses introduce students to principles of design, promotion, production of brochures and publications, media operations, broadcasting, and consumer behavior. You'll be taught how to plan, execute, and control advertising media campaigns and use case studies based on actual situations as a real-world basis for learning.

Advanced classes will hone your ability to develop creative strategies, deal with clients, understand how the public thinks, calculate and work within advertising budgets, and use new technologies. In the process, practical industry problems are integrated with theory. You should get experience designing ad campaigns for print and broadcast in both the private and nonprofit sectors. The legal and ethical aspects of advertising will be covered, as well as issues of how well the advertising industry regulates itself. Equally important, through coursework and work with clients, you'll pick up research skills essential to gather and gauge public opinion, consumer and voter preferences, and buying patterns.

Trends

Trends in advertising react to constantly evolving societal standards, including those that push the limits of traditional cultural values. While commercial advertising will remain the largest arena of operations, advertising professionals will be called on increasingly to work with nonprofit clients in fund-raising efforts. Advertising also will play a larger role in government as public agencies fight to compete with—and sometimes assist—the private sector in recreation, health, education, tourism, and other services. Interactive advertising will grow in importance as society relies more heavily on the Internet and other cyberspace media.

What You Need to Succeed

Creativity and a grasp of technology are two important attributes for success in the field. You'll need imagination to originate, analyze, and reshape a range of advertising ideas, and an ability to use design software and video and audio equipment to demonstrate those concepts. By definition, advertising is a communications field, so you have to be able to communicate effectively not only in writing, but also graphically and verbally with clients, co-workers, and the consumers who are the targets of the ads. Organizational, planning, and financial skills will help you better understand a client's operations and better develop advertising strategies to improve client performance and profits.

Also, you must be able to work in teams with other creative staff, to perform professionally under deadline pressure, and to understand a client's business needs and budget restrictions. At the same time, a competitive spirit will help propel you in the competitive atmosphere of advertising, marketing, and promotion.

Related Fields

Graphic Design
Journalism
Marketing
Public Relations
Technical Writing
Telecommunications

Typical Basic Courses

Ad Copy and Layout
Advertising Copywriting
Advertising Graphics and Production
Consumer Behavior
Creative Strategies
Media Planning
Media Relations
Principles of Advertising

An Array of Electives

Advertising and Society
Consumer Research
Direct Response Advertising
Electronic Media Technology
International Marketing
Marketing Ethics
Professional Selling
Promotion Management

On-Campus Opportunities

Ad sales for your college newspaper,
   magazine, and broadcast station
Fund-raising for your college

Job Opportunities

Adequate supply / Some oversupply

Reading to Explore

Behind the Scenes: The Advertising Process at Work (Advertising Educational Foundation Video)

David Ogilvy: An Autobiography, by David Ogilvy (John Wiley & Sons)

Going Negative: How Attack Ads Shrink and Polarize the Electorate, by Stephen Ansolabehere and Shanto Iyengar (Free Press)

Satisfaction Guaranteed: The Making of the American Mass Market, by Susan Strasser (Pantheon)

Where the Suckers Moon: The Life and Death of an Advertising Campaign, by Randall Rothenberg (Vintage)

To Learn More

American Advertising Federation
1101 Vermont Ave. NW, #500
Washington, DC 20005
(800) 999-2231; fax (202) 898-0159
E-mail: aaf@aaf.org
Internet site: http://www.aaf.org

Aerospace and Astronautical Engineering

To the universe and beyond.
—*Buzz Skywalker,* Toy Story

What to Expect

The field takes you into challenging problems encountered in the design and operation of aircraft, missiles, and space vehicles. The curriculum concentrates on the fundamental subjects necessary for the research, design, development, and operation of the aerospace industry, both commercial and military. In the beginning, you'll encounter propulsion, aerospace dynamics, physics, electronics, and thermodynamics. Throughout, you'll learn to apply the principles of physical science and mathematics. Not surprisingly, your work will involve computers and sophisticated software. You'll do laboratory experimentation, learn manufacturing and design techniques, recognize economic considerations, become familiar with industrial applications, and research materials used to construct aircraft and spacecraft. Classes can help you focus on a particular type of aerospace product, such as helicopters, spacecraft, rockets, or commercial transports. Most students prefer to specialize in either aircraft or spacecraft, but the advanced courses you take aren't restricted to one or the other. You'll refine and expand your knowledge while developing expertise in such topics as fluid mechanics, stochastics, aerodynamics, orbit and flight mechanics, guidance and control systems, the physics of fluids, acoustics, or solid mechanics.

Trends

Trends in aerospace and astronautical engineering reflect the increasing sophistication of tools such as computers, lasers, and laser holographic interferometry. There will be opportunities to apply your knowledge beyond the aerospace and aviation industries. For example, aerodynamics apply to high-speed ground transportation, hydrofoils, the mechanics of blood flow, and noise generation. At the same time, the aerospace industry may shrink as government expenditures for military aircraft, missiles, and other aerospace systems decline.

What You Need to Succeed

Mastery of scientific, mathematical, and computer principles is assumed in carrying out the duties of aerospace and astronautical engineers. You must be able to work well in teams with colleagues from a variety of other disciplines, ranging from electrical engineers, mechanical engineers, industrial engineers, and computer scientists to astrophysicists, mathematicians, metallurgists, and industrial technologists. Beyond that are less tangible but not less important skills such as a drive to solve complex puzzles, long-term planning skills, and an ability to envision creative alternative solutions, since projects may stretch over a period of years. A competitive spirit is a related asset because of the competitive nature of the industry.

Related Fields

Astronomy and Astrophysics
Material Science and Engineering
Military, Aerospace, and Naval Science
Physics

Typical Basic Courses

Aerospace Dynamics
Electronics
Experimental Physics
Fluid Dynamics
Foundations of Propulsion
Materials Science and Engineering
Systems Analysis
Thermodynamics

An Array of Electives

Aeroelasticity
Aerospace Systems Design
Aircraft Design
Astrodynamics
Flight Control Systems
Flight Systems Testing
Remote Sensing Systems Design
Spacecraft Systems

On-Campus Opportunities

Laboratory assistant
Research assistant

Job Opportunities

Surplus / Substantial oversupply

Reading to Explore

Deltoid Pumpkin Seed, by John McPhee (Farrar)

Flying Blind, Flying Safe, by Mary Schiavo with Sabra Chartrand (Avon)

No Downlink: A Dramatic Narrative About the Challenger Accident and Our Time, by Claus Jensen (Farrar, Straus and Giroux)

The Right Stuff, by Tom Wolfe (Farrar, Straus and Giroux)

Twenty-First-Century Jet: The Making and Marketing of the Boeing 777, by Karl Sabbagh (Scribner)

To Learn More

American Institute of Aeronautics and
   Astronautics
1801 Alexander Bell Drive, Suite 500
Reston, VA 20191
(800) 639-2422; fax (703) 764-7551
E-mail: wilv@aiaa.org
Internet site: http://www.aiaa.com

Aerospace Education Foundation
1501 Lee Highway
Arlington, VA 22209
(703) 247-5800; fax (703) 247-5853
E-mail: aefstaff@aef.org
Internet site: http://www.aef.org

African American Studies

Black people must redefine themselves, and only they can do that. Throughout this country, vast segments of the black communities are beginning to recognize the need to assert their own definitions to reclaim their history, their culture, to create their own sense of community and togetherness.
—*Stokely Carmichael, political activist, quoted in* A Political Dictionary of Black Quotations Reflecting the Black Man's Dreams, Hopes, Visions

What to Expect

As an academic field, African American studies presents a body of knowledge that not only surveys the experiences of African Americans in the United States but also explores their heritage, from Africa through the New World, including the Caribbean. You'll investigate multiple disciplines to develop a broad understanding of African American culture, politics, and economics. At an introductory level, courses survey African American history, literature, arts, values, and intergroup relations. Africa's history, geography, and traditions are covered as well. You'll also study the forces that consciously and unconsciously engendered and maintain racism in North American societies, plus the social cost of racism and approaches to curtail it. In advanced classes, you may focus on specific areas of interest, among them dance, poetry, economic development, religion, government, rural communities, educational philosophies, the history of social movements, the role of African American women, Pan-Africanism, or urban issues. Students often elect to do an independent research project on a topic of their choice.

Trends

Trends in African American studies include more attention to the relationships between African Americans and other ethnic groups and to developing strategies that use economic and political power to achieve social goals. The future of affirmative action programs within government and the private sector will continue to be heatedly debated. Another area of growing interest is the impact of immigration on educational, business, and financial opportunities for African Americans.

What You Need to Succeed

A cornerstone of African American studies is an interest in—and concern for—the roles African Americans play in contemporary society and how their past roles shape the present. Because African American studies encompass aspects of so many disciplines, you must be able to conceptualize beyond narrow categories such as "sociology" or "history" or "religion" and be able to analyze problems that cross those lines. You should be able to take a long view of problems and issues, because the field covers hundreds of years of history and, at the same time, looks into the future. Strong written and verbal communication skills are essential, as is a mastery of research skills using documents, statistical data, oral histories, even fiction, drama, music, and poetry. Conducting interviews, distilling divergent perspectives to find common threads, ignoring stereotypes, and drawing logical conclusions are important.

Related Fields

African Languages and Cultures
History
Public Policy and Administration
Sociology
Urban Studies

Typical Basic Courses

African American History
African American Literature
African People and Cultures
Black Community
Black Nationalism
Introduction to African American Studies
Introduction to African History
Race and Ethnic Relations

An Array of Electives

African American Theater
Black American Music
Black Politics
Black Religious Experience
Economic Development Programs
Harlem Renaissance
Race and Society
Research Methods in Ethnic Studies

On-Campus Opportunities

Admissions and recruiting office
Research assistant

Job Opportunities

Adequate supply / Some oversupply

Reading to Explore

Have No Fear: The Charles Evers Story, by Charles Evers and Andrew Szanton (John Wiley & Sons)

I Know Why the Caged Bird Sings, by Maya Angelou (Bantam)

The Autobiography of Malcolm X, by Malcolm X (Ballantine)

The Portable Harlem Renaissance Reader, by David Leveering Lewis (Penguin)

The Power of Black Music: Interpreting Its History from Africa to the United States, by Samuel A. Floyd, Jr. (Oxford University)

To Learn More

Association for the Study of Afro-
   American Life and History
1407 14th St. NW
Washington, DC 20005
(202) 667-2822; fax (202) 387-9802
E-mail: asalh@earthlink.net
Internet site:
   http://www.artnoir.com/asalh.html

National Council for Black Studies
California State University, Dominguez
   Hills
Carson, CA 90747
(310) 243-2169; fax (310) 516-3987
E-mail: ncbs@dhvx20.csudh.edu
Internet site: http://www.eiu.edu/~ncbs

African Languages and Cultures

There is always something new out of Africa.
—*Pliny the Elder, historian, in* Natural History

What to Expect

Africa may be a single continent geographically, but it's a potpourri of languages, tribes, nations, rivalries, religions, habitats, histories, races, media, political structures, and economies. Through your courses, you'll gain a better understanding of the continent's shared traditions, conflicts, problems, and potential. In the beginning, you'll confront a broad range of topics in literature, art, societal values, linguistics, history, architectures, and geography from desert to rain forests to savannas to cities.

Then you can pick one or more areas to concentrate on, perhaps sociology and development, or oral traditions, or conversational languages, or comparative economics, or spiritual systems, or gender roles. Throughout, your studies will enable you to trace the historic roots of current situations from colonialism, slavery, and economic exploitation to Pan-Africanism, border disputes, and the cultural clash between modernization and tradition. These lessons will help you more fully understand North American culture, too, which has been influenced for more than three centuries by African people, religions, foods, linguistics, concepts of kinship and collective responsibility, and music.

Trends

Trends in African languages and cultures include more emphasis on finding lessons from history and society that apply broadly, using African culture as a resource rather than as only a reference point or subject of intellectual inquiry. Knowledge of Africa's languages and cultural patterns will become more useful in a global economy and in a world where Europe and the United States pay more attention to genocide, civil unrest, wars, and political instability on that continent. Environmental concerns about habitat destruction, population growth, industrialization, and the elimination of plant and animal species in Africa will continue to spread.

What You Need to Succeed

To draw lessons and find patterns from a multidisciplinary field such as African languages and cultures requires an ability to analyze, think creatively, and extract well-reasoned conclusions from what you observe, study, and hear. Your reading and listening should become attuned to nuances, unspoken thoughts, and cultural contexts. Mastery of at least one—and hopefully more—African languages is a must. Verbal and written language skills are vital to communicate well with Africans and gain a realistic feeling for their literature and culture. You will also need a mind open to multiculturalism, as well as a willingness to accept the beliefs and practices of other cultures without being judgmental or feeling superior. Naturally, you should be interested in travel, in meeting people of sharply divergent backgrounds, and in exploring lifestyles and values different from your own. Look for practical ways to apply your knowledge in government, business, writing, and international organizations.

Related Fields

African American Studies
Anthropology
Economics
History
International Relations
Linguistics

Typical Basic Courses

African Development and Technology
African Languages
African Political Systems
Cultures of Africa
Foundation of African Studies
Geography of Africa
Sub-Saharan Africa
Survey of African Literature

An Array of Electives

African Cultural Identities
Central and East African Art
Comparative Economic Systems
Decolonizing Africa
Environment and Society in Africa
Literature and Film in Africa
Sociology of Development
Southern Africa Since 1910

On-Campus Opportunities

International student center
Study-abroad programs office
Translator for foreign visitors

Job Opportunities

Adequate supply / Some oversupply

Reading to Explore

African Studies in the United States: A Perspective, by Jane I. Guyer (African Studies Association)

Mountain People, by Colin Turnball (Simon & Schuster)

Season of Blood: A Rwandan Journey, by Fergal Keane (Viking)

Shaka's Children: A History of the Zulu People, by Stephen Taylor (HarperCollins World)

The Myth of Wild Africa: Conservation Without Illusion, by Jonathan S. Adams and Thomas O. McShane (University of California)

To Learn More

African Studies Association
Credit Union Building
Emory University
Atlanta GA 30322
(404) 329-6410; fax (404) 329-6433
E-mail: africa@emory.edu
Internet site:
   http://www.upenn.edu/African_Studies/
   Home_Page/ASA_Menu.html

Agricultural Engineering

Speak to the earth, and it shall teach thee.
—*The Bible, Book of Job*

What to Expect

Your education in agricultural engineering will teach you to integrate basic physical and biological sciences by applying engineering fundamentals to biological systems. In introductory classes, you'll become familiar with principles of soil science, mechanics, engineering applications, and biotechnology. Such studies will include work with field and machine systems, environmental engineering controls, computer vision, and system analysis. You'll learn about applications in surveying, hydrology, soil conservation, solar radiation, field machinery performance, and power transmission systems. In advanced courses, you'll use engineering techniques in a variety of practical applications, including production, storage, processing, handling, distribution, and use of food products and other biomaterials. Courses will cover hardware, such as fluid power circuits and hydrostatic transmissions, agri-industrial applications of electrical power, and the processing of grain and foods. On the environmental front, look for classes in natural resource conservation engineering, agricultural climatology, and water quality engineering. The curriculum includes resource and environmental economics, as well as applications of computerized design tools.

Trends

Trends in agricultural engineering will focus industry and research efforts on biotechnology. This array includes development of new products, more efficient production of raw commodities and processed foods, and finding ways to serve a growing world population. On an international level, you'll see a strong impetus to use technology and genetics to meet demands for more food and improved nutrition, often for countries with only limited economic resources. Throughout, agricultural engineers will pay attention to environmental considerations such as protection of watersheds, erosion prevention, less harmful pest and weed controls, and energy conversation.

What You Need to Succeed

You'll need a strong interest in working in a hands-on fashion, mastering the latest technological tools, and understanding machinery and mechanical systems used in farming, ranching, and food processing. You must be adept at using computers. Problem-solving and analytical skills are vital, since the agricultural engineer frequently confronts questions of how to use existing technology and how to create new technology, often within financial restrictions. In addition, anticipate a diversity of challenges, since you could move from agricultural equipment to construction to grain processing to soil and water resource protection to biotechnology to manufacturing. Within these realms are aspects of design, testing, research, production, sales, and consulting. Some projects may involve a large component of independent work, but more often you'll collaborate with other engineers, technicians, and business personnel within your company or organization. Expect pressure to meet deadlines and beat competitors.

Related Fields

Biochemistry
Biology
Botany
Chemical Engineering
Crop and Soil Science
Horticulture

Typical Basic Courses

Agricultural Waste Management Systems
Engineering Applications for Biological
  Systems
Food Engineering Technology
Fundamentals of Hydraulic Systems
Fundamentals of Thermodynamics
Introduction to Soil Science
Mechanical Power Units
Storm Water Management

An Array of Electives

Ecological Engineering
Instrumentation
Mechanics of Biological Tissues
Physiological Engineering
Plant Layout and Principles of Handling
Principles of Aquaculture
Principles of Navigation
Soil and Water Management Systems

On-Campus Opportunities

Research assistant

Job Opportunities

Near balance / Supply equals demand

Reading to Explore

A Garden of Unearthly Delights: Bioengineering and the Future of Food, by Robin Mather (Dutton)

Dream Reaper: The Story of an Old-Fashioned Inventor in the High-Tech, High-Stakes World of Modern Agriculture, by Craig Canine (University of Chicago)

John Deere Tractors Worldwide: A Century of Progress, 1893–1993, by Don Macmillan (American Society of Agricultural Engineers)

Making Hay, by Verlyn Klingenberg (Random House)

Who Will Feed China? Wake-Up Call for a Small Planet, by Lester R. Brown (Norton)

To Learn More

American Society of Agricultural
  Engineers
2590 Niles Road
St. Joseph, MI 48095-90659
(616) 429-0300; fax (616) 429-3852
E-mail: hq@asae.org
Internet site: http://www.asae.org

Tau Beta Pi
University of Tennessee
POB 2697
Knoxville, TN 37901-2697
(413) 546-4578; fax (413) 546-4579
E-mail: tbp@tbp.org
Internet site: http://www.tbp.org

American Studies and Culture

From the beginning, intellectual and spiritual diversity has been as characteristic of America as racial and linguistic diversity. From the beginning, Americans have known there were new worlds to conquer, new truths to be discovered. Every effort to confine Americanism to a single pattern, to constrain it to a single formula, is disloyalty to everything that is valid in Americanism.
—*Henry Steele Commager, historian and educator, in* Freedom, Loyalty, Dissent

What to Expect

American studies encompass the experiences, values, perspectives, concerns, contributions, encounters, and conflicts of the diverse groups that make up the United States. Your work will delve into a cross section of other fields, ranging from the arts and social sciences to history and literature. You'll learn to make comparisons, think more creatively and expansively, and write analytically. Introductory courses typically survey American culture from colonization to the present with resources as varied as film, fiction, music, history, art, photography, and architecture. While it began as a cross breeding of American literature and U.S. history, the field has broadened significantly to include both the knowledge and the analytical tools of anthropology, sociology, the arts, gender studies, ethnic studies, religion, education, and philosophy. Classes reflect that interbreeding. At a more advanced level, you may concentrate on a theme such as regionalism, law and society, or gender roles. American studies majors often go into teaching or work for museums, cultural organizations, arts agencies, or government.

Trends

Trends in American studies and culture include growing attention to international factors. For example, you may learn about the ways immigrants have shaped—and continue to reshape—U.S. culture. At the same time, you may assess the ways American popular culture reshapes foreign societies, especially when telecommunications and transportation make it so easy to "export" American culture, for better or for worse. A second trend reflects the continued effort to give deserved intellectual attention to—and appreciation of—the cultural influences of traditionally underrepresented people in American society: women, homosexuals, and ethnic and racial minorities.

What You Need to Succeed

You must be open minded to pursue a career in American studies. That means a capacity to set aside stereotypes, clichés, and traditionally narrow ways of approaching problems.

Analytical and writing skills and a willingness to read voraciously are essential because you'll be exploring differences and commonalities, trying to distill themes that can improve Americans' understanding of each other and the world. As you'll discover, each individual brings a slightly different perspective to cultural and social issues. That's why tolerance is critical as you better recognize the nation's ethnic, cultural, religious, gender, and economic diversity—and your place in it. Equally important are inquisitiveness and a love of the complex, of navigating intellectual twists and turns, and of working on issues for which there are no "right" or "wrong" answers. Any possible answer, you must recognize, is also affected by developments in other countries. Persistence, creativity, and diligence will strengthen your arguments, analyses, and conclusions.

Related Fields

African American Studies
English
History
Philosophy
Theater and Drama
Women's Studies

Typical Basic Courses

American Philosophy
American Political Thought
Community and Diversity in American
  Life
Introduction to Native American Studies
Periods in American Culture
Theater in America
Themes in American Culture
Women in America

An Array of Electives

American Autobiography
American Cultural Themes
American Ethnic and Racial Experience
Evolution of American Thought
Feminist Thought
Latino Literature of the United States
Music in America
New Worlds: Colonialism and Cultural
  Encounters

On-Campus Opportunities

Campus museum docent/guide
Research assistant

Job Opportunities

Surplus / Substantial oversupply

Reading to Explore

The Great Gatsby, by F. Scott Fitzgerald
(Cambridge University)

The Machine in the Garden, by Leo Marx
(Oxford University

The Majic Bus, by Douglas Brinkley
(Harcourt Brace)

*The Virgin Land: The American West as
Symbol & Myth*, by Henry Nash Smith
(Vintage)

Their Eyes Were Watching God, by Zora
Neale Hurston (University of Illinois)

To Learn More

American Studies Association
1120 19th St. N.W., Suite 301
Washington, DC 20036
(202) 467-4783; fax (202) 467-4786
E-mail: pp001366@mindspring.com
Internet site:
  http://www.georgetown.edu/crossroads

Animal Science

Animals are unpredictable things and often embarrass their doctors, but oh, those old black magic days with their exotic, largely useless medicines reeking of witchcraft.
—*James Herriot, veterinarian and author, in* Best of James Herriot

What to Expect

Traditionally, animal science has dealt primarily with livestock—cattle, horses, sheep, and pigs—and poultry. Today, however, it's also a foundation for careers in a variety of professions beyond farming and veterinary medicine, including caretaking, working in zoos and research laboratories, and protecting rare and endangered species. At the introductory level, you'll learn the fundamentals of animal physiology, genetics, nutrition, and management and have extensive opportunities to work directly with animals.

Advanced courses explore the scientific and the business aspects of the major. For example, you may study endocrinology, lactation biology, biotechnology, the physiology of particular types of animals such as poultry or swine, mating systems, and disease prevention. You also can take courses in marketing; equine, swine, sheep, cattle, or dairy cattle management; processed meats; and computer applications for animal science, among others. You'll refine laboratory skills as you conduct experiments and research on such topics as molecular reproductive endocrinology, protein metabolism, forage analysis, toxicology, and comparative nutrition.

Trends

Trends in animal science include issues of quality and safety of animal products, improvement of biological and management efficiency, sustainable agricultural systems, and environmental concerns. Biotechnology provides innovative approaches for confronting these challenges. There will be continued debate over how to provide safe, nutritious, and economical food, fiber, and recreation without compromising the welfare of animals or the environment. Other issues will involve government regulations, ranging from land use and zoning for farm production to safeguards for animal welfare and our food supply.

What You Need to Succeed

To begin with, you must enjoy working with and caring for animals. You also need a strong orientation toward the biological sciences, including anatomy, physiology, nutrition, and genetics. Depending on the type of animals you work with, you may spend a lot of time outdoors. The work is often physically demanding, you may work in far-from-sanitary conditions, and some duties, such as euthanizing hopelessly ill, aged, or injured animals, may prove emotionally stressful. Hours are often irregular because animals operate on different biological clocks than humans do. A patient nature is a very helpful attribute in this field.

An interest in new developments and research findings is important because you'll want to try advances in animal nutrition, veterinary medicine, sanitation, and breeding. Increasingly essential are business skills necessary to manage farms, kennels, ranches, and other operations. That includes a familiarity with accounting and bookkeeping, personnel management, and government regulations concerning animal care, veterinary medications, and zoning.

Related Fields

Biology
Crop and Soil Science
Entomology
Environmental Studies
Food and Nutrition
Zoology

Typical Basic Courses

Anatomy and Physiology of Farm
 Animals
Animal Reproduction
Food and Animal Toxicology
Introduction to Animal Agriculture
Introductory Animal Management
Livestock and Meats Judging
Principles of Feeding and Nutrition
Product and Livestock Marketing

An Array of Electives

Animal Biotechnology
Biology of Growth and Lactation
Enterprise Management
Farm Animal Genetics
Merchandising Livestock
Nonruminant Nutrition
Reproductive Endocrinology
Ruminant Nutrition

On-Campus Opportunities

Campus veterinary clinic
Laboratory assistant
Research assistant

Job Opportunities

Near balance / Supply equals demand

Reading to Explore

Deadly Feasts: Tracking the Secrets of a Terrifying New Plague, by Richard Rhodes (Simon & Schuster)

Hearts and Minds: The Controversy Over Laboratory Animals, by Julian M. Groves (Temple University)

Horse Power: A History of the Horse and Donkey in Human Societies, by Juliet Clutton-Brock (Harvard University)

The Best of James Herriot: Favourite Memories of a Country Vet, by James Herriot (St. Martin's/Reader's Digest)

The Last Ranch: A Colorado Community and the Coming Desert, by Sam Bingham (Pantheon)

To Learn More

American Society of Animal Science
1111 N. Dunlap Ave.
Savoy, IL 61874
(217) 356-3182; fax (217) 398-4110
E-mail: asas@asasochq.org
Internet site: http://www.asas.org

Anthropology and Archeology

If we are to achieve a richer culture, rich in contrasting values, we must recognize the whole gamut of human potentialities, and so weave a less arbitrary social fabric, one in which each diverse human gift will find a fitting place.
—*Margaret Mead, anthropologist, in* Sex and Temperament in Three Primitive Societies

What to Expect

From introductory survey courses to advance classes, you'll be exposed to four broad fields of study: cultural anthropology, physical anthropology, linguistics, and archeology. Each will teach you distinct skills, such as applying theories, using research methodologies, formulating and testing hypotheses, and developing data. The bottom line is the same: exploring the question of what it means to be human. To reach an answer, you'll study geographic differences, gender differences, cultural differences, language differences, biological differences, and differences throughout history. Classes could involve field work—interviewing people—as well as library research, computer analysis of data, and excavation of sites where long-dead people lived or worked. Upper-level courses let students focus on issues and research of particular interest, much of which crosses disciplinary lines. Options include primate and human evolution, magic and witchcraft, male-female conflicts, archeological exploration techniques, ethnicity and multiculturalism, native peoples in contemporary societies, and forensic identification of skeletal and dental remains. You may take courses dealing with a single geographic region such as Latin America, the Pacific and Oceana, the American West, or the Caribbean.

Trends

Trends in anthropology and archeology reflect an expansive definition of the field. More anthropologists will become involved in such areas as epidemiology, public health, health care, ecology, and community studies. Multiculturalism in American society and an increasingly global orientation in our economy will demand deeper understanding of foreign cultures and how they interact with our own. Laws designed to preserve evidence of past societies mean archeologists will play a bigger role when digging is required for highway and other construction projects.

What You Need to Succeed

Anthropologists must carefully observe humans, their behavior and their cultures. Archeologists must carefully observe the physical evidence of past human behavior and cultures. Members of both professions must be able to keep meticulous records and pay attention to the myriad details of data collection. Success requires a firm, broad background in math, statistics, science, biology, the arts, and history, as well as computer proficiency. Strong communications skills are mandatory as you conduct interviews and make your findings know to professionals and lay people. Be open minded about new areas, such as gender research.

For field work with foreign cultures—whether abroad or within the United States—language skills and social ease in strange situations are essential. Because you'll be called on to help solve intricate puzzles about life and society, a desire for intellectual stimulation is important. In addition, you must respect diversity in lifestyles and traditions, avoiding any attitude that your own culture is "superior" to the one you're studying.

Related Fields

African Languages and Cultures
Asian Languages and Cultures
History
Linguistics
Religious Studies and Theology
Sociology

Typical Basic Courses

Comparative World Cultures
Cultural Changes
Family and Kinship
Human Origins
Introductory Archeology
Survey of Cultural Anthropology
Survey of Physical Anthropology
World Prehistory

An Array of Electives

American Indians Today
Environmental Archeology
Introduction to Museums
Linguistic Anthropology
Magic, Witchcraft, and Religion
Maritime Peoples
Medical Anthropology
Peoples and Culture of Asia

On-Campus Opportunities

Campus museum guide/docent
Research assistant

Job Opportunities

Surplus / Substantial oversupply

Reading to Explore

Archaeology (magazine)

Kokopelli: Fluteplayer Images in Rock Art, by Dennis Slifer and James Duffield (Ancient City)

The Neanderthal Enigma: Solving the Mystery of Modern Human Savages, by Joe Kane (Vintage Departures)

Unraveling Piltdown: The Science Fraud of the Century and Its Solution, by John Evangelist Walsh (Random House)

To Learn More

American Anthropological Association
4350 N. Fairfax Drive, Suite 640
Arlington, VA 22203
(703) 528-1902; fax (703) 528-3546
E-mail: pevans@ameranthassn.org
Internet site:
  http://www.ameranthassn.org

Society for Historical Archaeology
P.O. Box 30446
Tucson, AZ 85751
(520) 886-8006; fax (520) 886-0182
E-mail: sha@azstarnet.com
Internet site:
  http://www.azstarnet.com/~sha

Architecture

When the architects are ghosts, the house is, of course, a nightmare.
—Alan Van Dine, designer and writer, in Unconventional Builders

What to Expect

Architecture's central concern is the quality of the human habitat and ways to design that habitat to accommodate a diverse, complex range of human activities. Courses start with the fundamentals of design and incorporate two divergent aspects that eventually unite. One looks back with a historical perspective on cultural, visual, natural, and constructed environments. The other looks forward into computer and other technological applications. You'll become familiar with construction materials, structural performance, and different architectural styles and philosophies. Tools of study include geographic information systems and acoustics labs. And you'll be exposed to sky and solar angle simulators, thermal testing chambers, weather stations, and testing equipment for materials and structural analysis.

As you progress, you'll expand your design abilities and may select specialized courses dealing with historic preservation, architectural history and criticism, computer-assisted design, or economic and social aspects of architecture. You'll also learn about legal requirements ranging from government permit regulations to the Americans with Disabilities Act.

Trends

Trends in architecture reflect innovative thinking, the availability of new technological tools to design buildings, and development of lighter and stronger construction materials that allow more alternatives for implementing those designs. As American society globalizes, architects will be influenced more by multicultural and international forces as they blend art and science in the design of environments for people. There will be growing attention to historic preservation and adaptive uses of historic structures for contemporary purposes, such as converting abandoned warehouses into condos or empty barns into retail shops while protecting their architectural integrity.

What You Need to Succeed

Begin with a sense of aesthetics, a desire to create, and an eagerness to work hard to transform your visions into tangible realities. You should be able to pay attention to fine details. Working in teams, making decisions, and communicating clearly are critical because architects don't work in a vacuum. They collaborate with colleagues within their own organizations and consult closely with clients, contractors and subcontractors, interior designers, mechanical engineers, landscape architects, product developers, and other professionals.

Imagination, freehand drawing skills, and a willingness to accept challenges are crucial, both in designing projects and in understanding the relationships between building design and human ecology—the psychological and cultural dimensions of a building. At the same time, recognize the fact that economics—project costs—may limit what your clients can afford to do. Finally, you must perform well under time pressure because delays and missed deadlines can prove costly—financially and professionally.

Related Fields

Art
Art History
Civil Engineering
Graphic Design
Landscape Architecture
Urban Planning

Typical Basic Courses

Architectural History
Architectural Theory
Building Construction
Design
Elements of Architecture
Graphics
Materials and Assembly
Structures

An Array of Electives

Architectural Criticism
Computer Applications
Construction Management
Contemporary Architecture Issues
Environmental Control Systems
Historic Preservation
Structural Innovations
Urban Design

On-Campus Opportunities

Campus buildings department
Campus planning department

Job Opportunities

Near balance / Supply equals demand

Reading to Explore

Rise of the New York Skyscraper, 1865–1913, by Sarah Bradford Landau and Carl W. Condit (Yale University)

The Power of Place: Urban Landscapes as Public History, by Dolores Hayden (MIT)

The Sand Dollar and the Slide Rule: Drawing Blueprints from Nature, by Delta Willis (Addison-Wesley)

The Unreal America: Architecture and Illusion, by Ada Louise Huxtable (New Press)

Unconventional Builders, by Alan Van Dine (J. G. Ferguson)

To Learn More

American Institute of Architects
1735 New York Ave. NW
Washington, DC 20006
(202) 626-7300; fax (202) 626-7587
E-mail: aia@aia.org
Internet site: http://www.aia.org

Art

We all know that art is not truth. Art is the lie that makes us realize truth—at least the truth that is given to us to understand.
—*Pablo Picasso, artist, quoted in the* New Yorker, *March 9, 1957*

What to Expect

The study of visual arts can help develop artistic and creative abilities, strengthen your analytical skills, and improve your ability to interpret the original work of others. Introductory courses lean toward the practical rather than the theoretical, helping you to develop aesthetic awareness and perceptual and inventive problem-solving abilities. You will get hands-on experience in drawing, painting, jewelry making, metalsmithing, sculpture, and other visual art disciplines. You'll gain exposure to a variety of mediums and materials, including oils, watercolors, pastels, pen and ink, pencils, plaster, metals, clay, silkscreen, film, paper, and even computers. Much of your time will be spent in art and design studios.

Advanced course work will polish your skills, expose you to more mediums, provide a deeper understanding of art theory and art history, and allow you to work closely with faculty who have professional as well as teaching credentials. Often, what you learn in one medium opens creative possibilities in other mediums. But art is more than a profession. Art studies can build life-long recreational interests, too, and you'll come to appreciate and understand the creativity and genius of past and present artists and artisans.

Trends

Trends in art include expanded use of computers, both as tools to assist in designing projects and as a medium to create art. Meanwhile, some artists will become increasingly involved in industrial and environmental design and the use of art and aesthetics in public places to improve the cultural quality of life. Another growth area is the use of art in therapy.

What You Need to Succeed

We communicate with images, and images that trigger ideas, thoughts, and feelings are created by artists. That's why you, as an artist, must be especially interested in what you see, regardless of medium. Colors, lines, and shapes must work for you. Relish the chance to invent new combinations of visual elements. In addition to imagination, creativity, and self-discipline, other assets are necessary. For example, scientific knowledge is necessary for a medical or scientific illustrator, and a growing number of artists use computer design techniques.

Often you'll work independently, choosing subjects and media that suit you, so become self-motivated and confident in your decision making. Become able to control your own time, since working hours are often unstructured. Inherently, artists' works are subject to public scrutiny and critiques, so you'll need a high level of self-worth and a realization that criticism of your work is not a personal attack. Be open to suggestions for improvement.

Related Fields

Architecture
Art History
Graphic Design
Photography and Cinema
Textiles and Apparel

Typical Basic Courses

Ceramics
Craft Design
Drawing
Introduction to Art Education
Principles of Art and Design
Printmaking
Visual Foundations
Watercolor Painting

An Array of Electives

Fiber and Fabric Design
Hand Papermaking
Jewelry and Metalsmithing
Life Drawing
Lithography
Sculpture
Weaving
Wood Design

On-Campus Opportunities

College museum or gallery

Job Opportunities

Surplus / Substantial oversupply

Reading to Explore

Painting as a Pastime, by Winston Churchill (Cornerstone)

Somehow a Past: The Autobiography of Marsden Hartley, by Marsden Hartley (MIT)

That's the Way I See It, by David Hockney (Chronicle)

The Art of Pottery, by Hugo Munsterberg (Viking Penguin)

The Letters of Vincent Van Gogh, by Ronald de Leeuw (Penguin)

To Learn More

College Art Association
275 Seventh Ave.
New York, NY 10001
(212) 691-1051; fax (212) 627-2381
E-mail: nyoffice@collegeart.org
Internet site: http://mufasa.mit.edu/caa

Art History

What we call "works of art" are not the results of some mysterious activity, but objects made by human beings for human beings. A picture looks so remote when it hangs glassed and framed on the wall. . . . But originally they were made to be touched and handled, they were bargained about, they were quarreled about, worried about."
—E. H. Gombrich, art historian and author, in The Story of Art

What to Expect

The history of sculpture, painting, crafts, and architecture from a range of geographical regions and cultural traditions is part of human history, part of creative development, and part of our values today. Even if you're not talented in creating art, you can study what the creativity of others has produced and find ways to share that knowledge with others. Introductory courses will familiarize you with a cross section of the physical results of human creativity in various eras, from prehistoric cave art through modern movements, such as Cubism.

From there, you'll move on to more advanced study, perhaps devoting your attention to the art of particular regions—the Far East, the American West, Southeast Asia—or particular times—the Renaissance, the Byzantine era, the Ming dynasty—or particular schools—Impressionism, Dadaism, the Hudson River School. You'll also become familiar with historic preservation methods, museum curatorship, theories of aesthetics, even the business and financial aspects of art sales, auctions, and collections.

Trends

Trends in art history draw from a growing awareness of society's multicultural roots and experiences. While study and appreciation of the so-called "Old Masters" won't disappear, more attention will be paid to the history of art from places other than Europe and North America. In addition, art historians will reach out to place a piece of art in the context of its times—to understand contemporary cultural, economic, and political forces and available materials that shaped the artist's or artisan's approach.

What You Need to Succeed

While art history by definition looks back, art historians also must look ahead to technology and science for preserving and restoring the past. You need an awareness that art was not created—nor is shown—in a vacuum. Instead, it's an integral component of a culture or mix of cultures, produced through imagination and talent with available materials. Whether or not you're an artist as well as an art historian, it's a field for nonjudgmental, tolerant thinking. There is no "wrong" reason to like a piece of art, and beauty is in the beholder's eye.

On a practical level, mastery of a foreign language will help in finding, interpreting, and displaying works of art. An understanding of museum and gallery curatorship is an asset, as is knowledge of restoration techniques. Many art historians are involved in acquisition and sales, so an interest in business may prove helpful.

Related Fields

Architecture
Art
Graphic Design
History
Photography and Cinema

Typical Basic Courses

Ancient Art
Art in America
Contemporary Art
Experiencing Art—Image, Artist, and Idea
Gothic and Renaissance Art
History of Visual Communication
Survey of Art History
Twentieth-Century Art

An Array of Electives

African Art
Art Historical Methods
Art of Islam
Latin American Art
Michelangelo
Museum Curatorship
Software Design in the Arts
Women in Art

On-Campus Opportunities

College museum and gallery

Job Opportunities

Surplus / Substantial oversupply

Reading to Explore

An Invitation to See: 150 Works from the Museum of Modern Art, by Helen M. Franc (Museum of Modern Art)

Beyond the Flower: The Autobiography of a Feminist Artist, by Judy Chicago (Viking)

Dawn of Art: The Chauvet Cave, by Jean-Marie Chauvet, Eliette Brunel Deschamps, Christian Hillaire, Paul G. Bahn, and Jean Clottes (Harry N. Abrams)

False Impressions: The Hunt for Big-Time Art Fakes, by Thomas Hoving (Simon & Schuster)

Painted Dreams: Native American Rock Art, by Thor Conway (NorthWord)

To Learn More

College Art Association
275 Seventh Ave.
New York, NY 10001
(212) 691-1051; fax (212) 627-2381
E-mail: nyoffice@collegeart.org
Internet site: http://mufasa.mit.edu/caa

American Association of Museums
1575 I St. NW, Suite 400
Washington, DC 20005
(202) 289-6575; fax (202) 289-6578
Internet site: http://www.aam-us.org

Asian Languages and Cultures

More attention to Asia and more light on Asiatic problems are crying needs of the day. It is not too much to say there can be no peace in the world without the cooperation of the peoples of Asia.
—*Herbert Adams Gibbons, historian and journalist, in* Asia *magazine (May 1924)*

Why to Expect

The Asia-Pacific region stretches over more than 30 countries, from Japan to Iran, from the former Soviet Union's Asian republics to New Zealand, and to the Pacific islands with their diverse, rich cultures and languages. The region has a rapidly growing economy and a population with close ties to peoples throughout the United States. Your classes will introduce you to many of the languages, religions, traditions, financial systems, politics, and languages of these nations. What you learn will mix aspects of linguistics, anthropology, history, economics, the arts, theology, foods, and international relations. You'll also become alert to stereotypes, develop an appreciation for different cultural values, and better understand Asian-American relationships and rivalries.

You can choose to concentrate your course work on a single nation—say, China, Korea, or India—or on a subregion, such as southeast Asia. More likely, you'll take a transnational approach and cross disciplines as well as national borders. For example, you could take advanced courses in the literature of different countries, or the history of several nations' music or art. You may want to focus on U.S. relations with the region, or on revolutionary movements, or on religions, or on comparative government.

Trends

Trends in Asian studies reflect the expanding commercial, political, technological, and cultural ties within Asia and between the region and the United States, Canada, and Europe. That includes not only trade and business, but also sensitive public-policy issues such as human rights and the conflicts between traditional values and feminism, minority rights, and religious freedom.

What You Need to Succeed

To study a region of the world like Asia, you need an open mind capable of absorbing and assessing information from traditional and nontraditional sources. Because nations evolve differently and maintain different standards and values, you need to think flexibly and not judgmentally. Your standards and way of thinking may be alien to people in this vast part of the world. Also, you should be willing to travel and to experiment with different customs and ways of life.

That open-mindedness must include enthusiasm for stepping over disciplinary lines so you can visualize connections between a society's music, theater, literature, political system, economics, educational institutions, and family relations. You need to address situations analytically, see patterns, and appreciate diversity so you can better draw accurate conclusions. Communication and observational skills are essential as you deal with people of varied heritages and values. Of course, you should become fluent in Asian languages.

Related Fields

Finance and Banking
Economics
History
Political Science
Religious Studies and Theology
South and Southeast Asian Studies

Typical Basic Courses

Arts of China
Asia: Social Sciences Perspectives
Asian Languages
Asian Political Systems
East Asian Cultures
Economic Development in Asia
Introduction to Asian History
Survey of Asian Religions

An Array of Electives

Ancient China
Ancient India
Asia Through Fiction
Asian American History
Asian Pacific Communities
Asian-U.S. Relations
Chinese Revolution
History of Japan

On-Campus Opportunities

International student center
Study-abroad programs office
Translator for foreign visitors

Job Opportunities

Surplus / Substantial oversupply

Reading to Explore

So Close to Heaven: The Vanishing Buddhist Kingdoms of the Himalayas, by Barbara Crossette (Vintage Departures)

The Age of Hirohito: In Search of Modern Japan, by Daikichi Irokawa (Free Press)

The Chinese Century: A Photographic History of the Last Hundred Years, by Jonathan D. Spence and Annping Chin (Random House)

The Great Game: The Struggle for Empire in Central Asia, by Peter Hopkirk (Kodansha Globe)

The Invisibles: A Tale of the Eunuchs of India, by Zia Jaffrey (Pantheon)

To Learn More

The Asia Society
725 Park Ave.
New York, NY 10021
(212) 288-6400; fax (212) 517-8315
E-mail: robertas@asiasoc.org
Internet site: http://www.askasia.org

Astronomy and Astrophysics

Born with the thirst of knowing about the stars.
—*Edgar Lee Masters, poet, in* Spoon River Anthology

What to Expect

Astronomy uses the principles of math and physics to explore the fundamental nature of the universe and can apply this knowledge to problems in navigation and space flight. Your studies will begin with an overview of the universe, including the celestial sphere, orbits, spectra, stars, asteroids, rings, the solar system, and stellar evolution. You'll also cover the interstellar medium, the Milky Way, galaxies, and the large-scale structure of the universe. Orbital mechanics, radiation laws, and thermal physics are part of the curriculum. From there, course work in basic astrophysics explores electromagnetic radiation, telescopes, and astronomical detectors, and you'll become familiar with various branches of astronomy—planetary, stellar, galactic, and extragalactic. Lab work is an integral part of the program.

More advanced courses teach astronomical observational techniques and how to do quantitative analysis of astronomical data. This involves practical experience with modern instrumentation and computer-based reduction, analysis, and data interpretation. Courses delve into multiwavelength studies of stars and galaxies, including distances, luminosities, masses, dynamics, and stellar populations. You can also explore high-energy astrophysics related to black holes, supernovae, gamma-ray bursts, and cosmic rays.

Trends

Trends in astronomy include working with information discovered by the Hubble Space Telescope, which enables us to see many galactic and extragalactic features previously unseen. Analysis of its findings will take decades. Astronomers will continue to pinpoint the age and the size of the universe and resolve contradictory evidence. At the same time, there's concern over cuts in government financial support for space and aerospace research and exploration.

What You Need to Succeed

Astronomy attracts people who combine a speculative spirit with a scientific bent. An inquisitive mind, imagination, diligence, and the capacity to work independently are important attributes. A great enthusiasm for stars, planets, and galaxies is vital, of course, but it's not enough. You'll also need analytical skills and a strong interest in research because virtually all astronomers conduct research, assess large amounts of data amassed by observatories and satellites, and prepare scientific reports and papers on their findings.

Computer skills are critical for research. Get a solid grounding in physics and math, as well as a mastery of optical telescopes, radio telescopes, and other instruments. Travel may be required. In addition, good communication skills will help you work in teams—with colleagues from your own country and abroad—and let you explain complex phenomena to lay people.

Related Fields

Aerospace and Astronautical Engineering
Mathematics
Physics

Typical Basic Courses

Frontiers of Astronomy
Geology of the Planets
Introduction to Astrophysics
Introduction to the Solar System
Observational Astronomy
Origin of the Elements
Quantum Mechanics
Stars and Galaxies

An Array of Electives

Fluid Dynamics
Galactic and Extragalactic Dynamics
Gravitational Astrophysics
High Energy Astrophysics
Instrumentation and Data Analysis
Modern Cosmology
Space Sciences Policy
Stellar Astrophysics

On-Campus Opportunities

Campus planetarium
Research assistant

Job Opportunities

Adequate supply / Some oversupply

Reading to Explore

Cosmos, by Carl Sagan (Random House)

Edwin Hubble: Mariner of the Nebulae, by Gale E. Christianson (University of Chicago)

Pale Blue Dot: A Vision of the Human Future in Space, by Carl Sagan (Random House)

Sky and Telescope (magazine)

The Planet Mars: A History of Observation and Discovery, by William Sheehan (University of Arizona)

To Learn More

The Planetary Society
65 N. Catalina Ave.
Pasadena, CA 91106
(818) 793-5100; fax (818) 793-5528
E-mail: tps@mars.planetary.org
Internet site: http://www.planetary.org

Atmospheric Science and Meteorology

There is no such thing as bad weather; every sky has its beauty, and storms which whip the blood do but make it pulse more vigorously.
—*George Gessin, author, cited in* The Crown Treasury of Relevant Quotations

What to Expect

In this field, you study the atmosphere—the air covering the earth—and the natural processes and forces responsible for how the air behaves. While the best-known application of the field is weather forecasting, your studies will also illustrate how weather information and meteorological research are used in agriculture, sea and air transportation, climactic trends, and air pollution. Initial coursework introduces you to the basics of radiation and energy budgets, thermodynamics, water vapor and clouds, winds, pressure, and circulation theory. You'll explore global dynamics and forecasting of large-scale weather events such as tornadoes and thunderstorms, plus learn to use thermodynamic diagrams and weather prediction software and do map analysis. You'll become familiar with sensors, Doppler radar, weather balloons, and other instrumentation used in climatology, research, and forecasting. Laboratory work is a key component of this program.

More advanced classes deal with weather dynamics, the planetary boundary layer, numerical weather predictions, and satellite meteorology. Computer modeling, air pollution predictions and controls, and atmospheric physics are among other options. Applications-oriented courses teach how to use climatological theory and computers to develop models for use in water resources, utilities, agriculture, construction, transportation, and recreation.

Trends

Trends in atmospheric science and meteorology include the drive to apply meteorological knowledge to environmental problems, such as ozone layer depletion, global warming, air pollution, and drought, and to further research solar energy and wind power. Computers will exert an increasingly potent influence in gathering and analyzing atmospheric information. And, atmospheric scientists will work even more closely with scientists and engineers in other disciplines.

What You Need to Succeed

As an atmospheric scientist, you may be expected to work long and often irregular hours, including weekends and holidays, because most weather stations operate 24 hours a day. The workload and stress are especially heavy during weather emergencies such as blizzards, hurricanes, tornadoes, floods, and thunderstorms. And there are time pressures, such as forecast deadlines, with which to contend.

Computer skills and a strong base in physics and mathematics are paramount, as is mastery of meteorological instruments and equipment. For instance, increasingly sophisticated computer models of the atmosphere are used for long-term, short-range, and local-area forecasts, and sophisticated equipment gathers data, transmits data, and monitors air emissions from factories. You should work to develop expertise in a related field such as engineering, physics, or agriculture. Also, build teamwork and communication skills, since meteorologists frequently work with other science professionals.

Related Fields

Biology
Environmental Studies
Geography
Geological and Earth Sciences

Typical Basic Courses

Atmospheric Thermodynamics and
   Hydrostatics
Basic Principles of Meteorology
Climate Dynamics
Evolution of the Earth System
Meteorological Observations and
   Instruments
Microclimatology
Physical Meteorology
Science of Earth Systems

An Array of Electives

Advanced Atmospheric Dynamics
Atmospheric Air Pollution
Biogeochemical Cycles, Agriculture, and
   the Environment
Environmental Biophysics
Mesoscale Meteorology
Modeling the Earth System
Natural Resources Management
Statistical Methods in Meteorology

On-Campus Opportunities

Campus museum
Research assistant

Job Opportunities

Adequate supply / Some oversupply

Reading to Explore

Beyond the Warning: The Hazards of Climate Predictions in the Age of Chaos, by Anthony Milne (Associated)

Braving the Elements, by David Laskin (Doubleday)

Laboratory Earth: The Planetary Gamble We Can't Afford to Lose, by Stephen H. Schreider (Basic)

The Heat Is On, by Ross Gelbspan (Addison-Wesley)

Twister, by Kay Davidson (Pocket Books)

To Learn More

American Meteorological Society
35 Beacon Street
Boston, MA 02108
(617) 227-2425; fax (617) 742-8718
E-mail: amspubs@ametos.org
Internet site: http://www.ametsoc.org/ams

Biochemistry

The microbial world and the world within our genes is always dynamic, and new threats appear or are discovered every year. For example, the threat of antibiotic-resistant microbial strains is no longer hypothetical—it is real. This and other threats to our nation's health demand our constant vigilance.
—*Susan Taylor, biochemist, letter in May/June 1995 newsletter of the American Society for Biochemistry and Molecular Biology*

What to Expect

An ever-growing arsenal of techniques helps researchers dissect the innermost secrets of the cell and develop new ways to detect and attack disease. As a biochemistry student, your introductory classes will build an understanding of those detection techniques and how to use them. You'll learn research methods in the lab and study life on every level, from individual molecules to the interconnected web of Earth's organisms—and all the bacteria, yeast, plants, and animals in between. Training will encompass molecular biology, chemistry, physics, and genetics, as well as the cultural and legal ramifications of biochemical discoveries. Higher-level classes will hone laboratory skills and teach you more about cell structure and such specialties as genetic engineering, X-ray crystallography, mass spectroscopy, and electron microscopy. Practical applications will sound a constant theme: how to apply this knowledge and these tools to solving biological, medical, pollution, agricultural, and pharmaceutical challenges.

Trends

Trends in biochemistry include linking the field to other disciplines—genetics, cell biology, and neurobiology, for example—because the science of biochemistry is the glue that holds everything in biology together. Beyond that, a major challenge will be confronting the limits of past breakthroughs. For example, some vaccines successful in the past have lost their effectiveness, and resistant strains of bacteria and viruses are evolving. There will be biochemical approaches to hereditary diseases, including Alzheimer's, heart disease, obesity, alcoholism, and some mental illnesses. Biochemists will also probe the nature of human thought and emotion. And if extraterrestrial organisms are discovered, biochemists will try to unlock the secrets of those alien life forms.

What You Need to Succeed

Attention to detail and precision are imperative. Biochemistry involves extensive laboratory work, an ability to plan strategies to transform theory into reality, and a patient, diligent, and detail-oriented personality. In other words, it's a form of high-stakes scientific detective work. You'll need an eagerness to learn, a natural curiosity about how life works, and an excitement about the opportunity to become an explorer in a microscopic world. You should enjoy hands-on work and have the self-confidence to persevere when one avenue of experimentation proves to be a dead end.

At the same time, your perspective should extend beyond the laboratory to weigh the ethical and societal impact of research on such problems as genetic defects, toxic chemicals, and genetically engineered crops. Issues such as these provoke intense public, moral, and political debates, so you should be able to articulate the reasons for your work, not merely the methodology and techniques you use.

Related Fields

Biology
Chemistry
Chemical Engineering
Micro and Molecular Biology
Pharmacy
Physics

Typical Basic Courses

Analytical Separations and Membranes
Biochemical Research Techniques
Chemistry of Life
General Genetics
Inorganic Chemistry
Introduction to Biochemical Activities
Introduction to Molecular Biology
Structure and Reactions in Biochemical
   Processes

An Array of Electives

Biochemical Techniques
Biophysics
Control of Gene Expression
Issues in Biochemistry
Medical Biochemistry
Metabolic Regulation
Nucleic Acids
Protein Structure

On-Campus Opportunities

Laboratory assistant
Research assistant

Job Opportunities

Near balance / Supply equals demand

Reading to Explore

Darwin's Black Box: The Biochemical Challenge to Evolution, by Michael J. Behe (Free Press)

Double Helix: Being a Personal Account of the Discovery of the Structure of DNA, by James D. Watson (Macmillan)

Force of Nature: The Life of Linus Pauling, by Thomas Hager (Simon & Schuster)

Free Radical: The Life of Albert Szent-Gyorgyi and the Battle over Vitamin C, by Ralph W. Moss (Paragon House)

Level 4: Virus Hunters of the CDC, by Joseph B. McCormick, Susan Fisher-Hoch, and Leslie Alan Horvitz (Turner)

To Learn More

American Society for Biochemistry and
   Molecular Biology
9650 Rockville Pike
Bethesda, MD 10814
(301) 530-7145; fax (301) 571-1824
E-mail: asbmb@asbmb.faseb.org
Internet site: http://www.faseb.org/asbmb

Biology

We will now discuss in a little more detail the struggle for existence.
—*Charles Darwin, scientist, in* On the Origin of Species

What to Expect

Biology is the science of life and offers many topics for study, including mammalogy, human and animal genetics, plant pathology, biological engineering, oceanography, cellular biology, environmental science, and conservation. That's why introductory courses survey a wide sweep of topics, from cell biology, applied botany, and human anatomy to bacteriology, ecology, and microbiology. This broad foundation integrates knowledge from different life sciences. You'll examine relationships among living organisms and their environments, cover basic concepts in physiology and molecular biology, and become familiar with cell functions and structure.

Laboratory work is at the core of many lower-level and advanced courses. By conducting experiments and using a variety of equipment and tools such as electron microscopes and computers, you can investigate processes such as enzyme action and the movement of substances through membranes, test contaminants, prepare biological specimens, and analyze research data. Field work may involve fisheries, forests, live specimen collection, and common organism identification. Other course options may deal with endocrinology, the biology of addictive drugs, molecular genetics, and wetlands ecology, among others. Research projects could involve medical parasites, reptiles and amphibians, birds, natural resource management, and aquaculture, among many topics.

Trends

Trends in biology are intimately tied to biotechnology, especially at molecular and genetic levels. Biotechnology is used in pharmaceuticals, medicine, and agriculture to make plants and animals more disease resistant or productive. For example, biologists in medical science may try to formulate a combination of drugs to reduce the effects of cancer, while those in agriculture may test genetic alterations to improve wheat or rice production.

What You Need to Succeed

You'll need to be curious about living things and want to learn scientific methods to observe and evaluate life processes. That involves developing a familiarity with scientific methods and equipment, as well as a willingness to keep current with new technological developments. You should be detail oriented in research, enjoy experimentation and hands-on lab and field work, and feel comfortable addressing what may be only a small part of a major problem, such as protecting species or combating diseases.

At times you may work independently, but at other times belong to a team. Either way, you must be able to communicate concisely and clearly, both in writing and verbally. Work in biology often involves field trips that feature physical activity and primitive living conditions. An interest in social and economic issues is valuable if you hope to play a role in decisions that require biological knowledge, such as debates involving health, natural resource management, education, and agriculture.

Related Fields

Botany
Crop and Soil Science
Environmental Studies
Forestry
Marine Biology and Oceanography
Zoology

Typical Basic Courses

Cell Biology
Environmental Biology
General Biology
Genetics
Human Anatomy
Human Biology
Introductory Bacteriology
Microbiology

An Array of Electives

Aquatic Ecology
Biology of Cancer
Biopolitics and Human Nature
Ecosystems
Evolution
Human Physiology
Mycology
Vertebrate Paleontology

On-Campus Opportunities

Laboratory assistant
Research assistant

Job Opportunities

Adequate supply / Some oversupply

Reading to Explore

A Natural History of the Senses, by Diane Ackerman (Vintage)

Life Itself: Exploring the Realm of the Living Cell, by Boyce Rensberger (Oxford University)

Lives of a Cell: Notes of a Biology Watcher, by Lewis Thomas (Viking Penguin)

Privileged Hands: A Scientific Life, by Geerat Vermeij (W.H. Freeman)

The Beauty of the Beastly: New Views on the Nature of Life, by Natalie Angier (Houghton Mifflin)

To Learn More

American Institute of Biological Sciences
1313 Dolley Madison Blvd.
McLean, VA 22101
(800) 992-2427; fax (703) 790-2672
E-mail: admin@aibs.org
Internet site: http://www.aibs.org

Botany

To his music plants and flowers ever sprung.
—*William Shakespeare, playwright, in* Henry VIII

What to Expect

Botanists are plant biologists, so your introductory courses will involve biology, evolution, genetics, and environmental interrelationships. Your studies will take you into the laboratory and outdoors, into the field. Tools include electron microscopes, radioisotopes, digital imaging analysis, polymerase chain reaction, cell and tissue culture, satellite imaging, and telemetry. You'll study processes that occur on a chronological scale ranging from fractions of a second to eons of evolutionary time. As a practical matter, you'll deal with a range of problems including food supply and production, plant pathology, and biological diversity.

If you have a mathematical mind, plant genetics, systems ecology, and developmental botany offer challenges. If chemistry is of interest, try courses in plant physiology and molecular biology. If you're concerned about food supply, pathology and plant breeding classes may appeal to you. And if you're interested in environmental issues, consider classes in ecology and evolutionary biology.

Trends

Trends in botany include an expanding emphasis on how plants fit into environmental protection concerns, including the design of safeguards for rare and endangered species. Another trend ties botanists to pharmacologists who research new medicinal uses of herbs and other plants for treatment and prevention of cancer and other diseases. Yet another trend involves the study of how genetic information in DNA controls plant development—knowledge that can improve crop yield and crop quality.

What You Need to Succeed

Plants—their diversity and the scientific mysteries they harbor—should intrigue you. You should harbor a sense of wonder about their varying complexity, their survival tactics, and their as-yet-undiscovered potential as sources of medicine, food, aromatics, even aesthetics. Beyond that, as a botanist, you need a solid foundation in the sciences, including chemistry, biology, geology, and physics, as well as in mathematics and computers. That foundation will help you understand the roles plant play in our ecosystems.

Attention to detail and precision are important attributes. Also important are verbal and written communications, so you can share your analysis and findings. Options within botany can accommodate a variety of orientations—toward laboratory research, teaching, field work, strategic planning, natural resource management, biotechnology, the theoretical, and the practical. Skills in hands-on work, in experimentation, and in analyzing environmentally related public and economic policies will help shape your success. It's important to be able to work cooperatively with other scientists.

Related Fields

Agricultural Engineering
Biology
Crop and Soil Science
Environmental Studies
Forestry
Horticulture

Typical Basic Courses

Aquatic Plant Biology
Dendrology
Ecology and Environmental Systems
Evolution
Fundamentals of Genetics
Introductory Plant Pathology
Plant Biology
Plants and Civilization

An Array of Electives

Biology of Fungi
Comparative Limnology
Diseases of Forest and Shade Trees
Plant Growth Regulation
Plant Physiology Metabolism
Plant Taxonomy
Principles of Mycology
Wetlands Ecology

On-Campus Opportunities

Campus grounds department
Laboratory assistant

Job Opportunities

Adequate supply / Some oversupply

Reading to Explore

An All-Consuming Passion: Origins, Modernity and the Australian Life of Georgiana Molloy, by William J. Lines (University of California)

Charles Darwin's Letters: A Selection, by Frederick Burkhardt (Cambridge University)

Preparing Scientific Illustrations, by Mary Helen Briscoe (Springer-Verlag)

The Medicinal Garden, by Anne McIntyre (Henry Holt)

The Private Life of Plants, by David Attenborough (Princeton University)

To Learn More

Botanical Society of America
1735 Neil Ave.
Columbus, OH 43210
(614) 292-3519; fax (614) 292-3519
E-mail: hiser.3@osu.edu
Internet Site: http://www.botany.org

Business Administration

Few people do business well who do nothing else.
—*Philip Dormer Stanhope, Earl of Chesterfield, diplomat and writer, in letter of Aug. 7, 1749 to his son*

What to Expect

As a prospective business manager, you need a solid grounding in economics, human relations, financial principles, accounting, and organizational behavior. Lower-level courses will expose you to purchasing, decision-making tools, human resource management, financial analysis, and management. You'll see how businesses interact with government, legal and political institutions, public policy, and each other. At a more advanced level, courses delve into entrepreneurship, taxation, marketing and logistics, retailing—even ways to use business administration concepts and practices in nonprofit, educational, and government agencies. You'll learn about business information systems as well. Undergraduate programs are increasing their emphasis on field-based learning opportunities—application of classroom theory to real-world problems—through internships and courses in which students act as consultants to local businesses. They're also encouraging students to think about quality management, ethics, and the management of innovation and technology in the workplace.

Trends

Trends in business administration reflect a global economy, the expansion of U.S. companies abroad, the operation of foreign companies in the United States, and a greater emphasis on diversifying the work force and opening career opportunities. A second strong trend is the continued move toward mergers, acquisitions, joint ventures, and corporate restructuring, which puts heavy pressure on business managers to adapt. A third is the ever-shifting degree of government regulation and oversight of business and industry, coupled with the use of business as a political ping-pong ball. And a fourth trend involves the changes—many driven by advertising and new technologies—in consumers' marketplace expectations.

What You Need to Succeed

The ability to work in teams, ease with computers and other technological tools, a bent toward planning, and strong communication skills are essential for success. Business organizations depend on teamwork rather than unilateral decisions as they develop and implement plans. Computers are necessary for financial analysis, asset and debt management, personnel and customer record keeping, and efficient research. Business strategies may take months or years to carry out, so long-term planning counts heavily. And you can't work well with colleagues and clients unless you can communicate clearly and persuasively. Finally, mastery of a foreign language will make you more useful as business operations cross borders, physically and electronically. Yet those attributes aren't enough. Your attention must extend beyond day-to-day duties to an awareness of governmental issues that affect your business, including environmental and safety regulations, tax and economic development policies, and international trade rules. And you must be able to analyze how those issues affect your operations.

Related Fields

Accounting
Economics
Finance and Banking
Human Resources and Personnel
   Management
Management
Public Policy Studies

Typical Basic Courses

Business Report Writing
Dynamics of Organizational Behavior
Fundamentals of Finance
Introductory Accounting
Law, Public Policy, and Business
Legal Environment of Business
Marketing Communications
Production/Operations Management

An Array of Electives

Entrepreneurship Law
Federal Income Taxation
Financial Markets
Health Services Administration
International Finance
Managerial Cost Accounting
Risk and Insurance
Small Business Management

On-Campus Opportunities

Business, bursar, controller's, and financial aid offices
Campus bookstore

Job Opportunities

Near balance / Supply equals demand

Reading to Explore

Built to Last: Successful Habits of Visionary Companies, by James C. Collins & Jerry I. Porras (Harper Business)

Company Man: The Rise and Fall of Corporate Life, by Anthony Sampson (Times/Random House)

Hard Landing: The Epic Contest for Power and Profits That Plunged the Airlines into Chaos, by Thomas Petzinger, Jr. (Times Business/Random House)

Managing in a Time of Great Change, by Peter F. Drucker (Truman Talley/Dutton)

The Chain Gang: One Newspaper Versus the Gannett Empire, by Richard McCord (University of Missouri)

To Learn More

American Assembly of Collegiate Schools
   of Business
600 Emerson Road, Suite 300
St. Louis, MO 63141
(314) 872-8481; fax (314-872-8495)
E-mail: sally@aacsb.edu
Internet site: http://www.aacsb.edu

Chemical Engineering

Whenever new fields of technology are developed, they will involve atoms and molecules. Those will have to be manipulated on a large scale, and that will mean chemical engineering will be involved—inevitably.
—*Isaac Asimov, scientist and science fiction author, in "The Future of Chemical Engineering,"* Chemical Engineering Prog., *Vol. 84, No. 1*

What to Expect

Chemical engineering blends the science of chemistry with the discipline of engineering. The goal: to link scientific knowledge to products created by the human mind. You will learn about the systems and technologies used to synthesize new materials and to transform combinations of elements safely, efficiently, and on a large scale. You'll start with the fundamentals, such as principles of chemical engineering and materials, learning about thermodynamics and energy balances, and laboratory experimentation in heat, mass transfer, and chemical reactor performance. From there, courses will explore biochemical engineering, process control, industrial applications, polymers, and other more technical topics. You may want to select an area to concentrate your studies, such as process engineering to learn how to create processes to meet a product's specific needs, or environmental control to develop pollution reduction strategies, or biomedical engineering to develop medical advances in biomaterials. Other courses can build skills in technical sales, consulting, and product development.

Trends

Trends in chemical engineering reflect the versatility of its professionals, who are moving into a range of growth areas including water and air pollution abatement, energy resources such as petroleum and solar power, recovery of natural resources, creation of cleaner fuels, and improved agriculture and food processing. In the future, chemical engineers will become more involved in manufacturing and developing medical supplies and pharmaceuticals, oceanographic and weather research, and developing biodegradable materials for packaging. Increasing numbers of chemical engineers are entering patent law and medicine.

What You Need to Succeed

As a chemical engineering student or professional, you'll rely on science, creativity, and ingenuity to produce and improve products economically. Problem-solving skills, an interest in experimentation and innovation, and an attention to detail are musts. So is the ability to work in teams with other engineers, as well as with production personnel and managers. Odds are that you'll spend at least some time overseeing and monitoring production, and that may require travel, especially if you work for a large corporation or as a consultant.

You also must feel comfortable in a lab setting, even if you're assigned primarily to a desk or to a factory. Mastery of math is very important in all areas, as is a mastery of computers. Knowledge of physics and business often proves helpful. Many chemical engineers also must understand laws and government regulations for environmental protection, control of toxic substances, and job health and safety.

Related Fields

Biochemistry
Chemistry
Materials Science and Engineering
Operations Research and Industrial
  Engineering
Petroleum Engineering

Typical Basic Courses

Chemical Engineering Materials
Chemical Engineering Principles
Chemical Reactor Design
Fluid Flow amd Heat Transfer
Introduction to Process and Design
Mass Transfer and Separations
Material and Energy Balances
Thermodynamics

An Array of Electives

Biochemical Engineering
Biological Transport Mechanisms
Catalysis and Kinetics
Chemical Reaction Engineering
Environmental Separations
Process Design
Process Dynamics and Control
Transport Phenomena

On-Campus Opportunities

Laboratory assistant
Research assistant

Job Opportunities

Good demand / Possible shortage

Reading to Explore

A History of the Dow Chemical Physics Laboratory: The Freedom to Be Creative, by Ray H. Boundy and J. Lawrence Amos (M. Dekker)

Chemical and Engineering News (Magazine)

Fifty Years Young: Products and Processes—The Future of Chemical Engineering, by J. Bridgwater (Cambridge University)

The Expanding World of Chemical Engineering, by John Garside and Shintaro Furusaki (Gordon and Breach Science)

The Making of an Engineer: An Illustrated History of Engineering Education in America, by Lawrence P. Grayson (Wiley)

To Learn More

American Institute of Chemical
  Engineers
345 E. 47th St.
New York, NY 10017
(212) 705-7338; fax (212) 705-3294
E-mail: xpress@aiche.org
Internet site: http://www.aiche.org

Chemistry

Chemists might sway, if they pleased, the destinies of humanity.
—*Wilkie Collins, novelist, in* The Woman in White

What to Expect

Chemists search for new knowledge about chemicals and put that knowledge to practical use. Your own studies can head in a wide-open range of career directions, from environmental chemistry, biotechnology, and materials science to medicinal chemistry, hazardous waste management, and agricultural chemistry. You'll start with the fundamentals by learning atomic and molecular theory, reactivities and properties of chemical substances, and the states of matter. These courses will introduce you to the basic subfields of organic, physical, analytical, and inorganic chemistry, as well as biochemistry. In the process, you'll acquire laboratory skills as well as familiarity with waste handling and safety equipment.

From there, courses tackle more advanced topics such as structure and bonding, chromatography, organic synthesis, molecular spectroscopy, lasers, photochemistry, and biochemical toxicology. Laboratory work will become more complex, and the problems more challenging as you build scientific apparatus and perform experiments. Experimental physical chemistry, for example, involves exploring chemical thermodynamics, statistical mechanics, and chemical kinetics. You'll also address societal and ethical aspects of chemistry.

Trends

Trends in chemistry include the continuing search for innovative and better products, including development of new industrial processes, cosmetics, synthetic fibers, and fuels. Environmental and health issues will continue to confront chemists from two directions. One challenge involves cleaning up past chemical contamination and preventing future public health problems and environmental consequences from exposure to chemical substances. The other challenge involves finding ways to use chemistry to solve environmental and health problems.

What You Need to Succeed

Chemists must be able to read, evaluate, and interpret information on a numerical, chemical, and general scientific level. You must enjoy working with your hands and be able to assemble experimental chemical apparatus, design experiments, and use appropriate instruments and technology to measure chemical properties and composition. You won't be able to rely on scientific knowledge alone, though. Without communication skills, you won't be able to instruct production workers and subordinates or make known the results of your scientific inquiries, findings, and conclusions. Attention to detail and a commitment to quality control are critical, especially given the potential hazards of some chemical materials. Perseverance, curiosity, and the ability to tackle procedures step-by-step are important. While you need the capacity to function independently, teamwork is important because many of your activities will involve fellow chemists, other scientists, engineers, technicians, and production workers. An understanding of business, marketing, economics, and increasingly complex government regulations might pay off.

Related Fields

Biochemistry
Chemical Engineering
Materials Science and Engineering
Micro and Molecular Biology
Nutrition and Food Science

Typical Required Courses

Chemistry in Modern Society
Chemistry in the Biosphere
Environmental Chemistry
Instrumental Analysis
Introductory Organic and Biochemistry
Modern Inorganic Chemistry
Physical Chemistry
Quantitative Analysis

An Array of Electives

Analytical Spectroscopy
Atmospheric Chemistry
Chemistry of Natural Waters
Chromatography and Analytical
  Separations
Electroanalytical Chemistry
Molecular Quantum Theory
Organic Synthesis
Structure and Bonding

On-Campus Opportunities

Laboratory assistant
Research assistant

Job Opportunities

Near balance / Supply equals demand

Reading to Explore

Bombardier Beetles and Fever Trees: A Close-Up Look at Chemical Warfare and Signals in Animals and Plants, by William Agosta (Addison-Wesley)

Braving the Elements, by Harry B. Gray, John D. Simon, and William C. Trogler (University Science)

Chemical Magic, by Leonard A. Ford and E. Winston Grundmeier (Dover)

Grand Obsession: Madame Curie and Her World, by Rosalynd Pflaum (Doubleday)

Our Stolen Future: Are We Threatening Our Own Fertility, Intelligence, and Survival?—A Scientific Detective Story, by Theo Colburn, Dianne Dumanoski, and John Peterson Myers (Dutton)

To Learn More

American Chemical Society
1155 16th St. NW
Washington, DC 20036
(202) 872-4600; fax (202) 872-4615
E-mail: education@acs.org
Internet site: http://www.acs.org

Civil Engineering

Stories in stone and steel.
—*Donald L. Miller, historian, in* City of the Century

What to Expect

From the pyramids of ancient Egypt to the Golden Gate Bridge to the "Chunnel" linking England and France, civil engineers have faced and helped solve challenges. Today, they confront a technological revolution, population growth, and problems ranging from pollution and urban redevelopment to energy needs and traffic congestion. Basic courses will introduce you to construction materials, structural analysis, and engineering applications for water systems, roads, buildings, transit systems, and other infrastructure. You'll learn to use computers and other sophisticated high-tech tools in project design, construction, scheduling, and cost control.

As you advance, specialized courses offer opportunities to probe structural, environmental, water resource, geotechnical, transportation, construction, and urban planning situations. You may take several higher-level courses in a single area, such as highways and pavement, where you'll learn about design, operations, traffic safety, and traffic flow theory. Transportation is another subfield, with courses on engineering for airports, railroads, and mass transit systems. You should emerge from the program with an understanding of construction-related business, law, and ethics, including legal liability issues and how to prepare contracts and specifications.

Trends

Trends in civil engineering will include increased gauging of environmental implications of construction and greater consideration of the human elements of projects. Those trends will require designs that minimize the adverse impact on natural habitats, use more recycled, energy-efficient, and nonhazardous materials in construction, and take into account the ramifications of a structure or system on neighborhoods. Civil engineers will be on the cutting edge of discoveries in such realms as solar power, high-speed rail lines, wastewater cleanup, and spacecraft.

What You Need to Succeed

Civil engineers are problem solvers who can apply technical and technological skills to major projects and have a strong drive for technical detail. A sense of community service, development, and improvement is important because public benefits and public costs are involved in the projects you'll tackle, including highways, water purification and hazardous waste treatment systems, and energy plants. Long-term vision is essential, because many projects take years to come to fruition and then last for decades, even centuries. Despite the long view, you also need to meet short-term deadlines, often with millions of dollars at stake.

Strong supervisory abilities and the capacity to weigh economic factors will enhance your career prospects, as will a broad understanding of design and construction techniques. Expect to be asked to present your ideas to clients, other decision makers, and the public, and be willing to incorporate suggestions and criticisms from other people.

Related Fields

Agricultural Engineering
Architecture
Environmental Studies
Landscape Architecture
Materials Science and Engineering
Urban Planning

Typical Basic Courses

Civil Engineering Materials
Construction Estimating and Scheduling
Fundamentals of Surveying
Introduction to Environmental
    Engineering
Introduction to Fluid Mechanics
Soil Mechanics
Structural Analysis
Transportation

An Array of Electives

Applied Hydraulics
Engineering Economics
Geotechnical Engineering
Hazardous Waste Management
Pavement Design and Analysis
Structural Mechanics
Transportation Planning
Water and Wastewater Treatment

On-Campus Opportunities

Campus buildings department
Campus grounds department
Campus physical plant

Job Opportunities

Good demand / Possible shortage

Reading to Explore

City of the Century, by Donald L. Miller (Simon & Schuster)

Engineers of Dreams: Great Bridge Builders and the Spanning of America, by Henry Petroski (Vintage)

Hoover Dam: An American Adventure, by Joseph E. Stevens (University of Oklahoma)

Rise of the New York Skyscraper, 1865–1913, by Sarah Bradford Landau and Carl W. Condit (Yale University)

To Engineer Is Human: The Role of Failure in Successful Design, by Henry Petroski (Vintage)

To Learn More

American Society of Civil Engineers
1801 Alexander Bell Drive
Reston, VA 20191
(800) 548-ASCE; fax (703) 295-6131
E-mail: student1@asce.org
Internet site: http://www.asce.org

Classical Languages and Classics

Ancient times were the youth of the world.
—*Francis Bacon, philosopher and essayist, in* De Dignitate of Augmentis Scientarium

What to Expect

To many, the study, preservation, and advancement of our classical inheritance from Greece and Rome seem unrelated to modern life. Not so. Classical languages and classics are closely tied to Western heritage and contemporary languages. As a student in the field, you'll become immersed in the tongues, the literature, and the cultures of ancient times. There will, of course, be Latin and Greek to master. In addition, classes will familiarize you with aspects of ancient history, religions, philosophy, government structures, drama, poetry, art, and archeology, from Homer to the end of classical antiquity. You'll also become familiar with other ancient civilizations, such as Minoa, Mycenaea, and the Byzantine empire.

From there, you'll advance into detailed studies of the works of ancient writers and how their writings reflect a scientific, sociological, cultural, and political world that is long gone but still influential. In the literary realm, you can focus on tragedy or comedy; in the religious realm, the transition from paganism to Christianity. Not all topics will be thousands of years removed from today's world. You'll have the opportunity to consider such current topics as sports, food, fashion, gender roles, and economics—but from a different perspective.

Trends

Trends in classical languages and classics include closer relationships with allied professions, particularly archeology and history, and research into patterns of ancient life that relate to contemporary issues, such as the role of women, slavery, homosexuality, and the genesis of literary traditions, scientific theories, and democratic thought.

What You Need to Succeed

You'll need a flair for foreign languages and history, and an enjoyment of intellectual challenges that generally don't carry immediate rewards. You'll need to communicate well verbally and in writing, tailoring your communication to your audience, whether students, lay people, or scholars. Aside from that, you need strong research skills, a willingness to work with complicated documents, diligence, and imagination, because this is not a field where dramatic, short-term "breakthroughs" and discoveries are typically made.

Remember, this is a field open to speculation and multiple approaches to reasoning. Despite centuries of study, debate, and interpretation, many questions remain unanswered about how ancient people lived, what they thought, and how they interacted. In addition, many writings disappeared, leaving gaps in the documentary record. You should be able to read and think critically and to love learning for learning's sake as well as for the intellectual challenge.

Related Fields

Anthropology and Archeology
History
Linguistics
Philosophy
Religious Studies and Theology

Typical Basic Courses

Ancient Philosophy
Greek
Greek and Roman Art
Greek Civilization
Introduction to Ancient Studies
Latin
Mythology
Roman Civilization

An Array of Electives

Ancient Athletics
Ancient Literary Criticism
English from Latin and Greek Roots
Food in the Ancient World
Greek and Roman Religions
Roman and Greek Drama
Topics in Latin Poetry
Women in Antiquity

On-Campus Opportunities

Campus museum

Job Opportunities

Surplus / Substantial oversupply

Reading to Explore

A Short History of Byzantium, by John Julius Norwich (Knopf)

Ancient Greece: From Prehistoric to Hellenistic Times, by Thomas R. Martin (Yale University)

Black Athena Revisited, by Mary R. Lefkowitz and Guy MacLean Rogers (University of North Carolina)

I, Claudius: From the Autobiography of Tiberius Claudius, by Robert Graves (Vintage)

Schliemann of Troy: Treasure and Deceit, by David A. Traill (St. Martin's)

To Learn More

American Classical League
Miami University
Oxford, OH 45056
(513) 529-7741; fax (513) 529-7742
E-mail:
    americanclassicalleague@muohio.edu
Internet site:
    http://www.umich.edu/~acleague

Cognitive Science

I think, therefore I am.
—*René Descartes, philosopher, cited in* Bartlett's Familiar Quotations

What to Expect

The solid foundation for this relatively new, interdisciplinary field is a tripod comprising computer science, cognitive psychology, and philosophy. In each of these three disciplines, you'll learn fundamental concepts and methods that help shed light on one of contemporary science's most baffling enigmas: the nature of human thought and consciousness. Basic courses will include computers and the mind, foundations of artificial intelligence, introduction to human memory, and philosophy of the cognitive sciences. You'll find useful allied classes in information-processing theory, developmental psychology, human perception, psycholinguistics, and semantics.

As you progress, advanced courses will allow you to explore deeply the philosophical underpinnings of computer functioning and design, human intelligence and learning, and the treatment of cognitive disorders in children, adults, and the elderly. Classes in human-machine interaction, robotics and machine vision, and bioengineering principles will be useful for theoretical views. To gain knowledge about applied fields, study brain anatomy, cognitive neuroscience, practical linguistics, and communication disorders.

Trends

Trends in cognitive science include a greater emphasis on computer simulation of human intelligence. As technology advances with stunning speed, the ability to function effectively with advanced software and hardware—and also to develop and refine computer-based models—will become crucial. There is also growing scientific interest in cognition and problem solving among primates and other nonhuman animals—both for the benefit such research can bring to the study of human intelligence, and also for its philosophical and ecological implications. As new findings rapidly emerge in genetics and embryology, neuroanatomy, and environmental medicine, cognitive scientists will offer their skills in multidisciplinary efforts to understand and treat Alzheimer's disease, autism, schizophrenia, aphasia, attention-deficit disorder, and other cognitive impairments.

What You Need to Succeed

In this rapidly evolving field bridging psychology, the life sciences, and computer science, it's imperative to have strong research skills. Not only do you need to be well versed in each of these disciplines—and such subspecialties as biochemistry and molecular biology—but you must think creatively, even boldly. Perhaps because cognitive science is so new, its participants routinely make leaps of intuition across chasms of knowledge concerning the mysteries of human thought, rationality, and problem solving. You'll use tools that include sophisticated computers, high-level statistics and probability, and sometimes medical, biological, and zoological instruments in laboratory settings. Not only should you enjoy broadly theorizing on unresolved questions about the human mind that have proven baffling for millennia, you should also possess the ability to handle highly specific data methodically and precisely. Because most cognitive scientists constantly share their findings with those in other disciplines, good communication as well as analytical skills are a must.

Related Fields

Biology
Computer Science
Philosophy
Psychology

Typical Basic Courses

Cognitive Processes in Development
Computers and the Mind
Foundations of Artificial Intelligence
Introduction to Cognitive Science
Introduction to Human Memory
Neurobiology and Behavior
Philosophy of the Cognitive Sciences
Thinking and Reasoning

An Array of Electives

Biocoustic Signals in Animals and Man
Cognitive Neuroscience
Comparative Cognition
Human-Machine Interaction
Information Processing: Conscious and
    Nonconscious
Robotics and Machine Vision
The Cognitive Psychology of Oral
    Traditions
Typical and Atypical Intellectual
    Development

On-Campus Opportunities

Campus museum
Research assistant

Job Opportunities

Surplus / Substantial oversupply

Reading to Explore

After Thought: The Computer Challenge to Human Intelligence, by James Bailey (Basic Books)

How Brains Think, by William H. Calvin (Basic Books)

Searching for Memory: The Brain, the Mind, and the Past, by Daniel L. Schacter (Basic Books)

The Emotional Brain, by Joseph LeDoux (Simon & Schuster)

The Thinking Ape: Evolutionary Origins of Intelligence, by Richard Byrne (Oxford University)

To Learn More

American Psychological Association
750 First Street NW
Washington, DC 20002
(202) 336-5500; fax (202) 336-5568
E-mail: webmaster@apa.org
Internet site: http://www.apa.org

Computer Science

The computer has the potential to be a tool to leverage human intelligence.
—*Bill Gates, computer entrepreneur, in* The Road Ahead

What to Expect

Computer science is a rapidly evolving field that involves the understanding and design of computers and computational processes. Students study digital computers and how to use them for effective processing of information. You'll be concerned with the representation of information and its transformation. Courses range from theoretical studies of algorithms—calculations used to solve problems—to practical issues related to hardware and software design. That means balancing practical skills with exposure to the underlying concepts, and learning to apply them to real-world situations. You'll study programming methodology and languages, database systems, networking and communication, parallel and distributed computation, computer-human interaction, software engineering, and artificial intelligence.

Through course work, you'll discover the inherent meshing of theoretical concepts of computability and algorithmic efficiency with the latest advances in processor and memory technologies. In addition, classes, research, and hands-on work will illuminate the interdependence of hardware and software and help you appreciate the challenges of large-scale software production and engineering principles. That knowledge can lead to careers in programming, systems analysis, data processing and database management, communications, and consulting.

Trends

Trends in computer science reflect a boom in information systems and the Internet as computers become faster, more affordable, more versatile, more prevalent, and more indispensable to our society. Their usefulness will become increasingly evident in areas from agriculture to science, from school rooms to the factory, from government to transportation, and from the arts and humanities to businesses. Increasingly, computer scientists will become more than mere techies; they'll need to master the substance of the information they work with, develop managerial skills, and contribute to making business decisions for their employers.

What You Need to Succeed

As a computer science student or professional, you'll need a firm foundation in mathematics and science. You'll also need a broad liberal studies education to understand the societal implications of your work and to understand your employer's operation, whether in business, science, manufacturing, engineering, education, or another field. You should be able to apply the fundamental concepts and techniques of computation, algorithms, and computer design to specific problems. That includes detailing specifications, analyzing problems, and providing a reliable design that functions as desired and meets cost criteria.

Do you enjoy working with ideas and people, not just machines? Although computer scientists frequently work independently, they also team up for large projects. Therefore, they must communicate effectively with other computer personnel and with staffers who lack technical computer backgrounds. Creativity and a sense of innovation provide an advantage in developing software, Web sites, and even computer games.

Related Fields

Business Administration
Cognitive Science
Electrical Engineering
Mathematics

Typical Basic Courses

Algorithms and Computing
Assembly Language Programming
Automata and Language Theory
Computer Applications
Data Structures and Programming
  Concepts
Discrete Computational Structures
File Organization
Introduction to Operating Systems

An Array of Electives

Artificial Intelligence
Compilers
Computer Architecture
Computer Graphics
Database Systems
Networks
Parallel and Distributed Computing
Software Specification and Design

On-Campus Opportunities

Computer centers and labs
Programming
Research assistant
Web page design

Job Opportunities

High demand / Limited supply

Reading to Explore

A History of the Information Machine, by Martin Campbell-Kelly and William Aspray (Basic Books)

Engines of the Mind: The Evolution of the Computer from Mainframes to Microprocessors, by Joel Shurkin (Norton)

High Noon on the Electronic Frontier, by Peter Ludlow (MIT)

Trust Me, I'm Your Software, by Nancy G. Leveson (Addison-Wesley)

Twenty-Four Hours in Cyberspace, by Rich Smolan and Jennifer Erwitt (Que/Macmillan)

To Learn More

Computing Sciences Accreditation Board
2 Landmark Square, Suite 209
Stamford, CT 06901
(203) 975-1117; fax (203) 975-1222
E-mail csab@csab.org
Internet site: http://csab.org/~csab

Criminal Justice

Unless justice be done to others it will not be done to us.
—*Woodrow Wilson, president, as quoted in* Peter's Quotations: Ideas for Our Time

What to Expect

Crime prevention, safeguarding life and property, preserving peace and civil rights, and maintaining social order with justice and freedom are essential to a democratic society. To prepare you to help accomplish those goals, the criminal justice curriculum merges topics in psychology, sociology, political science, geography, education, and anthropology. Courses will help you understand the causes of crime, how to control it, and how to administer criminal justice and corporate security agencies. You'll be introduced to criminology, juvenile justice, corrections, and policing, with attention to current issues and problems. You'll become familiar with the courts and legal system, as well as research methods. As an upper-class student, you may choose an area of specialization—most often law enforcement, corrections, juvenile justice, or private security. You will examine criminal justice programs and policies, prevention of crime and delinquency, substance abuse, and modern investigative, computer, and forensic tools to deter and detect crime. You'll discover how criminal justice interacts with sometimes-competing social and cultural values.

Trends

Trends in criminal justice include the development of alternatives to incarceration, especially for nonviolent offenders, as prisons and jails become more costly and crowded. Privately run jails, prisons, and juvenile facilities will become more common. Another area of change is technological, as investigators use increasingly sophisticated scientific tools to analyze DNA and other evidence. There will be more attention paid to prevention programs for at-risk youth. Finally, industry and business demand improved security systems for computers, trade secrets, and facilities, as well as protection against terrorism at home and internationally.

What You Need to Succeed

This is a demanding, high-pressure profession, often requiring long hours on the job, close teamwork, and extensive paperwork. Personal responsibility and a high standard of ethics are musts, as is a commitment to public service. Many jobs, such as law enforcement and corrections officers, have physical fitness and psychological standards as well. Good communication skills are vital because professionals interact—often in the public eye—with colleagues, community residents, lawyers, judges, journalists, witnesses, criminals, and inmates. Juvenile justice careers require skills in counseling and empathetic listening. For investigative positions, you're expected to have an analytical mind, strong interviewing skills, an interest in problem solving, and a willingness to persevere. That means following up often-ambiguous tips and information, understanding the sophisticated scientific tools available to investigators, and developing insights into the psychology of criminals, witnesses, victims, and even judges, lawyers, and fellow officers. Finally, law enforcement agencies are quasi-military, so you must feel comfortable within a highly disciplined structure.

Related Fields

Political Science
Psychology
Public Policy Studies
Social Work
Sociology
Urban Studies

Typical Basic Courses

American Judicial Process
Corrections
Criminal Law Process
Criminology
Introduction to Private Security
Juvenile Justice Process
Police Procedures
Survey of Criminal Justice

An Array of Electives

Asset Protection Management
Correctional Programming and Analysis
Crime and Social Policy
Delinquency and Treatment
Intelligence Operations
Introduction to Forensic Science
Investigative Procedures
Police Administration

On-Campus Opportunities

Campus police cadet
Parking enforcement
Security office

Job Opportunities

Adequate supply / Some oversupply

Reading to Explore

Cop: A True Story, by Michael L. Middleton (Contemporary)

Dead Man Walking, by Helen Prejean (Vintage)

Fist Stick Knife Gun: A Personal History of Violence in America, by Geoffrey Canada (Beacon)

The New Ethnic Mobs: The Changing Face of Organized Crime in America, by William Kleinknecht (Free Press)

The Oxford History of the Prison: The Practice of Punishment in Western Society, by Norval Morris and David J. Rothman (Oxford University)

To Learn More

American Correctional Association
4380 Forbes Blvd.
Lanham, MD 20706
(301) 918-1800; fax (301) 918-1900
E-mail: aca.org@corrections.com
Internet site:
  http://www.corrections.com/aca

International Association of Chiefs of
  Police
515 N. Washington St.
Alexandria, VA 22314
(800) 843-4227; fax (703) 836-4543
Internet site:
  http://www.internationalchiefs.org

Crop and Soil Science

To smell to a turf of fresh earth is wholesome for the body; no less are thoughts of mortality cordial to the soul.
—*Thomas Fuller, British minister and writer, in "The Virtuous Lady"*

What to Expect

Natural sciences, agriculture, and economics come together here. The goal of the soil scientist is to improve the fertility as well as the chemical, physical, and microbial characteristics of soil. The goal of the crop scientist is to increase plant production, quality, and profit through breeding, genetics, and physiology. Your basic courses will introduce you to all these aspects of the field. They'll sensitize you to relationships, too, such as those among soil, plants, and animals. There's a heavy emphasis on chemistry, plant biology, and genetics, with extensive laboratory work and field experience.

At a higher level, you'll see more cross-fertilization where biology and physics overlap, or where biology, geology, and chemistry join. You'll learn how many past crop production practices caused environmental problems, while the general decline in environmental quality has harmed crop production and the soil. Advanced courses will put crop and soil science into a broader context with environmental issues, recreational applications such as golf courses and parks, quality-of-life concerns, landscaping, and crop management.

Trends

Trends in crop and soil science reflect increasing societal demands to protect our soil and water resources, as well as an escalating need to remediate contaminated soil and water. Meanwhile, a population boom coupled with shrinking agricultural land—especially in developing nations—strains the ability of farmers to increase yield and produce enough crops to sustain that population. And environmental concerns and controls will make it tougher to use many chemical fertilizers and pesticides, putting pressure on crop and soil researchers to find nonhazardous alternatives.

What You Need to Succeed

Your foundation should be an interest in natural sciences, environmental issues, and appropriate uses of the earth's resources for productive purposes. Strong research and laboratory skills are essential for success, coupled with a yen to experiment and an ability to apply research findings systematically to actual problems. Technology will become a more potent weapon in the crop and soil scientist's arsenal, so you must be comfortable with advances in biotechnology, genetic redesign, computer analysis, and the use of high-altitude infrared photographic imagery. You should recognize that crops and soil are only part of a vast, complex ecosystem that varies from farm to farm, from region to region. That's why a cooperative approach and holistic thinking about complex problems are necessary to work effectively with other scientists, business representatives, farmers and growers, property owners, engineers, and government regulators. Finally, familiarity with principles of business and management pay off if you enter industry, agribusiness, or public service.

Related Fields

Biology
Botany
Entomology
Forestry
Geological and Earth Sciences
Horticulture

Typical Basic Courses

Computer Applications in Agronomy
Forage Crops
Introduction to Agronomy
Introductory Plant Genetics
Principles of Crop Production
Soil and Landscape Fundamentals
Turfgrass Management
Weed Science

An Array of Electives

Biogeochemistry
Crop Physiology
Crop Systems Management
Forest Hydrology
Microbial Ecology
Seed Production and Technology
Soil Biophysics
Soil Management and Environmental
  Impact

On-Campus Opportunities

Campus greenhouses
Campus grounds department
Research assistant

Job Opportunities

Near balance / Supply equals demand

Reading to Explore

Advance of the Fungi, by Ernest C. Lange (Henry Holt)

Dirt: The Ecstatic Skin of the Earth, by William Bryant Logan (Riverhead/Putnam)

Out of the Earth: Civilization and the Life of the Soil, by Daniel Hiller (University of California)

The Forgotten Pollinators, by Stephen L. Buchmann and Gary Paul Nabhan (Island Press/Shearwater)

The Last Harvest: The Genetic Gamble That Threatens to Destroy American Agriculture, by Paul Raeburn (Simon & Schuster)

To Learn More

American Society of Agronomy
677 S. Segoe Road
Madison, WI 53711
(608) 273-8080; fax (608) 273-2021
E-mail: lmalison@agronomy.org
Internet site: http://www.agronomy.org

Dance

Dancing is the loftiest, the most moving, the most beautiful of the arts because it is no mere translation of abstraction from life; it is life itself.
—*Havelock Ellis, psychologist and author, in* The Dance of Life

What to Expect

Dancers have always used their talents and their bodies to convey ideas, rhythm, stories, and sound, regardless of the form of the art they choose. Strenuous and time-consuming training in the studio under an instructor's supervision goes hand-in-hand with classroom lessons. Lower-level courses familiarize you with different genres: classical ballet, jazz, modern dance, tap, and ethnic dance. They also introduce you to production, composition, movement analysis, music theory, and dance history.

As you progress, courses and training build your skills. In addition, they instill a better understanding of the role dance plays in our cultures and of its relationships with other performing arts, including films, musicals, and even symphonic concerts. At this level you'll find opportunities for involvement in production, theatrical equipment and systems, lighting design, dance administration, and musical resources. An advanced choreography class will let you design and present a piece for public performance and critique.

Trends

Trends in dance reflect efforts to incorporate the performing arts into elementary and secondary school curricula more fully and to distill the myth that dance is an elitist—rather than a popular—form of entertainment. Increasingly, dance troupes will strive to build community support. They'll also stress physical fitness aspects to entice more recreational dancers. Attention to ethnic forms of dance will continue to expand, and the flow of immigrants to the United States will ensure that the mix of styles broadens as well. At the same time, dance companies and educators will be vigilant about potential cuts in government funding for the arts.

What You Need to Succeed

Patience, tenacity, diligence, and a devotion to dance are essential because your life as a dancer demands self-discipline and intensive rehearsing. Physical stamina and good health are necessary for practice, performance, and adherence to a rugged schedule that may require long hours, including weekends and holidays. Travel may be involved. You should be agile, flexible, graceful, and well coordinated, with a feeling for music, a sense of rhythm, and the creative capacity to express yourself through movement. An innovative nature and a willingness to experiment are essential in choreography.

You must be able to work cooperatively with other dancers, choreographers, musicians, directors, and performers. Many dancers develop additional performing skills, usually singing and acting. You must be amenable to constructive criticism, to adaptation, and to public appearances. To teach dance requires tolerance for the mistakes of others, as well as an inner drive to guide and inspire.

Related Fields

Music
Music History
Theater and Drama

Typical Basic Courses

Aspects of Rhythmic Movement and
   Dance
Ballet
Choreography
Dance as a Universal Language
Dance Improvisation
Jazz
Modern Dance
Movement Awareness and Injury
   Prevention for the Performing Artist

An Array of Electives

Ballroom Dancing
Concert and Theater Dance
Dance History and Philosophy
Dance Management
Dance Teaching Methods
Folk and Square Dance
Lighting and Staging for Dance
Teaching Children's Dance

On-Campus Opportunities

Campus theater

Job Opportunities

Surplus / Substantial oversupply

Reading to Explore

Diaghilev and the Ballets Russes by Boris Kochno (Harper and Row)

Nijinsky, Pavlova, Duncan: Three Lives in Dance, by Paul Magriel (De Capo)

Razzle Dazzle: The Life and Work of Bob Fosse, by Kevin Boyd Grubb (St. Martin's)

The Dance Through the Ages, by Walter Sorell (Grossett and Dunlap)

To a Young Dancer: A Handbook, by Agnes de Mille (Little, Brown)

To Learn More

Dance/USA
1156 15th St. NW, Suite 820
Washington, DC 20005
(202) 833-1717; fax (202) 833-2686
E-mail: danceusa@artswire.org
Internet site:
   http://artsnet.heinz.cmu.edu/~danceusa

Early Childhood Education

Make glad the heart of childhood.
—*Francis Pharcellus Church, editorial writer, in the* New York Sun, *Sept. 21, 1897*

What to Expect

From birth through the age of eight, children learn, change, and grow remarkably fast. Experiences during that period influence them throughout their lives. Competent and loving child care contributes to a child's development and the family's well-being. Through courses and real-world exposure, you'll learn elements of psychology, sociology, cognitive science, human biology, health, social work, and the creative arts, all in the context of helping young children mature.

A meaningful undergraduate curriculum should involve more than theory, so you should do field research, observation, and practicums at child care facilities, community centers, or kindergarten classrooms. Advanced courses deal in depth with such topics as children with special needs, public policy concerning child care, encouragement of language arts, day care philosophy, and instructional strategies. You'll gain familiarity with administrative and managerial requirements, as well as government regulations.

Trends

Trends in early childhood education reflect the large proportion of American households with only one parent or with two working adults. Tougher restrictions on welfare will force many recipients to find jobs or return to school, creating more demand for child care services. A growing number of employers will offer on-site child care, both as a convenience and as a tool to recruit and keep qualified employees. At the same time, more public school districts will add or expand early childhood programs for their communities. Within child care, you'll find a stronger emphasis on multiculturalism, on parental involvement, and on shaping programs to meet evolving community needs and concerns.

What You Need to Succeed

Start with a love of children and an eagerness to see them develop—emotionally, psychologically, and physically. You must have a commitment to their well-being and growth. Empathy, imagination, careful observation, and physical energy are all prerequisites for the field.

Patience counts, because youngsters perform and advance at varying paces. You'll work closely with children—and often their parents or other adult caregivers—from diverse ethnic, demographic, educational, and economic backgrounds. Therefore, you must communicate well with people of all ages. Be open-minded, creative, and flexible without being judgmental or imposing your own values on others. The ability to work in teams is another essential, since child care educators share responsibilities and work with other professionals, including nurses, social workers, psychologists, and counselors. Finally, recognize that early childhood education has a physical side, including active indoor play, outdoor play, and lifting, so fitness and stamina are important. Get ready to get down on the floor.

Related Fields

Cognitive Science
Elementary Education
Family and Child Development
Psychology
Special Education

Typical Basic Courses

Arts in Early Childhood Education
Child Development
Early Childhood Curriculum and
  Materials
Education of Children
Educational Psychology
Literacy Development
Observation and Assessment of Young
  Children
Young Children and Society

An Array of Electives

Cognitive and Psycho-Motor Experiences
Day Care Administration
Early Childhood Classroom Management
Instructional Strategies
Issues in Early Childhood Education
Play Development
Student Teaching
The Handicapped in Early Childhood

On-Campus Opportunities

Day care programs for children of staff
  and students

Job Opportunities

Adequate supply / Some oversupply

Reading to Explore

Art and Children: Using Literature to Expand Creativity, by Robin Works Davis (Scarecrow)

The Magic Years, by Selma H. Fraiberg (Simon & Schuster)

The Spiritual Life of Children, by Robert Coles (Houghton Mifflin)

The Uses of Enchantment: The Meaning and Importance of Fairy Tales, by Bruno Bettelheim (Random House)

Together and Equal: Fostering Cooperative Play and Promoting Gender Equity in Early Childhood Programs, by Carol Hilgartner Schlank (Allyn and Bacon)

To Learn More

National Association for the Education of
  Young Children
1509 16th St. NW
Washington, DC 20036
(800) 424-2460; fax (202) 328-1846
E-mail: naeyc@naeyc.org
Internet site: http://www.nayec.org

Economics

One of the soundest rules I try to remember when making forecasts in the field of economics is that whatever is to happen is happening already.
—*Sylvia Porter, financial writer, as quoted in* Peter's Quotations: Ideas for Our Time

What to Expect

In essence, economics is the study of the way societies satisfy their material desires and needs, with broad applications to finance, business, education, government administration, and other economic and political arenas. Introductory courses include surveys of microeconomics and macroeconomics, as well as overviews of U.S. and international monetary and banking systems and the collective bargaining process. To provide context, you will encounter economic history and comparative economics in your classes. In the process, you should develop an appreciation for the diversity of reasonable opinions about economic problems.

Most economists focus on practical applications of economic policy and use their understanding of economic relationships to advise businesses, public agencies, industry associations, and unions. So in advanced classes, you may study how economics relates to a specialized area such as health care, foreign trade, higher education, labor, natural resources and environmental protection, and government. You can also take classes in the realms of money, banking, securities, and public finance. At the same time, you'll build necessary technical skills in courses that involve econometrics, statistics, computers, and mathematics.

Trends

Trends in economics include a greater focus on regional and multinational finance and development, for example in Africa, the Pacific Rim, Europe, and the former Soviet Union. That emphasis reflects the globalization of the economy, a breakdown in barriers to trade, and the move to a free-market economy in former communist or one-party countries. In addition, legislative bodies such as Congress, state legislatures, and city councils increasingly demand economic analysis and financial projections for proposed new laws and government policies.

What You Need to Succeed

This field relies on strong analytical abilities, including the capacity to think abstractly and to use computers for modeling, analysis, and testing of hypotheses. You must be able to work accurately and pay attention to details because much of your time is devoted to data analysis. Persistence and patience are required, as are an interest in problem solving and competence to conduct independent studies and projects. Communication skills, both oral and verbal, are essential, and you must be able to explain economic concepts and analyses to lay audiences such as corporate executives and government officials. In addition, you should be able to use mathematics and statistics in your work. Many people are attracted to the field because it blends social sciences and math. At the same time, it provides an opportunity for involvement in the debate over important public issues such as monetary and employment policies, health care and school finance, and economic development initiatives.

Related Fields

Business Administration
Finance and Banking
International Relations
Labor and Industrial Relations
Management
Political Science

Typical Basic Courses

Comparative Economic Systems
International Economics
Introductory Microeconomics
Labor Economics
Money, Banking, and Financial Markets
Principles of Macroeconomics
Private Enterprise, and Public Policy
Survey of Public Economics

An Array of Electives

Advanced Monetary Theory
Distribution of Income
Economics of Health Care
Economics of Socialism
Environmental Economics
History of Economic Thought
Industrial Organization and Control
International Trade and Finance

On-Campus Opportunities

Campus business office
Research assistant

Job Opportunities

Near balance / Supply equals demand

Reading to Explore

Adam Smith Goes to Moscow: A Dialogue of Radical Reform, by Walter Adams and James W. Brock (Princeton University)

One World, Ready or Not: The Manic Logic of Global Capitalism, by William Greider (Simon & Schuster)

Peddling Prosperity: Economic Sense and Nonsense in the Age of Diminished Expectations, by Paul R. Krugman (W.W. Norton)

Poor Richard's Principle: Recovering the American Dream Through the Moral Dimension of Work, Business, and Money, by Richard Wuthnow (Princeton University)

Teachings from the Worldly Philosophy, by Robert Heilbroner (Norton)

To Learn More

American Economic Association
2014 Broadway, Suite 305
Nashville, TN 37203
(615) 322-2595; fax (615) 343-2595
E-mail: aeainfo@ctrvax.vanderbilt.edu
Internet site:
   http://www.vanderbilt.edu/aea

National Association of Business
   Economists
1233 20th St. NW, Suite 505
Washington, DC 20036
(202) 463-6223; fax (202) 463-6239
E-mail: busecon@cpcug.org
Internet site: http://www.nabe.com

Electrical Engineering

But what daring mortals you are! to rob the Thunderer of his Bolts—and for what?
—Josiah Wedgwood, artisan, in "The Capabilities of Electricity," letter of Oct. 9, 1766

What to Expect

From aircraft radar systems to home electronics, from bionic body parts to computer systems, electrical engineering leaves its mark. As a student, you'll become familiar with the theories and principles of the field and related sciences, plus learn to apply those theories and principles to practical—often futuristic—problems. Early courses will combine elements of physics, computing, chemistry, math, logic, electric circuits, and electronics with laboratory experience. Electronic analysis, design, and simulation will be covered, as will materials used by electrical engineers. You'll do computer modeling, design and construct digital logic circuits, program microprocessors, and use such equipment as oscilloscopes, transistors, and transformers.

From there, you'll do additional work with electronic circuits, electromagnetic and transmission theory, electrical machines and transformers, solid-state devices, mechanics, and thermodynamics. You can dig deeper into subfields like biomedical engineering, communications systems, energy and signal processing, electromagnetic fields, optical systems design, robotics, and power equipment. Much of your time will be spent in specialized labs equipped for holography and optics, ion implantation, crystal growing, vacuum deposition for thin-films research, energy conversion, and optical metrology. You should also become prepared for handling electrical engineering industrial assignments and developing engineering management tools and techniques.

Trends

Trends in electrical engineering involve its interaction with other areas such as computer science, biomedical engineering, aerospace, telecommunications, utilities, and geography. Challenges include finding ways to access information instantly, to provide ready access to cost-effective medical diagnoses, and to design new systems and products for consumer, industrial, and business use.

What You Need to Succeed

Everything in electrical engineering is teamwork. And because this is a look-ahead field, you must be able to take a long view and devise solutions that will last beyond tomorrow and next week. Computer mastery is expected, and so is experience in research and experimentation. You might be involved in designing and testing new products, so creativity is an asset. You might write performance requirements, so communication skills are necessary. You might estimate the time and cost of engineering products, so analytical ability provides an edge. You should understand mathematics and physics, but science isn't enough. A grounding in business is an asset because design and systems options often depend on financial and economic considerations, regardless of what technology may allow. You must also understand the specific industry you work in to put your engineering assignments into context effectively. In addition, you'll have to be able to weigh the societal impact of what you do.

Related Fields

Computer Science
Mechanical Engineering
Operations Research and Industrial
  Engineering
Physics

Typical Basic Courses

Digital Logic Fundamentals
Electromagnetic Fields and Waves
Electronic Circuits
Energy Conversion and Power
  Electronics
Instrumentation and Systems
Microprocessors and Digital Systems
Signals and Linear Systems
Statistical Thermodynamics

An Array of Electives

Biomedical Electronics
Digital Control and Robotics
Electro-Optics
Electronic Design Automation
Power System Analysis
Radar and Remote Sensing
Semiconductor Devices
Statistical Communication Systems

On-Campus Opportunities

Research assistant

Job Opportunities

Good demand / Possible shortage

Reading to Explore

Electrifying America: Social Meanings of a New Technology, 1880–1940, by David E. Ney (MIT)

Future Talk: The Changing Wireless Game, by Ron Schneiderman (IEEE Press)

The Invention That Changed the World: How a Small Group of Radar Pioneers Won the Second World War and Launched a Technological Revolution, by Robert Buderi (Simon & Schuster)

There Are No Electrons: Electronics for Earthlings, by Kenn Amdahl (Clearwater)

Thomas A. Edison: A Streak of Luck, by Robert Conot (DeCapo)

To Learn More

Institute of Electrical and Electronics
  Engineers
445 Hoes Lane
Piscataway, NJ 20191
(908) 562-5539; fax (908) 981-0225
E-mail: webmaster@ieee.org
Internet site: http://www.ieee.org

Elementary Education

A child miseducated is a child lost.
—*President John F. Kennedy, State of the Union Address, Jan. 11, 1962*

What to Expect

As the teacher's role evolves from lecturer or presenter to facilitator or coach, so too does the college curriculum for aspiring teachers change. You should prepare for an environment in which interactive discussions and hands-on learning are replacing memorization and repetitive drills and imaginative approaches to teaching are encouraged. Introductory courses will expose you to these changes in the context of educational philosophy, development of literacy, educational psychology, learning techniques, and understanding how children's minds develop. You'll become able to compare schools and consider diversity, inequality, and their ramifications for elementary school students.

At a higher level, classes cover particular disciplines—for example, social studies, math, language arts, or science—and an introduction to school administration. In addition, you'll learn more about diagnostic media, public education policy in the United States, and multicultural curriculums. A course on instructional technology, including computers and videos, may prove beneficial.

Trends

Trends in elementary education include challenges from two movements outside the traditional public and private school systems: home schooling and charter schools. Both put pressure on teachers, administrators, and boards of education to improve the performance of their children. A second important trend is multiculturalism and the move to introduce young children to a wider range of ethnic and cultural traditions. Also, expect more mixed-age groups—akin to the one-room schoolhouses of old—and more statewide and national standardized tests as society tries to find fair methods of measuring children's learning.

What You Need to Succeed

Do you enjoy working with young children and want to influence them for the better? Build on that foundation with knowledge of the subjects you teach and responsibility for constantly updating that knowledge. Add the capacity to communicate with children, inspire respect and trust, and motivate them to achieve. You must be able to understand their emotional and educational needs. Teaching is a two-way street; you should be willing to listen to your pupils' questions and learn from them. In addition, elementary education requires physical stamina and the capacity to react competently and confidently to crises and unanticipated events. Remember, teaching is a cooperative profession. You'll work with colleagues—teachers, counselors, aides, and administrators—and you'll have to reach out to parents and community members so that they are integral components of your students' support system. Creativity and a willingness to experiment with new techniques and materials are needed, too.

Related Fields

Early Childhood Education
Family and Child Development
Psychology
Secondary Education
Special Education

Typical Basic Courses

Adolescence and Student Learning
Classroom Management
Cognitive Development of the Child
Historical Foundations of Teaching
Human Development
Introduction to American Education
Literacy Development
Secondary School Teaching and Learning

An Array of Electives

Diagnostic Teaching Techniques
Educational Media and Technology
Educational Psychology
Multicultural Education
Philosophy of Education
School-Community Involvement
Student Teaching
Management, Measurement, and
    Curriculum

On-Campus Opportunities

On-campus schools for children of faculty
    and students

Job Opportunities

Adequate supply / Some oversupply

Reading to Explore

Hispanic Children and Youth in the United States: A Resource Guide, by Angela L. Carrasquillo (Garland)

How Children Learn, by John Holt (Dell)

Lucy Sprague Mitchell: The Making of a Modern Woman, by Joyce Antler (Yale University)

Radical Reflections: Passionate Opinions on Teaching, Learning, and Living, by Mem Fox (Harcourt, Brace)

The Dreamkeepers: Successful Teachers of African-American Children, by Gloria Ladson-Billings (Jossey-Bass)

To Learn More

American Federation of Teachers
555 New Jersey Ave. NW
Washington, DC 20001
(202) 879-4400; fax (202) 879-4556
E-mail: afteditor@aol.com
Internet site: http://www.aft.org

National Education Association
1201 16th St. NW
Washington, DC 20036
(202) 833-4000; fax (202) 822-7624
E-mail: cstowe@nea.org
Internet site: http://www.nea.org

English

A people's literature is the great textbook for real knowledge of them. The writings of the day show the quality of the people as not historical reconstruction can.
—*Edith Hamilton, novelist, in* The Roman Way

What to Expect

English is more expansive than prose and poetry, more than rigid rules of writing and grammar. Lower-level classes provide general outlines of the history of British and North American literature as well as an awareness of literary theories and of the social and historical contexts in which these traditions developed—and continue to evolve. Not all your reading will be devoted to the classical English language authors; professors also should introduce you to lesser-known but talented writers and to contemporary works. Expect heavy emphasis on improving your writing, thinking, and composition skills.

For perspective, you'll be taught about literary history and the writer's role in society, past and present. In advanced classes, you can study in depth a genre (such as satire or drama) or a time period (such as Victorian England or nineteenth-century United States) or an author (such as poet Edmund Spenser or playwright William Shakespeare) or a theme (such as film literature or Latino literature). Some high-level classes explore a single work in depth, such as *Beowulf* or the *Canterbury Tales*.

Trends

Trends in English reflect the emerging prominence of literature from previously overlooked or undervalued authors, such as women, homosexuals, and members of ethnic, racial, and religious groups. At the same time, more attention is being paid to works in English by writers from outside the United States and Great Britain, including Canada and Australia, and from former colonies in Africa, Asia, and Latin America.

What You Need to Succeed

Here's the bottom line: You must love to read and write. The ability to analyze and communicate are the cornerstones of success in English. You also need a broad knowledge of literary works in the major genres: fiction, poetry, playwriting, screenwriting, and nonfiction. Then you must be able to dig below the surface and go beyond the superficial by evaluating and interpreting literary works. Become adept at competently sharing those evaluations and interpretations. Be prepared to defend your ideas yet, at the same time, be willing to consider alternative theories.

Research skills are important. So is a mind open to new writers and new styles. Don't fall for the deceptively facile argument that all the "good" writers are dead, that literary styles cannot continue to evolve, and that only classical writing is worthy of transmission and studying. And don't let your focus on English literature cause you to ignore the literature of non-Anglo-American cultures.

Related Fields

American Studies and Cultures
Classical Languages and Classics
Journalism
Linguistics
Romance Languages
Theater and Drama

Typical Basic Courses

Classical Myths and Literature
Composition
Creative Writing
Expository Writing
Introduction to Poetry
Nature of Language
Survey of American Literature
Survey of British Literature

An Array of Electives

American Folklore
Comparative Drama
Fantasy for Youth
Literature of Nonwestern Cultures
Modern Critical Theory
Shakespeare
Technical and Professional Writing
Victorian Literature and Thought

On-Campus Opportunities

Library
Student newspaper or magazine
Writing center

Job Opportunities

Adequate supply / Some oversupply

Reading to Explore

Behind a Mask: The Unknown Thrillers of Louisa May Alcott, by Madeleine Stern (Quill/Morrow)

Emerson Among the Eccentrics: A Group Portrait, by Carlos Baker (Viking)

Letters to Alice on First Reading Jane Austen, by Fay Weldon (Taplinger)

Making the Alphabet Dance: Recreational Wordplay, by Ross Eckler (St. Martin's)

Woe Is I: The Grammarphobe's Guide to Better English in Plain English, by Patricia T. O'Conner (Grosset/Putnam)

To Learn More

College English Association
Department of English
Winthrop University
Rock Hill, SC 29733
(803) 323-2171; fax (803)
E-mail: sullivanwa@winthrop.edu
Internet site:
  http://lurch.winthrop.edu/cea

Entomology

Go to the ant, thou sluggard; consider her ways and be wise.
—*The Bible (Proverbs 6:6)*

What to Expect

The world as we know it would not exist without insects—those that plague us and those that help us survive, even prosper. Just as they are part of an interconnected world, so, too, does entomology interconnect with other natural sciences. You'll study insect anatomy, adaptations, and the practicalities and challenges of dealing with them. As course work progresses, you'll become familiar with the role insects play in biodiversity, as well as the benefits, drawbacks, and limitations of pest management. There will be lab experiments and field observations, with instruction in lab equipment and scientific observation techniques. These research methods will carry over into other scientific endeavors.

Once you master the basics, you'll learn more about genetics, toxicology, the classification and evolutionary history of insects, and which species are vectors of disease for humans and animals—everything from molecules to evolution. Some advanced undergraduate classes address real-world applications in turfgrass management, crop disease, epidemiology, DNA studies, food contamination, urban infestations, and forest and livestock health.

Trends

Trends in entomology emphasize the role insects play in biodiversity and the ecosystem and the search for insect control methods that don't threaten the environment with toxic chemicals. There is a need to develop and apply additional integrated pest management tactics for safe, effective, and affordable systems, such as encouragement of natural enemies, use of repellents or sterilants, and crop rotation. At the same time, there will be more attention paid to finding ways to channel insects' usefulness, such as pollination to improve crop productivity.

What You Need to Succeed

You need a strong interest in life sciences and an understanding of how insects relate to other life forms, both plants and animals, in the ecological web. Observation and research skills contribute significantly to success in entomology, whether it's in a natural habitat, on a farm or ranch, in a laboratory, or in an insect-infested building. That presumes the ability to use not only laboratory equipment, such as electron microscopes, but also machinery and equipment required in the field. An analytical mind coupled with a familiarity with computers are important to evaluate data, spot patterns, and plan strategies. You must be able to identify relationships between your work and that of scientists in allied disciplines. For example, entomologists are involved in spheres as diverse as genetics, economics, robotics, health, ecology, forensics, medicine, and international trade. Also, entomological research and implementation of management systems involve careful attention to detail and to recording the findings.

Related Fields

Biology
Crop and Soil Science
Environmental Studies
Forestry
Horticulture
Zoology

Typical Basic Courses

Agriculture and Pollination
Field Entomology
Forest and Shade Tree Insects
Insect Biology
Insects and Biodiversity
Insects and Our Health
Pest Management
Pests, Society, and Environment

An Array of Electives

Biological Control
General Nematology
Insect Behavior
Insect Ecology and Evolution
Insect Physiology
Integrated Pest Management Systems
Medical and Veterinary Entomology
Stream and Aquatic Insect Ecology

On-Campus Opportunities

Campus grounds department
Research assistant

Job Opportunities

Adequate supply / Some oversupply

Reading to Explore

Bugs in the System: Insects and Their Impact on Human Affairs, by May R. Berenbaum (Addison-Wesley)

Ninety-Nine Gnats, Nits, and Nibblers, by May R. Berenbaum (University of Illinois)

Pleasures of Entomology: Portraits of Insects and the People Who Study Them, by Howard Ensign Evans (Smithsonian Institution)

The Book of the Spider: From Arachnophobia to the Love of Spiders, by Paul Hillyard (Random House)

The Earth Dwellers: Adventures in the Land of Ants, by Erich Hoyt (Simon & Schuster)

To Learn More

Entomological Society of America
9301 Annapolis Road
Lanham, MD 20706
(301) 731-4535; fax (301) 731-4538
E-mail: esa@entsoc.org
Internet site: http://www.entsoc.org

Environmental Studies

O let them be left, wildness and wet / Long live the weeds and the wilderness yet.
—*Gerard Manley Hopkins, poet, in "Inversnaid"*

What to Expect

Today's and tomorrow's environmental problems require an understanding of natural science, economics, social policy, planning, and government. It's not enough to know biology or forestry or chemistry or engineering alone. Under the umbrella of environmental studies, they must fit into a broader setting. That's why many core courses are interdisciplinary in orientation, placing scientific principles in the context of public policies, political likelihoods, community concerns, and financial realities. Field and laboratory experiences are part of the curriculum.

Some higher-level courses deal with international issues, such as the cross-the-borders effects of nuclear waste disposal, overpopulation, air pollution, habitat destruction, overfishing, and ocean quality. Others focus on the economic and political aspects of conservation, use of non-renewable resources, and cleanup of polluted soil, air, and water. Still others concentrate on particular natural environments (watersheds, barrier islands, or forests, for example) or scientific applications (such as water quality management or solid waste engineering). You'll learn scientific and research techniques, statistical analysis, land use principles, and emerging technologies for locating and remedying contamination.

Trends

Trends in environmental studies reflect conflicts between citizen worries and economics, between costs and benefits, between what scientists can prove and what they merely believe to be true. There will be more emphasis on preventing problems, coupled with debate over who should pay—and can afford to pay—to correct past mistakes. Environmental scientists and policy analysts will find expanding opportunities within industry as companies attempt to avert future environmental crises, remedy existing problems, and deal with government regulations and agencies.

What You Need to Succeed

Do you like to apply science to social issues and living conditions, because that's what the field demands? Are you comfortable with teamwork, because the work involves scientists, resource managers, planners, policy makers, and financial experts? Can you take a long-range perspective, because environmental problems are rarely solved quickly, and environmental initiatives may take years, decades, or longer to come to fruition? Can you explain complicated scientific principles to lay audiences, because environmental experts interact with community residents, political and government leaders, and business managers? Do you have an open mind that can see multiple sides to an issue, and a cooperative spirit able to negotiate compromises, because competing interests are involved in these issues? In addition, you need to understand complex scientific processes, keep up with research findings, and be able to assess economic factors. At least some of your time may be spent outdoors and, for many environmental scientists, in the lab.

Related Fields

Biology
Chemistry
Fisheries and Wildlife
Geological and Earth Sciences
Marine Biology and Oceanography
Parks and Recreation

Typical Basic Courses

Atmosphere and Oceans
Diversity of Life
Environmental Chemistry
Environmental Planning
Introduction to Environmental Studies
Microbiology
Nature and Society
Principles of Ecology

An Array of Electives

Arctic and Alpine Ecology
Dynamics of Environmental Systems
Environmental Engineering
Environmental Law
Global Human Ecology
Great Environmental Writing
Media Coverage of Science and
    Environmental Controversies
Population and Society

On-Campus Opportunities

Campus recycling and energy conserva-
    tion offices
Research assistant

Job Opportunities

Surplus / Substantial oversupply

Reading to Explore

A Sand County Almanac, by Leopold Aldo (Oxford University)

Best of Edward Abbey, by Edward Abbey (Sierra Club)

Encounters with the Archdruid, by John McPhee (Noonday)

Heart of the Land: Essays on Last Great Places, by Joseph Barbato and Lisa Weinerman (Vintage)

Miracle Under the Oaks: The Revival of Nature in America, by William K. Stevens (Pocket)

To Learn More

Ecological Society of America
2010 Massachusetts Ave. NW, Suite 400
Washington, DC 20036
(202) 833-8773; fax (202) 833-8775
E-mail: esahq@esa.org
Internet site: http://www.sdsc.edu/~esa

Family and Child Development

Nobody who has not been in the interior of a family can say what the difficulties of any individual of that family can be.
—*Jane Austen, novelist, in* Pride and Prejudice

What to Expect

Family relationships—whether strong or weak, traditional or unconventional—underpin our society and shape the ways we interact with others. This field addresses those relationships from psychological, cultural, physiological, economic, sexual, and public policy perspectives. Classes will show you how individuals develop physically and emotionally. Much of the classroom emphasis is on early development, from birth until adulthood, but increasingly, courses cover adult relationships such as marriage and divorce, as well as the aging process. Health, counseling, diversity, and sociological factors permeate the curriculum.

Other course possibilities deal with family therapy techniques, male-female dynamics, gender roles, and coping with families under stress. Suicide prevention, death education, human sexuality, substance abuse, crisis intervention tactics, conflicts between generations, and family financial management also fall under the umbrella of family and child development. Hands-on opportunities may be part of your coursework.

Trends

Trends in family and child development mirror changes in contemporary society. Look around you to see why. The traditional definition of *family* continues to lose accuracy in this time of one-parent households, unwed heterosexual and homosexual couples living together, higher teen pregnancy and divorce rates, and media attention on assisted suicide. Professionals will experiment with alternative counseling techniques. The influx of immigrants with different family traditions will change the mix, as will the push to keep more elderly people with their families instead of in expensive nursing homes.

What You Need to Succeed

More than in most other fields of study, empathy and patience are crucial for success. Equally essential is tolerance of the viewpoints, uncertainties, and emotional conflicts of other people. That requires the ability to listen to what is expressed as well as to the undercurrents and tone of the words people use. In addition, communication skills are vital, whether you deal with children, young parents, spouses in conflict, or the elderly.

Your goal is to understand the limitless ways people interact with each other and to provide guidance, support, and recommendations so people can better lead their own lives. Beware of misleading people into believing you have all the answers, however. You cannot be judgmental when you disapprove, and you cannot lead other peoples' lives for them. Also, you must be trustworthy so that people will feel confidence in your professionalism and feel free to confide in you.

Related Fields

Early Childhood Education
Elementary Education
Psychology
Social Work
Sociology
Special Education

Typical Basic Courses

Adolescence
Child Growth and Development
Children, Youth and Family
Development and Guidance
Individual and Family Life Development
Parenting
Special Needs Children
Theories of Human Development

An Array of Electives

Abuse in Families
Aging and the Family
Assessment for Infants
Characteristics of Giftedness
Family Interaction Dynamics
Family Program Administration
Human Sexuality
Marriage and Family Therapies

On-Campus Opportunities

Crisis intervention center
Day care programs for children of staff
    and students

Job Opportunities

Adequate supply / Some oversupply

Reading to Explore

In My Room: Teenagers in Their Bedrooms, by Adrienne Salinger (Chronicle)

In the Name of the Family: Rethinking Family Values in the Postmodern Age, by Judith Stacey (Beacon)

She Works / He Works: How Two-Income Families Are Happier, Healthier, and Better Off, by Rosalind C. Barnett and Caryl Rivers (HarperSanFrancisco)

Sister to Sister: Women Write About the Unbreakable Bond, by Patricia Foster (Anchor/Doubleday)

The Third and Only Way: Reflections on Staying Alive, by Helen Bevington (Duke University)

To Learn More

National Council on Family Relations
3989 Central Ave. NE, #550
Minneapolis, MN 55421
(612) 781-9331; fax (612) 781-9348
E-mail: ncfr3989@ncfr.com
Internet site: http://www.ncfr.com

Finance and Banking

I am not in Wall Street for my health.
—*J. P. Morgan, capitalist, as quoted in* Money Talks

What to Expect

An understanding of finance is the bedrock for dealing with the stock markets, the banking system, the insurance industry, and U.S. and foreign economies. That's because finance involves the study of money management, acquisition of funds, and directing those funds to meet specific aims. As you start your studies, you'll begin to develop that understanding through courses that discuss financial markets and institutions, fundamentals of investment and insurance, and introductions to investment management, financial analysis, and personal finance. Higher-level courses take you more deeply into one or more finance-related disciplines such as corporate or international finance, banking, insurance, and financial planning. These courses are intended to build a knowledge base and to encourage managerial, analytical, planning, and strategic skills. They often use case studies to illustrate theories and computers to design long-term and short-term strategic and investment plans. The curriculum also covers aspects of the law and governmental regulation of securities, lending institutions, and international transactions, as well as their economic and social implications. Also, you'll work to absorb some of the psychological aspects of finance, including risk, speculation, and ethics.

Trends

Trends in finance and banking encompass the increasingly global elements of the economy, including exports, imports, foreign investments and stock markets, currency exchange rates, cartels, and electronic transfer of funds. Expect the continued evolution of new types of investment vehicles as alternatives to ordinary stocks, bonds, mutual funds, and commodities futures. In addition, the aging of our population will create more opportunities in the areas of professional financial management, estate planning, and retirement planning.

What You Need to Succeed

Can you look ahead and plan for the future, taking multiple contingencies into account and taking calculated risks? If so, you possess one characteristic key to success in this field. Are you comfortable with computers and able to master a variety of investment management and financial analysis software programs? If so, you have another essential characteristic. Do you have sales ability, patience, research skills, enthusiasm, discipline, problem-solving abilities, and self-confidence in a conservative work environment to assess alternatives and make decisions that potentially involve millions of dollars belonging to other people? Those, too, are necessary. Can you communicate well? You must work with clients, colleagues, and professionals in allied professions. Are you accurate, careful, and well organized? Sloppiness and negligence may trigger costly repercussions for your clients and your firm. Finally, are you honest and discreet? You must be worthy of trust, able to protect your clients' secrets, observant of the laws, and diligent in avoiding self-dealing, conflicts of interest, and misuse of inside or confidential information.

Related Fields

Accounting
Business Administration
Economics
Management
Marketing
Public Policy Studies

Typical Basic Courses

Corporate Finance
Entrepreneurial Finance
Financial Markets and Institutions
Fundamental Financial Analysis
Investment and Portfolio Management
Money and Capital Markets
Principles of Investment
Principles of Risk Management and
  Insurance

An Array of Electives

Capital Investment Analysis
Commercial Loan Management
Derivative Securities
Financial Futures and Options
International Finance
Management of Financial Institutions
Profiles in American Enterprise
Working Capital Management

On-Campus Opportunities

Faculty and staff credit union
Financial aid office

Job Opportunities

Near balance / Supply equals demand

Reading to Explore

The Bankers: The Next Generation, by
Martin Mayer (Dutton)

The Collapse of Barings, by Stephen Fay
(W.W. Norton and Co.)

The Education of a Speculator, by Victor
Niederhoffer (Wiley)

*Total Risk: Nick Leeson and the Fall of
Barings Bank,* by Judith H. Rawnsley
(Harper)

*Wriston: Walter Wriston, Citibank, and the
Rise and Fall of American Financial
Supremacy,* by Phillip L. Zweig (Crown)

To Learn More

American Bankers Association
1120 Connecticut Ave. NW
Washington, DC 20036
(800) 338-0626; fax (202) 663-7578
E-mail: kkelly@aba.com
Internet site: http://www.aba.com/aba

American Insurance Association
1130 Connecticut Ave. NW, Suite 1000
Washington, DC 20036
(202) 828-7100; fax (202) 293-1219
E-mail: webmaster@aiadc.org
Internet site: http://www.aiadc.org

Fisheries and Wildlife

In meadows one may remember ptarmigan chicks ignoring their mother's clucks and wandering in and out of camp, periodically exploding underfoot; on a summit, a distant hawk or eagle whose point of motion stresses how much air there is in the valley and sky.
—*Harvey Manning, writer, in* The Wild Cascades: Forgotten Parkland

What to Expect

Building on a base in biological and physical sciences, your courses will focus on science, public policy, and the economics of natural resources. You'll study ecology, conservation, and the policy aspects of fisheries and wildlife management. You may want to focus some electives on a particular area such as wildlife ecology, limnology, conservation biology, aquaculture, or environmental education. Due to growing concern about how hazardous substances affect wildlife health and survival, an introduction to toxicology will prove useful. Lab work and field work are important components of the major, and you'll come in contact with professionals who work for government agencies, national resources organizations, and environmental consulting firms. Because the field has significant economic aspects, you'll need classes in natural resources management and planning. Your studies can take you in a number of directions, both in college and afterwards. They include promotion and development of fisheries and wildlife resources, teaching, research, and public service.

Trends

Trends in the field of fisheries and wildlife reflect escalating public policy debates over balance: economics versus conservation, commercial fisheries versus recreational fishing, government versus business, health hazards versus acceptable risks, development versus habitat preservation. For example, professionals will become involved in devising and carrying out compromises between those who want to construct housing or dredge rivers on one side, and those who want to protect wetlands, woods, and other natural areas on the other. Another trend involves international debate over extraction of timber, minerals, and other resources from the rain forest and other sensitive habitats.

What You Need to Succeed

Enjoyment of the outdoors, an appreciation of biodiversity, and an understanding of competing pressures on environmental resources are key components for success, whether you work in the field, in a research setting, in a classroom, or in an office. Knowledge of statistics, math, and computers is increasingly essential because professionals analyze the relationships between fish and wildlife populations, their habitat, and human populations. You should be willing to tackle controversies because of frequent environmental, economic, and political clashes among government decision makers, business and development interests, citizen groups, agricultural advocates, and scientists. Verbal and written skills are important because you must know not only the scientific basis of your work but how to communicate that understanding to the public. Much of your contact may be with lay people who are concerned about these issues but who have little scientific training, while other contact will be with fellow resource management experts.

Related Fields

Biology
Environmental Studies
Forestry
Marine Biology and Oceanography
Parks and Recreation
Zoology

Typical Basic Courses

Conservation of Marine Resources
Ecosystem Processes
Ichthyology
Introduction to Fisheries and Wildlife
Mammalogy
Principles of Wildlife Management
Resources Ecology
Wildlife Biometry

An Array of Electives

Aquaculture
Comparative Limnology
Conservation Biology
Ecological Risk Assessment
Natural Resources Economics
Natural Resources Planning and Policy
Ornithology
Wildlife Nutrition

On-Campus Opportunities

Research assistant

Job Opportunities

Near balance / Supply equals demand

Reading to Explore

Darwin's Dreampond: Drama in Lake Victoria, by Tijs Goldschmidt (MIT)

Dead Reckoning: Confronting the Crisis in Pacific Fisheries, by Terry Glavin (Mountaineers)

Of Tigers and Men: Entering the Age of Extinction, by Richard Ives (Doubleday)

Sea of Slaughter, by Farley Mowat (Chapters)

The Wolves of Isle Royale: A Broken Balance, by Rolf O. Peterson (Willow Creek)

To Learn More

American Fisheries Society
5410 Grosvenor Lane, Suite 110
Bethesda, MD 20814
(301) 897-8616; fax (301) 897-8096
E-mail: main@fisheries.org
Internet site:
   http://www.esd.ornl.gov/societies/afs

The Wildlife Society
5410 Grosvenor Lane, Suite 200
Bethesda, MD 20814
(301) 897-9770; fax (301) 530-2471
E-mail: tws@wildlife.org
Internet site:
   http://www.wildlife.org/index.html

Forestry

This is the forest primeval. The murmuring pines and the hemlocks, bearded with moss, and in garments green, indistinct in the twilight.
—*Henry Wadsworth Longfellow, poet, in* Evangeline

What to Expect

Undergraduate forestry education blends the study of biological, economic, and social aspects of managing forest resources. You will gain a thorough understanding of ecosystem structure and function, and use hands-on laboratory exercises and field studies to develop management plans for proper stewardship of our forest resources. Coursework includes an overview of forestry techniques and issues, genetics, ecology, silviculture, and management that will help prepare you for work in forest conservation or as a professional forester. As a result, you'll expand your understanding of forest systems, forest dynamics, and human interactions with the environment and our ability to sustain, enhance, and conserve forests.

Toxicology, forest entomology, soils, hydrology, plant breeding, and wood science are part of the educational mix. And because the environment is a complex network, your traditional forestry education will expand to encompass training in such allied arenas as geography, environmental sciences, fisheries and wildlife, and parks and recreation.

Trends

Trends in forestry reflect our society's growing concern over environmental conservation and the highly charged political and economic debate over balancing "green" concerns with jobs and development. You will need to become familiar with other forestry-related controversies that could affect your studies and career. One controversy involves logging and forestry practices on publicly owned land, primarily state and national forests. A second controversy is international in nature: logging in the rain forests and other ecologically vulnerable habitats. And a third focuses on environmental practices within the United States, including clear cutting of land and paper mill pollution.

What You Need to Succeed

As a forester, you will need a sound, scientific understanding of ecology, as well as an appreciation for the increased demands society places on natural resources. You will be challenged by often-competing economic and environmental considerations. Jobs generally require both physical stamina and mental sharpness. Become familiar with the tools of the profession and with technological advances such as photogrammetry and remote sensing. Computer skills are used widely in the office and in the field to store, retrieve, and analyze information to manage forest land and resources.

Application of theory to practical problems counts heavily as you will have to integrate your knowledge of plants and animals with landowners' objectives to determine the most appropriate management strategy for the forest, wood lots, and even urban areas. People skills are important, too, as you interact with government agencies, property owners, industry representatives, environmental activists, and scientists. Naturally, you should enjoy being outdoors regardless of the weather.

Related Fields

Biology
Botany
Environmental Studies
Fisheries and Wildlife
Horticulture
Parks and Recreation

Typical Basic Courses

Forest and Agricultural Ecology
Forest Biometry
Forest Management
Forest Vegetation
Silviculture
Tenets of Forestry
Wood Technology
Woody Plant Genetics

An Array of Electives

Arboriculture
Forest Ecology
Forest Soils
Forestry in International Development
Plant Breeding and Biotechnology
Plant Evolution
Urban Forestry
Wood Plant Physiology

On-Campus Opportunities

Campus grounds department
Research assistant

Job Opportunities

Near balance / Supply equals demand

Reading to Explore

A Conspiracy of Optimism: Management of the National Forests Since World War II, by Paul W. Hirt (University of Nebraska)

A Sand County Almanac, by Leopold Aldo (Oxford University)

American Forests (magazine)

In a Dark Wood: The Fight Over Forests and the Rising Tyranny of Ecology, by Alston Chase (Houghton Mifflin)

The Sylvan Path: A Journey Through America's Forests, by Gary Ferguson (St. Martin's)

To Learn More

Society of American Foresters
5400 Grosvenor Lane
Bethesda, MD 20814
(301) 897-8720; fax (301) 897-3690
E-mail: safweb@safnet.org
Internet site: http://www.safnet.org

Geography

Geographers crowd into the edges of their maps parts of the world which they do not know about, adding notes in the margin to the effect that beyond this lies nothing but sandy deserts full of wild beasts, and unapproachable bogs.
—*Plutarch, biographer and moralist, in* Lives, Aemilius Paulus

What to Expect

There is a huge world around us for geographers to explore and map, literally from the earth to satellites. As you start in this field, you'll be exposed to three broad areas that merge natural and social sciences: physical and environmental geography, including climate; human geography, including population, culture, and politics; and technical geography, such as map making and remote sensing. Lab work will teach you to interpret and apply maps and remotely sensed imagery. These courses should provide a firm grounding in computer graphics, map design, distribution of economic resources, and air photo interpretation. They'll also familiarize you with research techniques and the rapidly evolving technology used in geography to identify and analyze the global patterns that shape our lives.

Higher-level courses will lead you in depth through selected geographic areas—perhaps in your own state or region, perhaps on another continent. At this point, you'll also work with advanced cartographic principles and applications. You will apply academic principles to real-world situations. For example, you may study the geography of transportation or agriculture, global weather or land use patterns, the geography of urban areas, and demographic issues related to environment, population, and development.

Trends

Trends in geography are dominated by technology. Maps are the geographer's fundamental graphic tools, and computers are revolutionizing map making. High-tech subfields will expand, including remote sensing with land and ocean images taken by satellite and high-altitude aircraft. Another booming subfield will involve geographic information systems that combine computer graphics, artificial intelligence, and high-speed communications for weather forecasting, emergency management, crime prevention, and land use planning.

What You Need to Succeed

Technical and research skills, combined with a solid background in geography, are essential for success. You must regard technology as an ally, not a foe to be wary of. You need an analytical mind to comprehend spatial problems that are often ill defined to develop strategies for attacking those problems, and then to use the technological tools of your trade to propose a solution (or often more than one alternative solution). Your assignments frequently will require teamwork and communication skills as you work with planners, business executives, economic development professionals, economists, government employees, scientists, community activists, and environmental experts. In addition, you should develop an awareness of and an ability to assess and address the social, political, and economic issues that affect what you can do. Depending on your job, you may also need to travel extensively.

Related Fields

Atmospheric Science and Meteorology
Environmental Studies
Geological and Earth Sciences
History
Marine Biology and Oceanography
Urban Planning

Typical Basic Courses

Cultural Geography
Environmental Systems
Geography of Recreation and Tourism
Geography of the United States and
  Canada
Introduction to Economic Geography
Introduction to Remote Sensing
Introductory Meteorology
Physical Geography

An Array of Electives

Agricultural Climatology
Geography of Transportation
Landscape Ecology
Map Production and Design
Remote Sensing of the Environment
Thematic Cartography
Urban Geography
Water Resources and Management

On-Campus Opportunities

Campus museum
Research assistant

Job Opportunities

Adequate supply / Some oversupply

Reading to Explore

Harm de Blij's Geography Book: A Leading Geographer's Fresh Look at Our Changing World, by Harm de Blij (Wiley)

How to Lie with Maps, by Mark Monmonier (University of Chicago)

Longitude: The True Story of a Lone Genius Who Solved the Greatest Scientific Problem of His Time, by Dava Sobel (Walker & Co.)

National Geographic (magazine)

Why in the World: Adventures in Geography, by George J. Demko, Jerome Agel, and Eugene Boe (Anchor)

To Learn More

Association of American Geographers
1710 16th St. NW
Washington, DC 20009
(202) 234-1450; fax (202) 234-2744
E-mail: gaia@aag.org
Internet site: http://www.aag.org

Geological and Earth Sciences

To stand virtually smack in the middle of the continent and find ripple marks left by waves of an ancient ocean, or to recognize the abundant evidence of the glaciers that once covered the Northeast is like having the power to look back in time.
—*Roger Tory Peterson, naturalist, as quoted in* A Field Guide to Geology: Eastern North America

What to Expect

Rocks, minerals, fossils, mountains, earthquakes, volcanoes, glaciers, water, and landforms are keys to the earth's past, present, and future. Basic courses introduce you to the earth's structure and composition, as well as to the natural forces that shape and reshape it. Laboratory work and field work are essential elements of the undergraduate curriculum, as are relationships between geology and other disciplines, including chemistry, botany, physics, engineering, environmental science, oceanography, and ecology. As you advance, you'll find courses in particular geoscientific realms such as energy and mineral resources, oceanography and marine geology, paleontology, geophysics, and the study of volcanoes, water, or glaciers. You can learn to investigate the movement and quality of surface water, to explore for oil and natural gas, and to decipher the earth's magnetic, electric, and gravitational fields. You'll also learn the importance of putting that scientific knowledge into the context of human impact, such as wise use of energy resources, selection of appropriate construction sites, and understanding of the economics of natural resources.

Trends

Trends in geological and earth sciences reflect society, business, and government concerns over dwindling energy, mineral, and water resources, environmental contamination, and policy-science issues such as rising sea levels and global warming. There will be a growing emphasis on environmental science and hydrogeology, mirroring the growing need to maintain the planet's natural environments and meet demands for natural resources (including finding geologically safe places to dispose of industrial wastes). Geoscience will also be called on to devise better ways to predict geological phenomena such as earthquakes and volcanic eruptions.

What You Need to Succeed

As a geoscientist, you should feel comfortable in a range of indoor and outdoor settings (the field is an outdoor laboratory filled with chances to observe the earth's processes in action). Travel is often involved, sometimes to remote areas in the United States and abroad, with difficult living conditions. Your work may involve preparing geologic maps, collecting samples, sampling the deep ocean floor, and exploring for new mineral or hydrocarbon resources. In the lab, you need technical and computer skills to conduct experiments or design computer models to test theories about geological phenomenon. In the office, you'll need a mastery of written and analytical skills to integrate field and laboratory data, and to prepare reports with maps and diagrams. Often, you'll find yourself working with professionals in allied fields, such as petroleum and transportation engineers, environmental scientists, economists, and urban or regional planners.

Related Fields

Atmospheric Science and Meteorology
Environmental Science
Geography
Petroleum Engineering

Typical Basic Courses

Engineering Geology
Environmental Geology
Global Change
Introduction to Geology
Introductory Mineralogy
Sedimentary Environments
Structural Geology
Vertebrate Life of the Past

An Array of Electives

Environmental Geochemistry
Glaciology
Great Geological Controversies
Hydrology
Invertebrate Paleontology
Order, Chaos, and Complexity
Petrology
Volcanology

On-Campus Opportunities

Campus museum
Research assistant

Job Opportunities

Adequate supply / Some oversupply

Reading to Explore

Basin and Range, by John McPhee (Noonday)

Naked Earth: The New Geophysics, by Shawna Vogel (Dutton)

The Bird in the Waterfall: A Natural History of Oceans, Rivers, and Lakes, by Jerry Dennis (HarperCollins)

The Evolving Coast, by Richard A. Davis (W. H. Freeman)

Why the Earth Quakes: The Story of Earthquakes and Volcanoes, by Matthys Levy and Mario Salvadori (Norton)

To Learn More

American Geological Institute
4220 King St.
Alexandria, VA 22314
(703) 379-2480; fax (703) 379-7563
E-mail: ehrinfo@agriweb.org
Internet site: http://www.agiweb.org/agi

Graphic Design

Nowadays, the growth of a graphic image can be divided into two sharply defined phases. The process begins with the search for a visual form that will interpret as clearly as possible one's train of thought. After this, to my great relief, there dawns the second phase, that is the making of the graphic print; for now the spirit can take its rest while the work is taken over by the hands.
—*M. C. Escher, graphic artist, in* The Graphic Work of M. C. Escher

What to Expect

Graphic design uses visual language to communicate ideas and messages, and training will help develop your skills necessary to accomplish that. In the process, you'll build a foundation in art history, an understanding of design theory, and a mastery of in-studio design methods. The curriculum should provide knowledge of color theory, visual aesthetics, and typography while developing your ability to apply design to real-world situations. Introductory courses cover elements of design theory, graphic form, photography, calligraphy, and technical drawing, and include experimental and practical projects.

From there, advanced courses deal with such topics as motion graphics, architectural detailing, and industrial design. You'll become familiar with the application of graphic design concepts to arenas ranging from photography, film, textiles, and packaging to theater, interior design, technical writing, and advertising. You need to know production and exhibition techniques, too. All this takes place in the classroom, in the studio, and in the campus computer center, where you'll use microcomputers, color laser printers, scanning equipment, and other state-of-the-art technology for compositional exercises and projects. Students also should understand the social and behavioral ramifications of graphic designs.

Trends

Trends in graphic design reflect changes in technology (including CD-ROM and the Internet) and in the field's relationship to art and society. Another growth area is computer animation—akin to high-tech puppeteering—which combines graphic art and computer skills into applications for television, movies, videos, commercials, and video games. Self-publishing and desktop publishing also will boom.

What You Need to Succeed

To the graphic artist, a sense of visual aesthetics and perceptual acuity are important, but so is technical competence. Master computer-assisted design software and related technological tools as helpers in making your visions tangible. Creativity is essential, but so is an ability to translate creative concepts—yours and your clients'—into appealing designs that meet their purposes: to sell, persuade, lure, excite, outrage, provoke, soothe. Can you fit comfortably into a creative team? Graphic designers sometimes work individually, but often join on projects with colleagues, copywriters, architects, product development experts, packaging engineers, artisans, and designers from other disciplines. That requires the capacity to communicate with words as well as with your art. Aside from the art, it also means you must understand the basics of the industries you work with, such as advertising, textiles, or publishing. Openness to constructive criticism and an ability to meet deadlines are key, too.

Related Fields

Advertising
Architecture
Art
Photography and Cinema
Textiles and Apparel

Typical Basic Courses

Basics of Computer Graphics
Design Applications
Design Theory and History
Graphic Form
Technical Drawing for Designers
Typography
Visual Aesthetics

An Array of Electives

Advanced Graphic Applications
Architectural Detailing
Desktop Publishing Graphics
Electronic Media Processes
Exhibit Design
Graphic Design Criticism
Industrial Design
Studies in Motion Graphics

On-Campus Opportunities

College news bureau
College publications office
Web page design

Job Opportunities

Good demand / Possible shortage

Reading to Explore

Creating Great Web Graphics, by Laurie McCanna (M.I.S. Press)

Creating Killer Web Sites: The Art of Third-Generation Site Design, by David Siegel (Hayden)

From Lascaux to Brooklyn, by Paul Rand (Yale)

The Art of the New Yorker, 1925–1995, by Lee Lorenz (Alfred A. Knopf)

The Graphic Work of M. C. Escher, by M. C. Escher (Ballantine)

To Learn More

American Institute of Graphic Arts
164 Fifth Ave.
New York, NY 10010
(212) 807-1990; fax (212) 807-1799
E-mail: aigaanswers@aiga.org
Internet site: http://www.aiga.org

History

History in general is a collection of crimes, follies, and misfortunes among which we have now and then met with a few virtues, and some happy times.
—*Francois Marie Arouet de Voltaire, philosopher, "Essay on the Morals and the Spirit of Nations"*

What to Expect

Dates to memorize? Facts to memorize? History's much more than that. It's a field in which you dig into the past, from antiquity to yesterday, and draw lessons about today and the future. What we glean from the cultural, intellectual, political, and economic life of past civilizations helps us understand the forces that buffet our own world. Introductory courses tend to focus on U.S. and Western European history, but should also expose you to the history of other geographic regions. You'll learn research methods and use of primary and secondary sources, and be encouraged to analyze arguments and assess interpretations of history.

Advanced courses allow you to acquire expertise. It could be thematic (such as the history of war, labor unions, or science), geographic (such as the Far East, American South, or Africa), or of an era (perhaps the Renaissance, Middle Ages, or post–World War II). You'll gain experience tracing the long-term impacts of historical events and developments, such as how the division of the Balkans after World War I led to regional warfare and "ethnic cleansing" more than 70 years later.

Trends

Trends in history include a stronger emphasis on the legacies and traditions of regions outside North America and Europe, including regions that are becoming more important economically to North America (such as the Pacific Rim and Latin America). Another trend focuses greater attention on previously underplayed aspects of our own history, including the role of women, ethnic groups, large corporations, and the environmental movement.

What You Need to Succeed

Are you fascinated with the past? Do you have the strong reading, writing, and analytical skills that are essential qualifications for success in history? Also essential is a mastery of research tools and techniques, from review of dusty documents and scrutiny of scratchy microfilms to delving into computerized databases and conducting interviews to gather oral histories. You'll need a perceptive mind and the capacity to weigh divergent and often conflicting accounts to draw reasoned and reasonable conclusions. Creativity and a compelling interest in open-ended puzzles should be part of your mindset. A touch of iconoclasm can induce you to take an unusual approach to a problem and potentially weave innovative, imaginative, yet reasonable solutions. Can you integrate history with psychology, politics, religion, and economics? Foreign language skills pay off, too.

Related Fields

American Studies and Culture
Anthropology and Archeology
International Relations
Political Science
Urban Studies
Women's Studies

Typical Basic Courses

Asian Civilizations
Early Western Civilization
European History Since 1500
History of Latin America
Introduction to Ancient Studies
U.S. Business and Economic History
U.S. Constitutional History
U.S. History to 1876

An Array of Electives

African History Since 1800
American and European Medicine
Heroes and Villains in the Middle Ages
Historic Preservation
History of the Holocaust
Modern France
U.S. Foreign Relations
Women in the United States

On-Campus Opportunities

Campus museum
Research assistant

Job Opportunities

Adequate supply / Some oversupply

Reading to Explore

Burr, by Gore Vidal (Random House)

Guns of August, by Barbara Tuchman (Macmillan)

How the Irish Saved Civilization: The Untold Story of Ireland's Heroic Role from the Fall of Rome to the Rise of Medieval Europe, by Thomas Cahill (Anchor/Doubleday)

No Ordinary Time: Franklin and Eleanor Roosevelt: The Home Front in World War II, by Doris Kearns Goodwin (Touchstone/Simon & Schuster)

The Best and the Brightest, by David Halberstam (Random House)

To Learn More

American Historical Association
400 A St. SE
Washington, DC 20003
(202) 544-2422; fax (202) 544-8307
E-mail: aha@theaha.org
Internet site:
   http://chnm.gmu.edu/chnm/aha

World History Association
Department of History and Politics
32nd and Chestnut Streets
Drexel University
Philadelphia, PA 19104
(215) 895-2471; fax (215) 895-6614
E-mail: rosenrl@post.drexel.edu
Internet site:
http://library.ccsu.ctstateu.edu/~history/
   wha/about.html

Horticulture

There's no mystery about gardening, just the wondrous fact that seed time and harvest time occur each year, generation after generation, wherever the soil is tilled. If gardeners do their part, they can confidently expect the miracle to continue as it has through all time.
—*James Underwood Crockett, gardener and writer, in* Crockett's Victory Garden

What to Expect

You'll find horticulturists in a variety of professional settings, including fruit and vegetable production, nursery and turfgrass management, golf courses and parks, landscaping, agribusiness, and the floral industry. That's why introductory courses expose you to a broad sweep of information about economic and ornamental plants. There's a mix of scientific and technical knowledge, research skills, and practical experiences in greenhouses, in gardens and—literally—in the field. You'll learn about concepts such as reproduction, water, growth and development, light, temperature, and plant anatomy. You'll also get a grounding in landscape principles, with training in reading blueprints, terrain, aesthetics, irrigation system design, and staking sites.

More advanced courses continue to stress science, including plant breeding, genetic engineering, and control of pests and disease. This is where you'll find classes covering postharvest technology—how to maintain the quality of plants, fruits, and vegetables after harvesting. At the same time, you'll learn business, sales, and managerial aspects of the field, augment research skills, and become familiar with technological advances.

Trends

Trends in horticulture reflect increased attention on three Es: environment, economics, and ethics. Expect more emphasis on plant and crop production systems that are resource efficient, environmentally sound, socially acceptable, and profitable. There will be continued pressure to reduce use of potentially dangerous chemicals, as well as opportunities to use horticulture to reclaim and rejuvenate damaged and devastated urban land, industrial sites, and wildlife habitats. Horticulturists will also confront pressure to justify spending money for beautification to bottom-line business and government executives.

What You Need to Succeed

Horticulture has shed its down-on-the-farm stereotype and moved high-tech with production and marketing of high-value plants and flowers. To go with that flow, you need research and business skills as well as knowledge about the processes for breeding and propagation of fruits, vegetables, flowers, and ornamental plants. At the same time, it remains a hands-on profession that often requires work outdoors, in greenhouses, and in nurseries. You must be able to communicate clearly with coworkers, scientists, customers, and suppliers of fertilizers and other products. Careful record keeping is important to track plant growth, test results, finances, weather patterns, and other variables. You'll have to keep up with new advances such as genetic engineering, integrated pest management, and stimulation of plant growth. For research jobs, you should enjoy experimentation and innovation. Finally, a sense of aesthetics is necessary for success in many areas of horticulture, including landscaping, plant selection, and garden design.

Related Fields

Biology
Botany
Crop and Soil Science
Forestry
Landscape Architecture
Parks and Recreation

Typical Basic Courses

Floral Design
Landscape Horticulture
Nursery Management
Ornamental Flowering Shrubs
Ornamental Trees
Plants and People
Principles of Horticulture
Turfgrass Maintenance

An Array of Electives

Floral Distribution and Marketing
Greenhouse Production
Horticultural Management
Pest Management
Plant Breeding and Biotechnology
Plant Evolution
Vegetable Production and Management
World Fruits and Vegetables

On-Campus Opportunities

Campus greenhouses
Campus grounds-keeping department
Research assistant

Job Opportunities

Near balance / Supply equals demand

Reading to Explore

In Search of Lost Roses, by Thomas Christopher (Summit)

My Weeds: A Gardener's Botany, by Sara B. Stein (Harper and Row)

Once Upon a Windowsill: A History of Indoor Plants, by Tovah Martin (Timber)

Tasha Tudor's Garden by Tovah Martin (Houghton Mifflin)

The 3,000 Mile Garden: from London to Maine — A Correspondence on Gardening, Food, and the Good Life, by Leslie Landt and Roger Phillips (Penguin)

To Learn More

American Horticultural Society
7931 East Boulevard Drive
Alexandria, VA 22308
(703) 768-5700; fax (703) 768-8700
E-mail: GardenAHS@aol.com
Internet site: http://eMall.com.ahs

Hotel/Restaurant Management

Be not forgetful to entertain strangers, for thereby some have entertained angels unawares.
—*Bible (Hebrews 13:2)*

What to Expect

As the service economy, business travel, and discretionary income for leisure expand, opportunities are growing in the restaurant, food service, resort, and lodging industries. Beginning courses provide an orientation to the principle elements of the field with a heavy emphasis on building business and managerial skills. The curriculum covers the impact of travel and tourism and provides an introduction to accounting, marketing, and sales, the operation and functions of different types of lodging and dining facilities, and standards of microbiology, sanitation, nutrition, and quality in food management. You'll learn about organizational behavior in the industry, including human resource management, interpersonal relations, and managing culturally diverse personnel.

At an advanced level, you'll improve your managerial and finance abilities, as well as your knowledge of how the industry works and changes. Courses offer training in such areas as information and computer systems, organization of food and beverage operations, menu development and recipe management, and strategies for financing hospitality ventures and expansion. In addition, you'll discuss policy and economic issues, as well as U.S. and foreign laws that regulate the industry.

Trends

Trends in hotel and restaurant management reflect greater travel and leisure spending. That's reflected in a growing proportion of meals eaten away from home, largely because more families have two working parents. A second trend involves the extension of U.S. hospitality corporations overseas and increased growth and competition among chains within the United States. Another trend is the increased reliance on computer information systems for planning, management, market research, and daily operations of restaurants, clubs, catering services, and hotels.

What You Need to Succeed

Hospitality is a people-oriented field. Strong person-to-person skills and a commitment to service are crucial, since most of your work will involve guests, clients, suppliers, co-workers, and managers. Be willing to accommodate diverse tastes and demands, and be excited by the chance to meet people from different cultures and to learn about their ways of life. You need self-discipline and the capacity to solve problems and make logical decisions—under time pressure and under the scrutiny of anxious guests—while managing your own stress. You must be able to communicate clearly, in writing and verbally. Command of at least one foreign language is an asset in light of international travel to the United States and the spread overseas of U.S. hospitality companies. Expect to work long hours, often on weekends, nights, and holidays. In addition, a comprehensive understanding of business, management, and supervision is necessary, as is familiarity with computers.

Related Fields

Business Administration
Management
Marketing
Parks and Recreation
Travel and Tourism

Typical Basic Courses

Beverage Management
Hospitality Information Systems
Hospitality Managerial Accounting
Hospitality Sanitation and Safety
Introduction to the Hospitality Industry
Lodging Facilities Management
Private Club Operations
Quality Food Management

An Array of Electives

Advanced Food Service Management
Catering
Convention and Meeting Planning
Food Purchasing
Hotel, Restaurant, and Tourism
  Marketing
Legal Aspects of Hospitality Services
Quality Food Production Systems
Wines of the World

On-Campus Opportunities

Campus dining services
Campus health club and restaurants

Job Opportunities

Good demand / Possible shortage

Reading to Explore

Be My Guest, by Conrad Hilton (Prentice Hall)

Dave's Way: A New Approach to Old-Fashioned Success, by R. David Thomas (G. P. Putnam's Sons)

Exploring Wine, by the Culinary Institute of America (Van Nostrand Reinhold)

Simply the Best: A Celebration of the First 50 Years in the Life and Times of Best Western International, by William H. Boyer (Heritage)

"Spotted Dick, S'il Vous Plait:" An English Restaurant in France, by Tom Higgins (Fawcett Columbine)

To Learn More

American Hotel and Motel Association
1201 New York Ave. NW
Washington, DC 20005
(202) 289-3100; fax (202) 289-3199
E-mail: comments@ahma.com
Internet site: http://www.ahma.com

National Restaurant Association
1200 17th St. NW
Washington, DC 20036
(800) 424-5156; fax (202) 331-5946
E-mail: isal@restaurant.org
Internet site: http://www.restaurant.org

Human Resources Management

Treat employees like partners, and they act like partners.
—*Fred Allen, corporate executive, as quoted in* Quotable Business

What to Expect

People make business, government, and nonprofit organizations work. Introductory courses will illuminate the interrelated nature of this field, combining psychology, employer-employee dynamics, affirmative action, society's diversity, and economics. You'll learn about organizational behavior and structure, how to determine fair and appropriate pay and benefit levels, how to motivate employees, and how to help those with alcohol, drug, or emotional problems remain productive. Classes will demonstrate how personnel patterns vary between private and government employers, the effects of civil service on public employment, the changing role and influence of unions, and the use of lawsuits to affect employment practices. The goal is to prepare you for jobs that involve career counseling, hiring and training employees, managing salaries and benefits, evaluating job performance, and guiding employees who need to improve their substandard performance.

Trends

Trends in human resources and personnel management reflect rapid changes in our national and international economies. For example, as companies merge, downsize, consolidate, and contract out for services, human resource managers will confront an array of hot issues. They range from designing severance packages and layoff procedures to developing retraining incentives and outplacement programs for workers who lose their jobs. Globalization of the economy will require you to learn about personnel practices and labor laws in other countries where your employer may add or expand operations. In addition, expect more attention on ways to implement nondiscrimination laws and policies that encourage equal employment opportunity regardless of gender, age, race, religion, ethnicity, national origin, or sexual preference.

What You Need to Succeed

By definition, personnel and human resource management involves interaction with people — job applicants and employees, managers and supervisors, and benefits staff. Therefore, you need a mix of abilities: written and verbal communications skills, computer skills, financial and business management skills, and leadership skills. You must be outgoing and feel comfortable with group decision making—being part of a chain of command rather than an ultimate decision maker. Your duties will have serious economic implications for your employer, whether a private business, a government agency, or a nonprofit organization. But never forget the human beings your work affects. You'll deal with many people under stress about job seeking, promotions, demotions, raises, parental leave, health problems, and working conditions. You'll also find yourself in the midst of conflicts between co-workers, supervisors, unions, and group insurance companies. You'll have to behave with sensitivity, patience, and politeness even in tough situations.

Related Fields

Business Administration
Labor and Industrial Relations
Management
Psychology
Public Policy Studies

Typical Basic Courses

Dynamics of Interpersonal Behavior
Hiring and Retaining
Human Resource Planning
Human Resources Management
Introduction to Personnel Management
Labor Relations
Organizational Behavior
Training and Development

An Array of Electives

Compensation and Reward Systems
Diversity in the Workplace
Individual and Team Development
Management of Compensation
Organizational Staffing
Organizational Theory
Personnel Selection and Evaluation
Redefining the Employer-Employee
  Relationship

On-Campus Opportunities

College personnel office
Job placement center

Job Opportunities

Adequate supply / Some oversupply

Reading to Explore

Mission Possible by Ken Blanchard and Terry Waghorn (McGraw-Hill)

Productive Workplaces: Organizing and Managing for Dignity, Meaning, and Community, by Marvin R. Weisbord (Jossey-Bass)

Proversity: Getting Past Face Value and Finding the Soul of People: A Manager's Journey, by Lawrence Otis Graham (Wiley)

Sacred Cows Make the Best Burgers: Developing Change-Ready People and Organizations, by David Brandy (Warner)

The Individualized Corporation: A New Doctrine for Managing People, by Christopher A. Bartlett and Sumantha Ghoshal (HarperCollins)

To Learn More

International Personnel Management
  Association
1617 Duke St.
Alexandria, VA 22314
(703) 549-7100; fax (703) 684-0948
E-mail: ipma@ipma-hr.org
Internet site: http://www.ipma-hr.org

Industrial Technology

Gee, we can develop a theoretical base for technology, but do we have the people available to actually make, manufacture, and utilize the technology?
—*Dan Manthei, educator, in newspaper interview*

What to Expect

This field prepares technical and technical management professionals for careers in business, industry, education, and government. Introductory courses provide extensive laboratory work and a close physical relationship with tools, electrical equipment, and moving machinery, plus a crucial awareness of industrial and occupational safety. In lower-level courses, for example, you can develop basic drafting competency, experiment with thermal, chemical, electrical, and mechanical properties of industrial materials, and work with transistor circuits, oscillators, and operational amplifiers. You'll use computers and other technology to design, plan, and control industrial and mechanical processes. At an advanced level, you'll learn about automotive, aviation, and manufacturing technologies, as well as electronics, graphics, design, construction, and materials ranging from wood and metals to plastics and composites. Course work also will build your planning and analytical capabilities and help you better apply theory to real-world situations encountered in the workplace. Because industrial technologists often specialize, you can take higher-level courses in such areas as production, polymers, robotics, metallurgy, automotive, aerospace, and packaging. Safety-oriented courses include fire protection and prevention, construction safety, and hazardous material handling.

Trends

Trends in industrial technology reflect society's expanding dependence on computers and computer-interfaced equipment and components to maintain reliable operations, to tackle problems, and to develop alternative approaches that are both efficient and economical. Vocational education and training programs, in schools and the workplace, will draw more attention as industry demands more skills from employees, who must be better prepared to deal with rapid technological changes, more sophisticated equipment, and global operations.

What You Need to Succeed

Industrial technologists must solve complex problems while working individually or as members of a team, perhaps with millions of dollars at stake and a deadline pressing. Written and

120

verbal communication skills are essential, as is your ability to interact with team members and people inside and outside your organization. Math and laboratory-oriented science skills are valuable. So are enjoyment of hands-on work and experimentation as well as an ability to think innovatively. In addition, you must be a self-motivated learner because change comes so rapidly in technological disciplines. What you learn in school might be quickly outdated, so plan to spend time tracking and testing new developments and equipment that can help you perform better. Finally, you need a broad range of knowledge and insight about the technological systems you manage, and you must be able to use the expertise of specialists to keep systems operating.

Related Fields

Civil Engineering
Computer Science
Electrical Engineering
Graphic Design
Materials Science and Engineering
Mechanical Engineering
Operations Research and Industrial
  Engineering

Typical Basic Courses

Applied Electronics
Engineering Design Graphics
General Drafting
Industrial Safety
Interior Design Drafting
Introduction to Industrial Technology
Metal Technology
Power and Energy Technology

An Array of Electives

Automotive Electrical Systems
Computer-Assisted Drafting
Construction Safety
Industrial Robotics
Linear Electronics
Manufacturing Quality
Metallurgy and Materials Testing
Student Teaching

On-Campus Opportunities

Campus physical plant
Campus workshops
Laboratory technician assistant

Job Opportunities

Near balance / Supply equals demand

Reading to Explore

Aramis, or the Love of Technology, by Bruno Latour (Harvard University)

Electrifying America: Social Meanings of a New Technology, 1880–1940, by David E. Ney (MIT)

Imagined Worlds, by Freeman Dyson (Harvard University)

Popular Mechanics (Magazine)

Why Things Bite Back: Technology and the Revenge of Unintended Consequences, by Edward Tenner (Alfred A. Knopf)

To Learn More

National Association of Industrial
  Technology
3300 Washtenaw Ave., Suite 220
Ann Arbor, MI 48104
(313) 677-0720; fax (313) 677-2407
E-mail: nait@nait.org
Internet site: http://nait.org

121

International Relations

Their goal is a world made safe for differences.
—*Ruth Pelton Benedict, anthropologist, in* The Chrysanthemum and the Sword

What to Expect

Colleges are adding a real-world focus to their traditional preoccupation with theory, and that's one reason virtually every major from accounting to dance to secondary education to parks and recreation now encompasses more international aspects than ever before. The study of international relations crosses disciplinary borders, just as professionals in the field cross national borders. That's evident from your beginning classes in foreign politics, world cultures, and economics, where you learn to spot and analyze national differences and, increasingly, similarities. You'll also work to develop and improve mastery of foreign languages. At an advanced level, the integration of humanities, business, social science, and the natural sciences continues. You might choose to focus in detail on a particular region and its relationships with the United States and other parts of the world. You might select several courses that follow a theme such as development, international organizations, peace and conflict studies, or comparative politics. You might opt to analyze foreign policy and diplomacy, that of the United States or other countries. You might decide on multinational trade and economic relationships. Study abroad is a virtual necessity.

Trends

Trends in international relations reflect how more attention will be paid to the role of private, nonprofit, and nongovernmental institutions in foreign affairs, rather than the past fixation on the official activities and formal policies of national governments and multilateral organizations such as the United Nations, NATO, and the World Bank. In addition, there will be more attentiveness to the impact of human rights policies on foreign aid, trade, and diplomatic alliances.

What You Need to Succeed

You must be able to combine theoretical, analytical, and research-related skills because problems don't have simple, self-evident, and universally acceptable solutions. Without tolerance and open-mindedness, you're certain to smash into brick walls. Be open to non–North American lifestyles, business and diplomacy methods, governmental operations, approaches to human rights, and systems for managing social conflicts—even if you disagree with them. Strong written and verbal communications skills are required, whether you go into business, public service, cultural exchange, international education, or tourism. Become comfortable using computers and the Internet. Part of the excitement of this field is the opportunity to travel and explore new places, but your work might take you away from home for long periods of time. Although English remains the common tongue in world business and diplomacy, you'll be expected to have fluency in one—and preferably more than one—other language.

Related Fields

African Languages and Culture
Asian Languages and Culture
Latin American Studies
Middle Eastern and Near Eastern Studies
Russian and East European Studies
South and Southeast Asian Studies

Typical Basic Courses

Changing World Political Economy
Foreign and Comparative Politics
Foreign Policy Decision Making
International Economics
International Politics: Stability and Change
International Relations
National Security Policy
Politics of Developing Areas

An Array of Electives

African Political Systems
Antarctic Marine Ecology and Policy
Foreign Policy of the Western European Powers
International Business and Marketing
International Law and Organization
Middle East Politics
Problems in World Population, Food, and the Environment
Russian Foreign Policy

On-Campus Opportunities

International student center
Study abroad programs office

Job Opportunities

Adequate supply/ Some oversupply

Reading to Explore

Changing Differences: Women and the Shaping of American Foreign Policy, 1917–1994, by Rhodri Jeffreys-Jones (Rutgers University)

Preventative Diplomacy: Stopping Wars Before They Start, by Kevin M. Cahill (Center for International Health and Cooperation/Basic)

The Clash of Civilizations and the Remaking of World Order, by Samuel P. Huntington (Simon & Schuster)

The Road to Hell: The Ravaging Effects of Foreign Aid and International Charity, by Michael Maren (Free Press)

United Nations: The First 50 Years, by Stanley Meisler (Atlantic Monthly Press)

To Learn More

International Studies Association
324 Social Sciences Building
University of Arizona
Tucson, AZ 85721
(520) 621-7715; fax (520) 621-5780
E-mail: isa@arizona.edu
Internet site: http://www.isanet.org

Journalism

The reporter is a stone skipping on a pond, taking an instant to tell one story and ricocheting to the next, covering a lot of water while only skimming the surface.
—*Charles Kuralt, radio and television journalist, in* A Life on the Road

What to Expect

Introductory courses focus on the basics of reporting and news writing, including broadcast news. You learn to ask questions, conduct interviews, and do research with documents and records. You gain a better grasp of grammar and style. In addition, you're taught to craft stories that will grab and hold a reader's or viewer's attention, and to unite spoken or written words with photos or video for more impact. Journalism students learn to perform under deadline pressure, to sift facts from opinion, and to make fair and balanced presentations.

Professional ethics, an understanding of libel and privacy laws, and knowledge of freedom-of-information laws will be part of your education. So will exposure to specialized types of coverage, such as environmental, health, legal, business, sports, and arts reporting.

Trends

Trends in journalism reflect two principal factors: exploding new technologies and economics. Newspapers, magazines, and broadcast stations increasingly cruise the electronic highway. That means you'll need to develop a broad array of skills, including an ability to use the Internet, CD-ROM, video, desktop publishing software, and computer design tools. Meanwhile, economics are reshaping the media industry with mergers of print and broadcast companies, the elimination of some publications, and the frequent launch of new ones. As staffs shrink, more work will shift to freelance writers, editors, photographers, and graphic artists. At the same time, many businesses in and outside traditional news organizations are developing specialized newsletters, which require journalists with writing, reporting, desktop design, and sometimes marketing skills.

What You Need to Succeed

Journalists go nowhere without a sense of curiosity, a touch of skepticism, an open mind, a love of communication, and a fascination with controversy. They must think creatively, gather facts diligently, ask potentially embarrassing questions, work with little over-the-shoulder supervision, meet deadlines, and frequently deal with people who are under emotional or financial stress.

You'll have to be able to express yourself clearly, often under time pressure, whether you choose print, broadcasting, or new media such as the Internet. You also must be able to understand—and reflect—the need for fairness and balance. Cooperation and teamwork with other reporters, photographers, graphic artists, and editors are essential. Journalists also must be familiar with computers as writing, research, and design tools. Some reporting is done over the phone, but much of it involves face-to-face interviews and attending news events, so self-confidence and a professional attitude are essential.

Related Fields

Advertising
English
Photography and Cinema
Public Relations
Technical Writing
Telecommunications

Typical Basic Courses

Introduction to Mass Media
Media Ethics
Media Law
News Editing
Newswriting and Reporting
Photojournalism
Press and Contemporary Issues
Writing for Broadcast

An Array of Electives

Computer-Assisted Journalism
International Media
Magazine Feature Writing
Media Management
New Media and the Internet
Opinion and Interpretive Writing
Publication Design
Sports Reporting

On-Campus Opportunities

Academic department newsletters
College newspaper, magazine, television
station, or radio station

Job Opportunities

Surplus / Substantial oversupply

Reading to Explore

A Life on the Road, by Charles Kuralt (Ivy)

All the President's Men, by Bob Woodward and Carl Bernstein (Simon & Schuster)

Murdoch, by William Shawcross (Simon & Schuster)

On Writing Well, by William Zinsser (HarperPerennial)

The Corpse Had a Familiar Face, by Edna Buchanan (Random House)

To Learn More

Accrediting Council on Education in
    Journalism and Mass Communications
School of Journalism
Stauffer-Flint Hall
University of Kansas
Lawrence, KS 66045
(913) 864-3973; fax (913) 864-5225
Internet site: http://www.aejmc.sco.edu

Society of Professional Journalists
16 S. Jackson St.
Greencastle, IN 46135
(765) 653-3333; fax (765) 653-4631
Internet site: http://www.spj.org

Judaic Studies

To be a Jew is a destiny.
—*Vicki Baum, author, cited in* The Crown Treasury of Relevant Quotations

What to Expect

Judaic studies encompasses the humanities and social sciences. The goal is not to produce clergy but rather to offer a broad education to prepare students for careers in sectarian or nonsectarian settings. Introductory courses such as "The Bible and Archaeology," "Elementary Hebrew," "Ancient and Medieval Jewish Civilization," and "Judaism and Christianity in Dialogue" impart a broad sweep of culture, history, and theology. You'll learn about Judaism's historically and socially unique aspects—and also what it has shared with other faiths around the globe. Advanced courses offer you the opportunity to delve more deeply into topics such as Jewish mysticism, the Holocaust in the context of Europe's enduring legacy of anti-Semitism, the Bible as literature, modern Hebrew poetry, Jewish music, and women in Jewish law. Not only will you acquire a firm base in the ethical and spiritual wisdom of this 4,000-year-old tradition, but you'll gain an ability to see the world through the eyes of great Jewish theologians, scholars, writers, musicians, artists, and storytellers. You might spend a semester or two furthering your studies in Israel.

Trends

Trends in Judaic studies include a growing interest in the role of women—historically and at present—in Jewish theology, culture, community, and family dynamics. The rapid increase in the number of female rabbis, cantors, and lay educational leaders reflects this development. There is also greater focus on the achievements and struggles of Sephardic (North African and Middle Eastern) Jewry, including Jewish people from Iran, Yemen, and Syria, generally ignored until recently by scholars in this field. The subject of Jewish mysticism—known as the Kabbalah—is also gaining attention among people of diverse faiths and backgrounds, interested in applying the wisdom of arcane texts to daily life today.

What You Need to Succeed

Are you fascinated by the sweeping drama of Jewish history, literature, music, philosophy, and theology? Certainly, such enthusiasm helps in this interdisciplinary field. But Judaic studies demands more than just interest or even pride in one of the world's oldest, influential religious-social groups. The ability to analyze historical documents, including primary sources—written in Hebrew, Aramaic, Yiddish, and other languages—is your foundation. Because such texts often express philosophical and religious concepts in abstruse symbolism, an ability to think broadly, yet with an eye to fine shades of meaning, is crucial. So is a tolerance for diversity of opinions on religious and ethnic matters and a willingness to reconsider traditional beliefs. You'll need a capacity to assess modern events—such as the social transformation of American Jewry, the Holocaust, and global politics embroiling Israel—through a powerful historical lens. To share your findings with colleagues and the general public interested in Jewish affairs, you'll need to write well. Increasingly, those in Judaic Studies are finding careers in education and community service, so interpersonal skills are a definite asset.

Related Fields

Archaeology and Anthropology
Classical Languages and Classics
History
Middle Eastern and Near Eastern
  Studies
Philosophy
Religious Studies and Theology

Typical Basic Courses

Ancient and Medieval Jewish Civilization
Bible and Archaeology
Elementary Hebrew
Introduction to Jewish Literature
Judaism and Christianity in Dialogue
Modern Jewish Civilization
Rebirth of Israel
The Jew in American Popular Literature

An Array of Electives

Analysis of Jewish Liturgical Texts
Holocaust and Modern Man
Islamic Philosophy
Israeli Politics and the Middle East
Jewish Ethics and Values
Jewish Mysticism
Women in Jewish Law
Yiddish Literature in Translation

On-Campus Opportunities

Campus museum
Research assistant

Job Opportunities

Surplus / Substantial oversupply

Reading to Explore

Gabriel's Palace: Jewish Mystical Tales, by Howard Schwartz (Oxford University Press)

Hitler's Willing Executioners: Ordinary Germans and the Holocaust, by Daniel Goldhagen (Knopf)

Living Judaism: The Complete Guide for Jewish Belief, Tradition, and Practice, by Wayne Dosick (HarperCollins)

Opening the Inner Gates: New Paths in Kabbalah and Psychology, by Edward Hoffman (Shambhala)

Sages and Dreamers: Biblical, Talmudic, and Hasidic Portraits and Legends, by Elie Wiesel (Simon & Schuster)

To Learn More

Association for Jewish Studies, MB 0001
Brandeis University
POB 9110
Waltham, MA 02254
(617) 736-2981; fax (617) 736-2982
E-mail: ajs@brandeis.edu
Internet site:
  http://www.acls.org/ajewishs.htm

Coalition for the Advancement of Jewish
  Education
261 West 35th Street, Suite #12A
New York, NY 10011
(212) 268-4210; fax (212) 268-4214
E-mail: 5008447@mcimail.com
Interet site: http://www.caje.org

127

Labor and Industrial Relations

Labor in this country is independent and proud. It has not to ask the patronage of capital, but capital solicits the aid of labor.
—*Daniel Webster, orator and diplomat, from a speech on April 2, 1824*

What to Expect

Labor relations is a dynamic field wrapped up in conflict and compromise, negotiation and tension, and located at the heart of our economic system. In early courses, you'll survey the historical and legal frameworks of the labor movement, learning about major labor-management laws, the structure of unions, economics, and the collective bargaining process. You'll become familiar with wage and benefit issues, administration of labor contracts, strikes, lockouts, grievance procedures, and workplace psychology. Classes also will cover unionization strategies adopted by unions and anti-unionization strategies used by employers. Labor laws, including court decisions, congressional actions, and National Labor Relations Board rulings, are part of the curriculum. Advanced courses dig more deeply into negotiation tactics, the role of arbitration, unfair labor practices, and contract enforcement. You can also explore key public policy issues such as workers' rights, the role of government in labor-management disputes, and occupational safety and health regulations.

Trends

Trends in labor and industrial relations include contracting out—the use of independent contractors rather than employees to perform work—and the development of worker-management councils to cooperatively address job concerns such as quality, occupational safety, working conditions, and implementation of new programs and technologies. Among government employers, there's momentum to privatize traditionally public services, including jails, schools, and health services, often at the cost of unionized jobs. Still another trend involves the move to unionize low-paid blue collar workers. Federal and state laws requiring welfare recipients to find jobs will also impact labor-management relations.

What You Need to Succeed

Whether you work in a labor union, in management, or as a neutral participant, such as an arbitrator or mediator, a solid foundation in economics will be essential. Beyond that, you should have an interest in problem solving and conflict resolution, because both sides prefer a win-win solution to the financial and personal disruption of a strike, lock-out, or slow-down. That requires an openness to negotiation and compromise, as well as an ability to focus on long-term goals, not merely a short-term edge. Certainly, you must be capable of clearly communicating your side's position and rationally assessing other points of view. In addition, you need self-confidence and media savvy to deal with press questions about potential or ongoing controversies. Other essential attributes for the labor relations professional include an interest in public affairs and the versatility to apply knowledge from multiple fields (for example, sociology, psychology, history, political science, business administration, and economics).

Related Fields

Economics
Human Resources and Personnel
  Management
Management
Psychology
Public Policy Studies

Typical Basic Courses

Collective Bargaining
Compensation and Benefits Systems
Employment and Unemployment
Income Maintenance and Health Care
Labor and Employment Law
Labor Markets
Quality of Work Life
Trade Union History and Organization

An Array of Electives

Collective Bargaining in Public
  Employment
Comparative Industrial Relations
Equal Opportunity Employment
Grievance Administration and
  Arbitration
Human Resource Information Systems
Human Resource Strategies and
  Decisions
Negotiation and Conflict Resolution
Organizational Behavior in Labor
  Relations

On-Campus Opportunities

Personnel office

Job Opportunities

Near balance / Supply equals demand

Reading to Explore

Can Unions Survive: The Rejuvenation of the American Labor Movement, by Charles B. Craver (New York University)

Rights at Work: Employment Relations in the Post-Union Era, by Richard Edwards (Brookings Insitution)

The New Unionism: Employee Involvement in the Changing Corporation, by Charles C. Heckscher (Basic Books)

The Transformation of American Industrial Relations, by Thomas A. Kochan, Harry C. Katz, and Robert B. McKersie (Basic Books)

Which Side Are You On? Trying to Be for Labor When It's Flat on Its Back, by Thomas Geoghegan (Plume)

To Learn More

Industrial Relations Research Association
4233 Social Science Building
1180 Observatory Drive
University of Wisconsin
Madison, WI 53706
(608) 262-2762; fax (608) 265-4591
E-mail: kbhutchi@facstff.wisc.edu
Internet site:
  http://www.ilr.cornell.edu/irra

Landscape Architecture

Ever charming, ever new / When will the landscape tire the view?
—*John Dyer, poet, in "Grongar Hill"*

What to Expect

As a student, you'll learn how to design the environment of neighborhoods, towns, and cities while protecting and managing the natural environment and enhancing the quality of life for the residents. Introductory courses provide a foundation in design theory, landscape horticulture, garden design, and construction. You'll gain perspective and an understanding of the field's influence through a landscape history course. As you advance, you can focus on more specialized topics ranging from site planning, urban planning, and regional landscape planning to ecological design, historic reclamation and preservation, and park and recreation planning. The social and behavioral aspects of landscape design also are important because the landscape architect's work is not done in an aesthetic vacuum. There are human dimensions to design, such as meeting the special needs of the elderly or disabled, so you should learn to evaluate existing environments and their effects on people. And because landscape architecture by definition involves manipulating the environment, classes should familiarize you with laws dealing with wetlands, clean water, and other environmental and natural resources issues.

Trends

Trends in landscape architecture will increasingly involve professionals in environmental protection and land reclamation, while rural concerns may attract you to farmland preservation, small town revitalization, and energy resource development and conservation. Innovations in computer technology are broadening the realm of computerized design, and there is a booming interest in landscape architecture for indoor settings such as atriums, malls, and enclosed pedestrian spaces.

What You Need to Succeed

You should appreciate nature and enjoy working with your hands and in the field. In addition, you'll need a working knowledge of architecture, civil engineering, horticulture, and urban planning, because elements from each of those fields are used to design aesthetic and practical relationships with the land. You must also be able to visualize alternatives to develop appropriate solutions for landscape architectural problems. Creativity might provide an edge. Technical skills and mastery of computer-assisted design software are essential, and so is a willingness to keep up with other technology, including video simulation to help clients envision your ideas and geographic information systems for mapping. Also essential are verbal and written communication skills, because the work requires you to confer with clients, explain and demonstrate their options, and work with construction personnel, gardeners, and other people who will physically implement your concepts and design. Be flexible, because you might need to make many changes before a design is finalized.

Related Fields

Architecture
Civil Engineering
Forestry
Horticulture
Parks and Recreation
Urban Planning

Typical Basic Courses

Design of Gardens and Parks
Fundamentals of Planting Design
Fundamentals of Site Grading and
    Construction
Land Use Planning
Landscape Architectural Design
Landscape Design History
Shaping the American Landscape
Urban Landscape Design

An Array of Electives

Comprehensive Landscape Planning
Environmental Art
Environmental Land Planning Theory
Golf Course Planning and Design
Land Surveying
Landscape Horticulture
Site Construction and Structures
Vernacular Landscape and Popular
    Culture

On-Campus Opportunities

Campus greenhouses
Campus grounds department
Campus planning office

Job Opportunities

Near balance / Supply equals demand

Reading to Explore

Frederick Law Olmsted: Designing the American Landscape, by Charles Beveridge (Rizzoli)

Gray World, Green Heart: Technology, Nature, and the Sustainable Landscape, by Rob Thayer (Wiley)

One Hundred English Gardens: The Best of the English Heritage Parks and Gardens, by Patrick Taylor (Rizzoli)

Taking Measures Across the American Landscape, by James Corner and Alex S. MacLean (Yale)

The Inward Garden: Creating a Place of Beauty and Meaning, by Julie Moir Messervy (Little, Brown)

To Learn More

American Society of Landscape
    Architects
4401 Connecticut Ave. NW, 5th Floor
Washington, DC 20008
(202) 686-2752; fax (202) 686-1001
E-mail: landnet@asla.org
Internet site: http://www.asla.org/asla

Latin American Studies

In diverse ways, the nations of Latin America are moving beyond their traditional roles as bit players on the world stage to claim leading parts in its economic, political, and cultural dramas.
—Peter Winn, author, in Americas: The Changing Face of Latin America and the Caribbean

What to Expect

A program in Latin American studies combines regionally oriented courses in economics, political science, history, literature, anthropology, religion, and other fields with Spanish and Portuguese language training. You'll study Latin American government systems from democracy to dictatorship to communism, the history of the region before and after European colonialism, and its arts and music. Most courses focus on Latin America itself, but learn about the history and heritage of Spain and Portugal, as well as the roles of Latinos and Latinas in the United States. If you're interested in literature, take advanced courses in the Latin American novel, drama and essay, and poetry and short story, plus classes in Spanish literature and Latino literature. If history and political science excite you, explore Latin American revolutions, the colonial era, or the history of individual countries such as Mexico, Peru, or Cuba. Language courses continue throughout the program. Foreign study experiences build linguistic fluency, cultural sensitivity, and substantive knowledge.

Trends

Trends in Latin American studies reflect the expanding business, political, and financial ties between the region and the United States. The North American Free Trade Agreement opened opportunities in Mexico, and pressure continues by other Latin American nations for similar treaties with the United States. Meanwhile, people of Latin American heritage are a fast-growing proportion of the U.S. population, making society, schools, and culture more diverse. At the same time, some governments in the region are under pressure to improve human rights, spur free market economies, and protect the environment from exploitation.

What You Need to Succeed

You need a genuine interest in the region's peoples, cultures, and history, plus the ability to identify common themes as well as differences in how each country or ethnic group developed. That will help you use your knowledge in a variety of arenas including international business and trade, government, diplomacy, education, tourism, journalism, and the arts. Take a multidisciplinary approach to assessing issues and potential solutions. Certainly, you must be able to speak, read, and write fluently in Spanish. Mastery of Portuguese, which is dominant in Brazil, is an asset, too. In one or both of those languages, you should be able to conduct research and interviews, use computerized databases, and discuss technical matters within your area of expertise or business. Interest in travel, in experiencing different cultures, and in meeting people of divergent backgrounds is valuable.

Related Fields

Geography
History
International Relations
Political Science
Romance Languages
Sociology

Typical Basic Courses

Art of Hispania
Colonial Latin American to 1810
Introduction to Spanish American
 Culture from the Discovery of America
 to the Present
Latino Cultures in the United States
Modern Latin America Since 1810
Portuguese
Spanish
Women in Latin America

An Array of Electives

Anthropology of Developing Nations
Modern Brazilian Literature and Culture
Modern Latin American Fiction in
 Translation
Political Economy of Latin America
Pre-Columbian Art: Ancient Mexico and
 Peru
The Economics of Development
The Invention of Spanish American
 Tradition
Third World Images in Film

On-Campus Opportunities

Campus museum
International student center
Translator for foreign visitors

Job Opportunities

Adequate supply / Some oversupply

Reading to Explore

Cracking Latin America: A Country-by-Country Guide to Doing Business in the World's Emerging New Markets, by Allyn Enderlyn and Oliver C. Dziggel (Probus Publishing)

Eva Peron, by Alicia Dujovne Ortiz (St. Martin's)

Guerilla Prince: The Untold Story of Fidel Castro, by Georgie Anne Geyer (Little, Brown)

Latin American Art in the Twentieth Century, by Edward J. Sullivan (Phaidon)

The Latino Reader: An American Literary Tradition from 1542 to the Present, by Harold Augerbraum and Margarite F. Olmo (Houghton Mifflin)

To Learn More

Center for Latin American Studies
University of Pittsburgh
4E04 Forbes Quadrangle
Pittsburgh, PA 15260
(412) 648-7392; fax (412) 648-2199
E-mail: clas@pitt.edu
Internet site: http://www.pitt.edu/~clas

Consort. of Latin American Studies
 Programs
Center for Latin American Studies
Tulane University
New Orleans, LA 70118
(504) 865-5164; fax (504) 865-6719
E-mail: rtsclas@mailhost.tcs.tulane.edu
Internet site: http://www.tulane.edu/~clas/
 clashome.html

Linguistics

The limits of my language stand for the limits of my world.
—*Ludwig Wittgenstein, philosopher, cited in* The Crown Treasury of Relevant Quotations

What to Expect

Language is a cornerstone of every society, every civilization. Languages evolve differently, some are more structurally complex than others, and some of the more than 5,000 known languages are spoken by only a small number of people. You'll begin by examining language as a system of human communication and by studying the differences and universal elements of language, including sound systems and patterns, word structure, and grammar. Because languages exist in social context, introductory courses will explore language and gender, language and social identity in the United States, and language in various cultures. You should become familiar with the research and data-gathering techniques linguists use. As you progress, courses will cover elements of linguistics in depth, including phonetics, syntax, morphology, and semantics. Psycholinguistics electives explore language acquisition and high-level language processing—what happens in the mind when you read or hear speech—including word recognition and the processing of sentences and conversations. Sociolinguistics describes and explains language in a social context, including elements of gender, ethnicity, and social class. You'll also learn field methods.

Trends

Trends in linguistics encompass greater sensitivity to the relationship between language and social problems, such as racial discrimination and inadequate public school systems. Debates also rage today over African American vernacular English and whether students who don't speak English at home should be taught in their native languages. In an era of telecommunications, satellite transmissions, VCRs, and easy international travel, linguists are under pressure to record and preserve "dying" languages before their dwindling number of speakers disappears entirely.

What You Need to Succeed

Are you fascinated by human language in all its incredible diversity? Do you enjoy exploring the changes that "living" tongues like English undergo in vocabulary, local dialect, syntax, and daily use? Are you interested in how such changes relate to movements in politics, social demographics, the sciences, fine arts, music, and literature? If so, a career in linguistics may prove satisfying. Employment opportunities in education, international business and marketing, public relations, and telecommunications and computer software development all expect strong analytic and research skills, a solid background in linguistic fundamentals, verbal precision, and self-starting ability. Linguists are called upon frequently for their expertise on specialized topics, including artificial intelligence, the history of the English language, second-language acquisition, and the growth of particular linguistic systems (such as those employed by lawyers, clergy, and physicians). Also important is a flair for translating and working with differing languages—ancient and contemporary—and adeptness in communicating orally and in writing to colleagues, business people, scientists, and the lay public.

Related Fields

Classical Languages and Classics
Cognitive Science
Philosophy
Psychology
Romance Languages
Speech Science and Audiology

Typical Basic Courses

Historical Linguistics
Introduction to Language and Linguistics
Language Acquisition
Phonetics and Phonology
Psycholinguistics
Sociolinguistics
Syntax
The Structure and Meaning of Words

An Array of Electives

Artificial Intelligence and Human
  Cognition
History of Legal Terminology
History of the English Language
Language and Culture
Philosophy of Language
Applied Linguistics: Second Language
  Acquisition
The Structure of Modern English

On-Campus Opportunities

Campus museum
Campus speech, hearing, and language
  clinic
Research assistant

Job Opportunities

Surplus / Substantial oversupply

Reading to Explore

Language and Human Behavior, by Derek Bickerton (University of Washington)

The Cambridge Encyclopedia of Language, by David Crystal (Cambridge University Press)

The Language Instinct: How the Mind Creates Language, by Steven Pinker (HarperPerennial)

The Origin of Language: Tracing the Evolution of the Mother Tongue, by Merritt Ruhlen (Wiley)

You Just Don't Understand: Women and Men in Conversation, by Deborah Tannen

To Learn More

Center for Applied Linguistics
1118 22nd Street NW
Washington, DC 20037
(202) 429-9292; fax (202) 659-8712
E-mail: info@cal.org
Internet site: http://www.cal.org

Linguistic Society of America
1325 18th Street NW, Suite 211
Washington, DC 20036
(202) 835-1714; fax (202) 835-1717
E-mail: lsa.lsadc.org
Internet site: http://www.lsadc.org

135

Management

Management now is where the medical profession was when it decided that working in a drug store was not sufficient training to become a doctor.
—*Lawrence A. Appley, American Management Association, cited in* Money Talks: The 2500 Greatest Business Quotes from Aristotle to DeLorean

What to Expect

Think of management as the study of decision making about how to allocate an organization's resources to achieve particular objectives. Be aware that although it's generally associated with business administration, managerial principles can also be applied to education and health care operations, religious and nonprofit organizations, and government. You'll become familiar with managerial concepts, techniques, and processes, and then move on to specific applications, including personnel, production, communications, and purchasing. Explore the dynamics of organizational behavior, computer applications, procurement, and analysis of management problems. Classes also address the role of business and society, legal and ethical restraints on business behavior, and diversity in the workplace. Advanced courses provide an opportunity to explore subjects in depth. For instance, if you're interested in personnel, take classes in compensation administration, human resources training, employment law, and labor relations. Other options include transportation management, logistics policy, multinational business management, entrepreneurship, and principles of retailing. Field studies and workplace observation should be part of the curriculum so you can watch professional managers in action.

Trends

Trends in management reflect the changing dynamics of the workplace, including downsizing, re-engineering, contracting out for services, corporate mergers and acquisitions, a rising self-employment rate, and aggressive organizing drives by labor unions. These developments will require managers to be creative and adaptable in making budgetary and personnel decisions. It also means that managers will find themselves changing duties and jobs more often—and sometimes involuntarily. Finally, managers will be pressed harder to demonstrate how their efforts are cost effective for their businesses, government agencies, or nonprofit organizations.

What You Need to Succeed

With rampant corporate and government downsizing, right-sizing, and re-engineering today, managers are under unprecedented pressure to meet organizational goals in an effective, timely manner. More than ever, you'll be expected to work well under stressful deadlines, put in long hours as necessary, participate fully as a team player, and communicate clearly with subordinates, colleagues, and executive officers. To succeed in management, you'll also need to combine analytic and social skills with computer literacy. It's vital to understand both the advantages and limitations of computer-based decision making. Those in management will rely especially heavily on the tools of mathematics, statistics, communications, and economic analysis. Throughout the American workplace, managers are becoming increasingly sensitive to legal considerations involving gender, race, sexual orientation, and ethnicity—as well as to the importance of accommodating physically and mentally impaired employees, protected by recent federal laws. Learn how to motivate others, instill confidence, avoid jargon, and solve problems cooperatively.

Related Fields

Business Administration
Human Resources and Personnel
    Management
Labor and Industrial Relations
Marketing
Operations Research and Industrial
    Engineering
Psychology

Typical Basic Courses

Business and Society
Computers in Business
Database Management
Financial Management
Labor-Management Relations
Leadership and Motivation
Organizational Development
Principles of Management

An Array of Electives

Compensation and Performance
    Appraisal
Decision Making and Negotiation
International Management
Male and Female Experiences in
    Organizations
Management Leadership and
    Organizational Productivity
Selection and Staffing
Strategic Management
The Sociology of Entrepreneurship

On-Campus Opportunities

Campus business office
Research assistant

Job Opportunities

Adequate supply / Some oversupply

Reading to Explore

The Dilbert Principle, by Scott Adams (HarperBusiness)

The Discipline of Market Leaders, by Michael Treacy and Fred Wiersema (Addison-Wesley)

The One-Minute Manager, by Kenneth Blanchard and Spencer Johnson (Berkley)

The Witch Doctors: Making Sense of the Management Gurus, by John Micklethwait and Adrian Woodridge (Times Books/Random House)

Thriving on Chaos: Handbook for a Management Revolution, by Tom Peters (HarperCollins)

To Learn More

American Management Association
1601 Broadway
New York, NY 10019-7420
(212) 586-8100; fax (212) 903-8168
E-mail: amapubs@aol.com
Internet site: http://www.amanet.org

Sigma Iota Epsilon
214 Wescott Building
Florida State University
Tallahassee, FL 32306
(904) 644-1750; fax (904) 644-4447
E-mail: mhankin@admin.fsu.edu
Internet site: http://www.fsu.edu/~sie

Marine Biology and Oceanography

The attractions, fascinations there are in sea and shore! What is it in us, aroused by those indirections and directions—so indescribably comforting, striking emotional, impalpable depths?
—*Walt Whitman, poet, cited in* The Crown Treasury of Relevant Quotations

What to Expect

Although marine biology is an offshoot of zoology while oceanography is linked to earth sciences, these two fields are strongly connected. Their foundation courses build familiarity with the physical and biological sciences, research techniques, and laboratory tools. You'll learn how oceans and their inhabitants fit the environmental picture. You'll survey ocean systems, resources and technology, the marine environment and principles of marine ecology, special roles and adaptations of marine plants and animals, and major marine communities. Classes cover physical, biological, chemical, and geological aspects of the oceans, including the development and structure of ocean basins. Advanced courses explore marine species in depth, including the evolution, taxonomy, behavior, physiology, and distribution of fish and marine mammals. You can study the effects and relationships of natural forces such as volcanoes and rock types on the oceans' physical features and resources. Marine ecology courses may focus on a particular region—such as Antarctica or the Gulf of Maine—and management of ocean resources.

Trends

Trends in marine biology and oceanography reflect concerns over marine habitats and both natural and human threats to the oceans, their plant life, and their wildlife. Those concerns range from destruction of coral reefs to tanker spills to overfishing and airborne pollutants. In addition, changing weather patterns, such as global warming, may affect shoreline erosion, the survival of marine species, and the food supply. Exploration and extraction of under-the-ocean and off-shore resources such as oil and minerals have wide ramifications, including pollution.

What You Need to Succeed

Develop strong research skills, which should encompass a mastery of computers, laboratory equipment, and high-tech instrumentation, including remote-sensing devices in satellites and electronic tracking equipment. Then you'll need to analyze that information and draw reasonable conclusions with economic, political, and environmental ramifications. Whether you go into research, service with a government or nonprofit organization, business, or education, you must be able to communicate scientific concepts and viewpoints effectively to a variety of audiences. Such domains include lectures, speeches, community meetings, articles, press releases, and books. You should enjoy the outdoors, field work, and travel because your career is apt to involve all three. Marine biologists and oceanographers may find themselves in remote areas of the world, but many also spend considerable time in laboratory settings. These fields frequently unite scientists from different countries in joint projects, such as exploring for new sources of oil or protecting endangered species.

Related Fields

Animal Science
Biology
Environmental Studies
Fisheries and Wildlife
Zoology

Typical Basic Courses

Biology of Fishes
Coastal Ecology and Bioclimates
Ecology of Animal Behavior
Introduction to Field Marine Science
Introduction to Nautical Science
Neurobiology of Animal Behavior
Practical Oceanography
Wetland Resources

An Array of Electives

Adaptations of Marine Organisms
Archaeology of Marine Communities
Coastal and Oceanic Law and Policy
Fisheries Management
Marine Biology for Teachers
Marine Botany: Ecology of Marine
    Plants
Marine Pollution
Volcanology

On-Campus Opportunities

Campus museum
Research assistant

Job Opportunities

Adequate supply / Some oversupply

Reading to Explore

Among Whales, by Roger Payne (Scribner)

Fire Under the Sea: The Discovery of Hot Springs on the Ocean Floor and the Origin of Life, by Joseph Cone (Morrow)

Ocean Enough and Time: Discovery of the Waters Around Antarctica, by James Gorman (HarperCollins)

The Universe Below, by William J. Broad (Simon & Schuster)

The Wealth of Oceans: Environment and Development on Our Ocean Planet, by Michael L. Weber and Judith A. Gradwohl (Norton)

To Learn More

American Society of Limnology and
    Oceanography
Virginia Institute of Marine Science
Route 1208
Gloucester Point, VA 23062
(804) 684-7000; fax (202) 357-0422
E-mail: zealon@vims.edu
Internet site: http://www.vims.edu

Marine Technology Society
1828 L Street NW, Suite 906
Washington, DC 20036-5104
(202) 775-5966; fax (202) 429-9417
E-mail: mtspubs@aol.com
Internet site:
    http://www.cms.udel.edu/mts

Marketing

Be everywhere, do everything, and never fail to astonish the customer.
—*(motto of Macy's department store) Margaret Getchell, cited in* Money Talks: The 2500 Greatest Business Quotes from Aristotle to DeLorean

What to Expect

As you'll soon recognize, marketing is about a lot more than sales. It embraces logistics, consumer behavior, and business management, too. Beginning courses introduce you to buyer behavior, determination of market segmentation and positioning, assessment of demand, and development of pricing strategies. You'll see how to apply behavioral principles to customer satisfaction, market planning, and the mix of products. And you'll study the role of manufacturing, operations, purchasing, and transportation of products in determining whether a business organization is competitive. A marketing research course will teach about survey design, data collection, and interpretation of information to analyze customer preferences and demand. Electives in personal selling, retail management, and sales management help build practical skills, ranging from analysis of sales territories and motivation of personnel to retail budgeting and promotional techniques. You can choose highly focused courses such as food marketing or mail-order techniques. To prepare for the global economy, take a course in international marketing management. A common thread in basic and advanced courses should be sensitivity to ethical practices, legal compliance, and diversity issues.

Trends

Trends in marketing mirror the telecommunications explosion, the growing acceptance of multiethnic values, and the ease of travel. Also, the Internet and cable television will become increasingly popular tools for selling products, services, and ideas. Traditional marketing avenues—among them direct mail, telephone solicitation, newspaper and magazine advertisements, and radio commercials—will become better targeted and more sophisticated to attract buyers. In addition, the globalization of the economy will open foreign markets to U.S. goods and services, creating vast marketing opportunities.

What You Need to Succeed

The field of marketing offers tremendous opportunity professionally, financially, and creatively to those with the right blend of skills. What are these? Start with a solid grasp of computer and statistical tools for measuring consumer attitudes, and combine that with a background in finance, sales, distribution, operations, and increasingly, social psychology. You should enjoy selling ideas, products, and services, and influencing the way people behave. The ability to think creatively—even along unusual, unconventional lines—in designing effective marketing campaigns can catapult you to success and influence in the business world. As an expert marketing products or services, you'll spend much of your professional time working as part of a team, along with those in advertising, finance, sales, and management. The more you can attack often-complex marketing issues from a multifactor and multidisciplinary viewpoint—for example, in motivating Baby Boomers to save for their retirement, or persuading Generation Xers to have greater brand-name loyalty—the more successful you're likely to be. Likewise, the ability to forecast trends through both quantitative and qualitative methods is a valued asset.

Related Fields

Advertising
Business Administration
Human Resources and Personnel
  Management
Public Relations

Typical Basic Courses

Consumer Behavior
International Marketing
Marketing Research
Principles of Marketing
Psychology of Selling
Quantitative Analysis for the Marketing
  Decision Maker
Retailing
Social Marketing

An Array of Electives

American Demographics
International Marketing Management
Manufacturing, Planning and Control
Marketing Fruits, Vegetables, and
  Ornamental Products
Marketplace Regulation and Consumer
  Protection
Procurement and Supply Management
Product and Price Planning
Sales Management

On-Campus Opportunities

Campus fund-raising and development
  office
Campus bookstore

Job Opportunities

Near balance / Supply equals demand

Reading to Explore

From Concept to Market, by Gary S. Lynn
(Wiley)

Inside the Tornado, by Geoffrey A. Moore
(HarperBusiness)

*Roadside Empires: How the Chains Franchised
America,* by Stan Luxemberg (Penguin)

*Selling the Invisible: A Field Guide to Modern
Marketing,* by Harry Beckwith (Warner)

*Service Edge: Inside 101 Companies That
Profit from Customer Care,* by Ron Zemke
and Dick Schaaf (New American
Library)

To Learn More

American Marketing Association
250 South Wacker Drive, Suite 200
Chicago, IL 60606
(312) 648-0536; fax (312) 993-7542
E-mail: info@ama.org
Internet site: http://www.ama.org

Pi Sigma Epsilon
6560 South 27th Street, Suite 203
Oak Creek, WI 53154
(414) 761-9350; fax (414) 761-9351
E-mail: pse@execpc.com
Internet site: http://www.execpc.com/~pse

Materials Science and Engineering

Where begin? With mechanistic processes like weaving? Printing? Stamping? Or with casting? Or with plastic, chemicalized materials like concrete, plastering, steel-making, paper-making, ceramics? Time was when the hand wrought. [But the] time is here when the process fabricates instead.

—*Frank Lloyd Wright, architect, in* Essays by Frank Lloyd Wright for Architectural Record, 1908–1952

What to Expect

Material engineers and scientists develop new types of metal alloys, ceramics, composites, and other materials to meet commercial needs. These range from ceramic tiles on the Space Shuttle to alloy turbine blades for jet engines to graphite golf club shafts. Throughout your studies, you'll apply the principles of mathematics and the physical sciences to tackle—and hopefully solve—such real-world problems. Beginning classes introduce you to the principles of materials science, including the structure, properties, and bonding of solids, thermodynamics, corrosion of metals, and the role of defects. You'll move on to overviews of processing and fabrication of materials, formation and processing technology for ceramics, and how to use phase diagrams and transformation kinetics to control the structure and mechanical properties of different materials. Higher-level courses become increasingly technical, whether they deal with the electronic properties of materials, pyrometry and thermal processing, thermochemistry, mechanical metallurgy, or polymers and composites. Look for options to help you specialize in an area of interest, such as aerospace applications, nuclear materials, or ceramic engineering design. Plan to spend a lot of time doing hands-on work in the laboratory to learn processing and fabrication, physical metallurgy, nondestructive testing, and other industrial techniques.

Trends

Trends in materials science and engineering reflect a response to industrial demands for the rapid development of stronger, more energy-efficient, more versatile materials. One expanding area involves biomaterials and biocompatability—designing materials for use in human implants. There will be continued attention to development of materials that can be manufactured and used in environmentally safe ways.

What You Need to Succeed

In creating new materials or enhancing already existing substances for specific scientific purposes, you'll need an array of essential skills. You'll be expected to be proficient in computer applications and applied mathematics. It's also important to demonstrate expertise in electronic instrumentation, mellaturgical properties, manufacturing systems, and of course, the specific chemical, biological, and engineering aspects of widely different materials. Because this field is one of the most rapidly changing today in all engineering, it's imperative to adapt quickly to new developments and enjoy learning long after you finish college. Professionals in materials science and engineering typically work in teams with other scientists, such as agricultural, civil, electrical, mechanical, and petroleum engineers as well as chemists and physicists, on solving problems.

Related Fields

Chemical Engineering
Electrical Engineering
Industrial Technology
Mechanical Engineering

Typical Basic Courses

Manufacturing Systems
Materials Science and Engineering
Mechanical Behavior of Materials
Mechanics of Deformable Solids
Physical Metallurgy
Polymeric Materials
Thermochemistry of Materials

An Array of Electives

Biological Transport Mechanics
Biomedical Electronics
Computational Mechanics
Dynamics
Environmental Effects on Materials
Experimental Mechanics
Failure Analysis
Physical Processing of Materials

On-Campus Opportunities

Laboratory assistant
Research assistant

Job Opportunities

Good demand / Possible shortage

Reading to Explore

A Place of My Own: The Education of an American Builder, by Michael Pollan (Random House)

American Plastics: A Cultural History, by Jeffrey L. Meikle (Rutgers University)

American Steel: Hot Metal and the Resurrection of the Rust Belt, by Richard Preston (Prentice-Hall)

Stuff, by Ivan Amato (Basic Books)

The Book of Bamboo, by David Farrelly (Sierra Club)

To Learn More

American Society for Metals
  International
9369 Kinsman Road
Materials Park, OH 44073-0002
(216) 338-5151; fax (216) 338-4634
E-Mail: asmfer@po.asm-intl.org
Internet site: http://www.asm-intl.org

The Minerals, Metals, Materials Society
420 Commonwealth Drive
Warrendale, PA 15086-7514
(800) 966-4867; fax (412) 776-3770
E-mail: csc@tms.org
Internet site: http://www.tms.org

Mathematics

Mathematics takes us into the region of absolute necessity, to which not only the actual world, but every possible world must conform.
—*Bertrand Russell, philosopher, cited in* The Reader's Digest Treasury of Modern Quotations

What to Expect

As a math student, you'll be immersed in one of the oldest and most fundamental fields of knowledge, yet you'll be learning how to create new theories and techniques involving up-to-the-minute technology. Your goal is to apply academic learning and computational tools to contemporary economics, engineering, business, and scientific problems. The building blocks are courses in algebra, trigonometry, probability and matrices, and calculus, along with differential equations and analytical geometry. You must master mathematical investigative techniques such as collecting data, searching for patterns, conjecturing, verifying, applying, and finding connections. Computers will be your indispensable tools, and you should be trained to use high-quality software to solve systems of linear and nonlinear equations, fixed-point iteration, and Newton's methods in several variables.

At a higher level, you'll hone analytical skills and explore topics in depth, including abstract and linear algebra, algebraic coding, numbers theory, and axiomatic and differential geometry. Geometric topology deals with the mathematical features of surfaces and higher dimensional manifolds, for example, and mathematical logic teaches logic and formal systems, syntax, and semantics. Other options encompass courses focusing on specific applications, such as mathematics for teachers, economists, biological scientists, and business administrators.

Trends

Trends in mathematics encourage mathematicians to use theories and techniques, including modeling and computational methods, to solve practical problems. Those could relate to analyzing the mathematical aspects of telecommunication systems, the effects of new drugs on diseases, the manufacturing processes, or production expenses. Professionals will be increasingly challenged by society's broad "math phobia" and mathematical illiteracy.

What You Need to Succeed

Not surprisingly, you need solid reasoning ability and persistence to identify, analyze, and apply basic principles of math to technical problems. Substantial knowledge of computer programming is mandatory, since most complex computation and much modeling are accomplished by computers. Written and verbal communication skills will help not only as you work with other math professionals but also when you interact with nonmathematicians and discuss proposed answers to their problems. You must be accurate, precise, and pay close attention to detail.

Competence with research tools is vital. Mathematicians frequently work on teams with experts in other disciplines, especially engineering, computer science, economics, government and business administration, statistics, actuarial science, physics, operations research, and even military strategy. That type of partnership requires an understanding of the allied fields and the ability to put math principles into a specific context. Finally, you must keep up with technological and computational advances that strengthen your capacity to solve technical problems.

Related Fields

Accounting
Computer Science
Finance and Banking
Statistics and Probability

Typical Basic Courses

Calculus
Introduction to Analysis
Introduction to Computer Science
Introduction to Modern Algebra
Linear Algebra
Multivariate Calculus
Ordinary Differential Equations
Probability Theory

An Array of Electives

Advanced Logic
Artificial Intelligence and Symbolic
 Programming
Complex Variables for Applications
Elementary Mathematical Physics
Evolution of Mathematical Concepts and
 Humanistic Studies
Mathematical Statistics
Number Theory
Topology

On-Campus Opportunities

Campus computer center
Research assistant

Job Opportunities

Adequate supply / Some oversupply

Reading to Explore

A Mathematician Reads the Newspaper, by John Allen Paulos (Anchor)

Mathematical Experience, by Philip J. Davis and Reuben Hersh (Birkhauser)

Mathematical Mysteries, by Calvin C. Clawson (Plenum)

Mathematical Tourist: Snapshots of Modern Mathematics, by Ivars Peterson (W. H. Freeman)

A Tour of the Calculus, by David Berlinski (Vintage)

To Learn More

Mathematical Association of America
1529 18th Street NW
Washington, DC 20036
(202) 387-5200; fax (202) 265-2384
E-mail: maahq@maa.org
Internet site: http://www.maa.org

Mechanical Engineering

The higher the technology, the higher the freedom. Technology enforces certain solutions: satellite dishes, computers, videos, and international phone lines force pluralism and freedom onto a society.
—*Lech Walesa, former president of Poland, cited in* The Executive's Book of Quotations

What to Expect

This is the broadest engineering discipline, spanning a variety of interdependent specialties. Through the curriculum, you'll learn to plan and design tools, machines, engines, and mechanical equipment ranging from robots, tools, and turbines to systems for refrigeration, air-conditioning, and materials handling. You'll rely on a broad foundation of mathematics, physics, and chemistry as you study how to apply solid mechanics, fluid mechanics, thermodynamics, heat transfer, materials, and electricity in industrial and commercial projects. You'll learn to design experiments and conduct engineering analysis in the laboratory and with computers. Typical introductory courses cover mechanical systems, mechanical behavior of materials, and basic solid and fluid mechanics. Technical electives encourage specializations such as energy conversion and utilization, machines and systems, nuclear engineering, thermal and environmental engineering, and vehicle propulsion. For example, you can choose courses in power plant design, nuclear reactor theory, or land vehicle dynamics. Look for classes in computer graphics and geometric modeling, computer modeling and simulation, and computer-aided design of components and systems. You should also learn about legal, regulatory, and environmental considerations in product design.

Trends

Trends in mechanical engineering reflect an expected growing demand for machinery and machine tools, as industrial machinery and processes will become increasingly complex. Also, construction and service sectors of the economy will need more mechanical engineering skills. At the same time, however, reductions in military spending and the nuclear energy industry are likely. More international opportunities will open as industrialization arrives in developing countries and as former communist nations build free-market economies. Certainly, environmental concerns will continue.

What You Need to Succeed

Fundamental for success in this field are strong abilities in mathematics and computer applications, coupled with an inquisitive mind and an interest in solving practical problems. It's not enough simply to know the various kinds of software and hardware for tackling particular tasks. You've got to be aware of their specific advantages and limitations. A solid grasp of physics—and the relevant principles that underlie the scientific problems you're addressing—is also an important asset. Whether developing new guidance systems for rockets or submarines, expanding a hospital's operating rooms, or improving the energy-efficiency of a regional power station, mechanical engineers always work as integral members of a team. You might be heavily involved in developing funding proposals, producing reports, and researching prior scientific efforts. So the sharper your communication skills—both oral and written—the more likely you are to succeed.

Related Fields

Aerospace and Aeronautical Engineering
Agricultural Engineering
Electrical Engineering
Materials Science and Engineering
Physics

Typical Basic Courses

Descriptive Geometry/Computer Graphics
Elements of Mechanical Design
Fluid Mechanics
Heat Transfer
Manufacturing Processes
Mechanical Vibrations
Mechanics of Materials Laboratory
Thermodynamics

An Array of Electives

Aerodynamics
Computer-Aided Design
Dynamics of Machines
Environmental Engineering
Fundamentals of Bio-Medical
   Engineering
Principles of Combustion
Solar Energy Design
Transducers, Sensors, and Computer
   Interfacing

On-Campus Opportunities

Laboratory assistant
Research assistant

Job Opportunities

Near balance / Supply equals demand

Reading to Explore

Innovators: The Discoveries, Inventions, and Breakthroughs of Our Times, by John Diebold *(Dutton)*

Levitating Trains and Kamikaze Genes: Technical Literacy for the 1990s, by Richard P. Brennan (Wiley)

The Evolution of Useful Things, by Henry Petroski (Knopf)

The Invention That Changed the World, by Robert Buderi (Simon & Schuster)

The Way Things Work, by David Macaulay (Houghton Mifflin)

To Learn More

American Society of Mechanical Engineers
345 East 47th Street
New York, NY 10017
(212) 705-7722; fax (212) 705-7739
Internet site: http://www.asme.org

Tau Beta Pi
University of Tennessee
POB 2697
Knoxville, TN 37901-2697
Internet site: http://www.tbp.org

Medical Technology

The machine does not isolate us from the great problems of [life], but plunges us more deeply into them.
—*Antoine de Saint-Exupéry, French author, cited in* The New International Dictionary of Quotations

What to Expect

On the cutting edge of patient care and new technologies, you'll be challenged to build a solid foundation of knowledge, then monitor and use the new methods in life-or-death situations. Plan to start with the fundamentals of laboratory analysis—biological, chemical, and instrumental—and the application of clinical laboratory principles, such as microscopy, specimen collection and handling, and quality control. At a higher level, you'll focus on the application of laboratory techniques to particular human and veterinary problems. You'll learn immunological methods to detect diseases, diagnostic biochemistry, and diagnostic assessment of blood cells and hemostatic functions. Another option is toxicology and therapeutic drug monitoring. Extensive hands-on laboratory work is involved, with some actual patient contact. You can specialize as well. For example, you might train to become a surgical technologist working in operating rooms or a radiologic technologist who takes x-rays and gives imaging tests, ultrasounds, and radiation treatment. Another concentration is nuclear medicine technology, with courses in radio-pharmaceuticals, nuclear imaging, and radiation safety. Consider a course in clinical laboratory management.

Trends

Trends in medical technology focus on technological advances to sustain human life from before birth through old age, the changing makeup of our population, and economics. Scientific advances such as fiber optics, laser technology, and radio-pharmaceuticals make possible new surgical and treatment procedures. The aging of the population means that there will be more elderly people who need diagnostic procedures, radiation therapy, and surgery. Financial pressures from insurance companies will shift some medical technology services out of hospitals and into less expensive physicians' offices and clinics. Cost considerations might delay some new technological applications as well as promising but extremely expensive nuclear medicine procedures.

What You Need to Succeed

This booming field today requires professionals with a practical mind-set, sensitive to the power of high-tech devices to diagnose and heal—and also to their current limitations. It's essential that you be comfortable with precise laboratory procedures, computer software and hardware, statistical data, and analysis techniques. Because new equipment, diagnostic techniques, and therapeutic services are constantly emerging and gaining widespread medical acceptance, you'll need to learn state-of-the-art instrumentation quickly and accurately—and undergo frequent retraining. With a career in medical technology, you'll be expected to acquire a solid understanding of technology's interface with the human body throughout the life-span, including ways to minimize risks during various medical procedures. Good oral and written communication skills are important for collaborating with other health care professionals in potentially life-or-death situations.

Related Fields

Industrial Technology
Nursing
Occupational Therapy
Physical Therapy

Typical Basic Courses

Cell Biology
Clinical Laboratory Computer Applications
Clinical Physiological Chemistry
Hematology
Immunology
Introduction to Medical Technology
Medical Parasitology
Principles of Medical Technology
    Education

An Array of Electives

A Case Study Appproach to Medical
    Technology
Body Fluids and Urinalysis
Clinical Immunology and
    Immunohematology
Clinical Laboratory Instrumentation
Diagnostic Microbiology
Integrating Clinical Laboratory Sciences
Introduction to Radioisotopes
Medical Technology Laboratory
    Management

On-Campus Opportunities

Campus health service
Lab assistant
Research assistant

Job Opportunities

Good demand / Possible shortage

Reading to Explore

Bitter Medicine: Greed and Chaos in American Health Care, by Jeanne Kassler (Carol Publishing)

Guns, Germs, and Steel: The Fate of Human Societies, by Jared Diamond (Norton)

Health Century, by Edward Shorter (Doubleday)

Prayer Is Good Medicine, by Larry Dossey (HarperCollins)

They All Laughed at Christopher Columbus: Tales of Medicine and the Art of Discovery, by Gerald Weissmann (Random House)

To Learn More

American Health Information
    Management Association
919 North Michigan Avenue, Suite 1400
Chicago, IL 60611-1683
(312) 787-2672; fax (312) 787-9793
E-mail: info@ahma.org
Internet site: http://www.ahima.org

American Society of Clinical Pathologists
2100 West Harrison Street
Chicago, IL 60612-3798
(312) 738-1336; fax (312) 738-1619
E-mail: info@ascp.org
Internet site: http://www.ascp.org

Medieval and Renaissance Studies

Some say that the age of chivalry is past, that the spirit of romance is dead. The age of chivalry is never past, so long as there is a wrong left unredressed on earth.
—*Charles Kingsley, novelist and minister, cited in* A Dictionary of Military Quotations

What to Expect

The Middle Ages and Renaissance in Europe were eras of creative genius among a few, wealth and power among a few, and abject ignorance among most. They were eras of cultural influences that shaped the Western world for centuries. They were also epochs of plague, despair, and poverty. As you enter this multidisciplinary field, you'll discover the vastness of its legacies in the arts, literature, sciences, and religions. Classes will survey the formation of medieval Europe from the decline of the ancient world through the renewal of town life, the age of scholasticism, and the development of monarchies and parliaments that followed. The curriculum also covers history, music, and the fine arts through the Renaissance, comparative religions and literatures, and the development of political theory. You can concentrate your studies. If your interest lies in literature, for example, there are offerings on Norse mythology, the growth of modern English, detailed studies of major writers such as Chaucer and Dante, and readings from an array of Middle English, Old English, and continental poets, playwrights, and authors. Advanced topics tackle specialized topics, such as Celtic and Nordic legends, the techniques monks used to illuminate medieval manuscripts, and High Renaissance artists of Italy.

Trends

Trends in medieval and renaissance studies include research and writing about the lives of ordinary people, from serfs and peasants to merchants and artisans. In contrast, past studies focused on the nobility, knights, prominent artists, and powerful figures in religion and government. There is also far more attention being paid to the role of women.

What You Need to Succeed

You must start with a broad, inquisitive mind and a strong desire to find solutions to unanswered questions about the past—particularly those helping to explain life and values in today's world. To research, probe, and interpret history, you'll use a variety of sources, including unpublished manuscripts, physical artifacts, works of art, and records kept by governments and religious bodies. Analytical skill and a finely honed sense of intuition are necessary as you strive to understand the thinking, achievements, and failures of the people of medieval and Renaissance Europe, and to draw logical conclusions from incomplete data. A familiarity with archaeological techniques and their limitations is important. You must be able to communicate lucidly in writing and orally to discuss issues, debate theories, and explain conclusions. Mastery of foreign languages—in forms far different from today's versions—is definitely required.

Related Fields

Art History
English
History
Music History
Romance Languages

Typical Basic Courses

Aspects of Medieval Culture
Aspects of Renaissance Culture
English Constitutional History
God and Salvation: The Drama of
    Human Redemption
History of Science to Newton
Knighthood and Chivalry
Medieval and Renaissance Arthurian
    Literature
Medieval Art and Architecture

An Array of Electives

Canterbury Tales
Castles, Courts, and Courtliness
History of Prints and Printmaking
Jews, Muslims, and Christians in the
    Middle Ages
Medieval Manuscript Illumination
Medieval Philosophy
Nobility in Medieval Europe
Words and Music: Love Songs of
    Medieval Europe

On-Campus Opportunities

College magazine
Research assistant

Job Opportunities

Surplus / Substantial oversupply

Reading to Explore

Ancient Ireland: From Prehistory to the Middle Ages, by Jacqueline O'Brien (Oxford University)

The Autumn of the Middle Ages, by Johan Huizinga and Ulrich Mammitzsch (University of Chicago)

The Mystery of King Arthur, by Elizabeth Jenkins (Dorset)

The New Knighthood: A History of the Order of the Temple, by Malcolm Barber (Cambridge University)

The Renaissance, Maker of Modern Man, by Paul M. Kendall (National Geographic)

To Learn More

TEAMS (The Consortium for the
    Teaching of the Middle Ages)
c/o Professor Paul E. Szarmach
Medieval Institute
Western Michigan University
Kalamazoo, MI 49008-3801
(616) 387-8745; fax (616) 387-8750
E-mail: ksaupe@calvin.edu
Internet site:
    http:/www.calvin.edu/~ksaupe/
    teams.html

Micro/Molecular Biology

To see a world in a grain of sand / And a heaven in a wild flower
Hold infinity in the palm of your hand / And eternity in an hour.
—*William Blake, artist and engraver, cited in* The New International Dictionary of Quotations

What to Expect

In the booming field of micro and molecular biology, your cornerstone will be a basic knowledge of the biological and physical sciences, and a detailed understanding of cellular biology, biochemistry, genetics, and developmental biology. Introductory classes will cover microbal structure and function, nutrition, growth, and control. Laboratory work begins with methodology, including microscopy, staining, culture media, aseptic technique, and laboratory safety. You'll gain expertise in the latest developments in DNA structure and protein sequencing—and their ramifications in fields such as medical microbiology—through course work in sophisticated computer programming, laboratory procedures, scientific terminology, and research methods. As you progress in micro and molecular biology, advanced courses will enable you to specialize in such subjects as environmental microbiology, bacterial genetics, strategy and tactics to fight viruses, industrial microbiology, molecular pathogenesis, and antibiotic medicine. Allied courses in bioengineering, food science, pharmacy, statistics, and business management will prove useful.

Trends

Trends in micro and molecular biology reflect an explosion of research—theoretical as well as applied—in genetics and genetical engineering. As an affluent American society seeks to prolong life and reverse the process of aging through techniques including gene splicing, transplants, and artificial organs, scientists with expertise in DNA functioning, gene regulation, and cell biology will be in the forefront. A growing medical interest in the structure of viruses—certainly fueled by but not limited to the global search for cures for AIDS and genetic disorders such as cystic fibrosis—will also strengthen scientific efforts to understand and combat diseases throughout the human life cycle. As part of this trend, there will be increased reliance on advanced computer modeling to unravel how bacteria and viruses originate, grow, and take over host organisms.

What You Need to Succeed

Are you interested in biological research on the cutting edge of science today? Do you have strong analytic skills and enjoy tackling both theoretical and applied problems? Such traits—combined with the intellectual patience needed to complete long-range projects and a tolerance for countless hours of meticulous, laboratory work—are essential for success in this expanding field. You'll not only need to acquire expertise in biotechnological instrumentation and advanced computer applications, but also know the fundamentals of allied fields such as biochemistry and physical chemistry, genetics, pharmacology, and physics. You might also need to become familiar with toxicology, plant pathology, bioengineering, and other rapidly changing scientific specialties.

Related Fields

Biochemistry
Biology
Pharmacy
Zoology

Typical Basic Courses

Biology
Cell Biology
Cells and Molecules
Evolutionary Ecology
Introduction to Microbiology and
    Immunology
Medical Microbiology
Microrganisms on the Planet Earth
Principles of Animal Development
Principles of Molecular, Cellular, and
    Developmental

An Array of Electives

Bacterial Genetics
Biotechnology and Its Social Impact
Computational Aspects of Molecular
    Biology
Environmental Microbiology
Food Microbiology
Industrial Microbiology
Molecular Pathogenesis
Viruses: Strategy and Tactics

On-Campus Opportunities

Lab assistant
Research assistant

Job Opportunities

Good demand / Possible shortage

Reading to Explore

Eleven Blue Men and Other Narratives of Medical Detection, by Berton Roueche (Little, Brown)

Life Itself: Exploring the Realm of the Living Cell, by Boyce Rensberger (Oxford University)

Lives of a Cell: Notes of a Biology Watcher, by Lewis Thomas (Penguin)

Virus Hunting: AIDS, Cancer, and the Human Retrovirus, by Robert Gallo (Basic)

Virus X: Tracking the New Killer Plagues: Out of the Present and into the Future, by Frank Ryan (Little, Brown)

To Learn More

American Society for Biochemistry and
    Molecular Biology
9650 Rockville Pike
Bethesda, MD 20814-3996
(301) 530-7145; fax (301) 571-1824
E-mail: asbmb@asbmb.faseb.org
Internet site: http://www.faseb.org/asbmb

American Society for Microbiology
1325 Massachusetts Avenue NW
Washington, DC 20005-4171
(202) 737-3600; fax (202) 942-9346
E-mail: webmaster@asmusa.org
Iternet site: http://www.asmusa.org

Middle Eastern and Near Eastern Studies

[T]he Middle East has been a rich and diverse region of enormous cultural significance. It has spawned three of the world's great religions . . . and has provided many other contributions to civilization. . . . [But] . . . the Middle East is afflicted with major conflicts that seem to defy solution.
—*from "The Middle East,"* Congressional Quarterly

What to Expect

In Middle Eastern and Near Eastern studies, you'll acquire an interdisciplinary perspective about one of the world's most volatile regions. With courses in economics, geography, history, international relations, political science, the arts, and religion, you'll understand how events including government upheavals, boycotts, terrorist acts, and threats of war are often rooted in centuries-old and seemingly insoluble ethnic and religious conflicts. You'll also gain familiarity with encouraging new trends in economic development, education, and social equality occurring in this region. You'll take specialized classes on topics such as the confluence and conflict of Arab and Jewish cultures, Near Eastern literature in translation, and music of the Middle East. To gain an edge in this field, you'll need to become proficient in one—and possibly two—foreign languages, such as Arabic, Turkish, Farsi (Persian), Hebrew, Kurdish, and Armenian. Foreign study may also be required. For a career in business, allied classes in economics, finance, or international marketing would be valuable.

Trends

Trends in Middle Eastern and Near Eastern studies reflect a growing interest in the history and current economic, social, and political status of ethnic and religious minorities. These include Palestinians living in Israel and Jordan, Iraqi Kurds, and Christian Arabs. There is also a mounting effort to relate current tensions and conflicts among Middle Eastern nations to long-standing historical and ethnic factors. The multifaceted contribution of women to diverse Middle Eastern cultures—as well as changes in their familial, sexual, and socioeconomic roles—is also gaining increased attention. On the religious front, there is growing interest in how age-old Middle Eastern texts such as those of Greek Orthodoxy, Islamic Sufism, and Jewish mysticism can offer the world spiritual guidance today.

What You Need to Succeed

Regardless of your college program's particular emphasis, you'll need top-notch verbal-analytic ability, an ease in merging knowledge from varied disciplines in the humanities and social sciences to arrive at meaningful conclusions, and a flair for foreign languages. The Middle East is filled with seeming contradiction and paradox. Whether your major leads you into education, business, or a career in government service, you'll need a genuine openness to attitudes about religion, politics, gender, and culture that often conflict sharply with accepted viewpoints in the United States. Preparation in finance and marketing, political science, public administration science, or international relations may prove beneficial. Extensive foreign travel is part-and-parcel of this challenging field.

Related Fields

Anthropology and Archaelogy
Asian Studies
Classical Languages and Classics
Geography
Judaic Studies
Political Science

Typical Basic Courses

Arabs and Jews: Cultures in Confluence and Conflict
Elementary Arabic
Elementary Hebrew
Elementary Persian
Elementary Turkish
Introduction to the Middle East
Music of the Middle East
Near Eastern Literature in Translation

An Array of Electives

Ancient Seafaring
International Relations of the Middle East
Islamic Civilization in Africa Since 1750
Palestinian Nationalism
Problems of Urbanization in the Middle East
The History and Archaeology of Ancient Egypt
Turkish Culture
Women, Men, and the Law in Muslim Court

On-Campus Opportunities

Campus newspapers, magazines, and radio and television stations
International student center

Job Opportunities

Surplus / Substantial oversupply

Readings to Explore

Beyond the Promised Land: Jews and Arabs on a Hard Road to a New Israel, by Glenn Frankel (Simon & Schuster)

Constantinople: City of the World's Desire, 1453–1924, by Philip Mansel (St. Martin's Press)

Desert Wisdom: The Middle Eastern Tradition from the Goddess to the Sufis, by Neil Douglas-Klotz (HarperCollins)

God Has Ninety-Nine Names: Reporting from a Militant Middle East, by Judith Miller (Simon & Schuster)

This Side of Peace: A Personal Account, by Hanan Ashrawi (Simon & Schuster)

To Learn More

Middle Eastern Studies Association of North America
1232 North Cherry Avenue
University of Arizona
Tucson, AZ 85721
(602) 621-5850; fax(602) 626-9095
E-mail: mesa@ccit.arizona.edu
Internet site:
  http://www.acls.org/mesa.htm

155

Military, Aerospace, and Naval Science

Let every nation know, whether it wishes us well or ill, that we shall pay any price, bear any burden, meet any hardship, support any friend, oppose any foe, to assure the survival and success of liberty.
—*John F. Kennedy, inaugural address as president, 1961*

What to Expect

You'll begin with an overview of the Army, Navy, or Air Force—depending on the Reserve Officer Training Corps branch you choose—and its officer corps, organization, and traditions. You'll examine the Defense Department, its war-fighting doctrines, and customs. Courses are also aimed at developing character, confidence and leadership, including decision making and time management. Training emphasizes skills such as physical fitness, sharpshooting, rappelling, map reading, and air, water, and land-terrain navigation. The advanced program covers military communication techniques, educational psychology, and logistics. You'll learn tactics and the principles of offensive and defensive combat operations, troop leadership procedures, planning and coordinating techniques, and combat intelligence. Field training exercises are required.

Trends

Trends in military, aerospace, and naval science reflect dramatic changes in international relations and alliances, including the democratization of former communist nations and the breakup of countries along ethnic, tribal, or religious lines—often accompanied by tensions that threaten regional and even world peace. At the same time comes a growing use of multinational peace-keeping forces, often using U.S. military personnel. Within the armed forces are high profile debates over sexual harassment, downsizing the Pentagon, and limitations on the roles of women and homosexuals.

What You Need to Succeed

Patriotism, a belief in your own leadership ability, and a willingness to make sacrifices for the country are part-and-parcel of the field. To be such a leader requires self-confidence, assertiveness, and the capacity to inspire others to follow you—even into dangerous situations. Analytical, strategic, and problem-solving skills are essential, including the ability to make decisions and implement them under pressure, amidst confusion, and within deadlines. Verbal and written communication skills and attention to detail are equally vital. Above all, you must feel comfortable functioning in a highly disciplined and highly structured organization where you're expected to give orders—and follow orders—always as part of a coordinated team. Mastery of sophisticated computers, state-of-the-art weaponry, and military vehicles, ships, and aircraft is required. So is physical fitness—even for positions not directly related to combat and its training. Foreign travel is often involved, both on a temporary and a long-term basis.

Related Fields

Aerospace and Aeronautical Engineering
Geography
History
International Relations
Political Science
Public Policy Studies

Typical Basic Courses

American Air Power
Fundamentals of Naval Science
Introduction to the Air Force
Leadership and Management
Management in the Armed Forces
Mapping: Land Navigation
Principles of Sailing
U.S. Organization for Defense

An Array of Electives

Air Force Leadership and Management
Contemporary Military Environment
Evolution of War
History of Amphibious Warfare
Leadership in Small-Unit Operations
National Security Forces in
  Contemporary American Society
Naval Operations
Theory and Dynamics of the Military
  Team

On-Campus Opportunities

College newspaper, magazine, and radio
  and television stations

Job Opportunities

Good demand / Possible shortage

Reading to Explore

My American Journey, by Colin L. Powell and Joseph Persico (Random House)

Patton: A Genius for War, by Carlo D'Este (HarperCollins)

The Battle for History: Re-Fighting World War II, by John Keegen (Vintage)

The Reader's Companion to Military History, by Robert Cowley and Geoffrey Parker (Houghton Mifflin)

Women Warriors: A History, by David E. Jones (Brassey's)

To Learn More

U.S. Air Force, Department of
  Recruitment
550 D Street West, Suite 1
Randolph Airforce Base, TX 78150
(800) 423-USAFfax (210) 652-6397
E-mail: webmaster@airforce.com/
Internet site: http://www.airforce.com

U.S. Army Recruiting Command
  Headquarters
Fort Knox, KY 40121
Washington, DC
(800) USA-ARMY; fax (502) 626-0914
E-mail: kelleyk@emh2.usarec.army.mil
Internet site: http://www.goarmy.com

U.S. Navy Recruiting Command
Ballston Center Tower #2
801 North Randolph Street
Arlington, VA 2203
(800) USA-NAVY; fax (703) 696-8957
E-mail: 857_at_cnr@fmso.navy.mil
Internet site: http://www.navyjobs.com

157

Music

It is better to make a piece of music than to perform one, better to perform one than to listen to one, better to listen to one than to misuse it as a means of distraction or entertainment.
—*John Cage, composer, cited in* The Crown Treasury of Relevant Quotations

What to Expect

Your education will be based solidly on three legs: theory and composition, music literature and history, and performance. In each domain, you'll gain proficiency through basic courses in music theory and sight singing, music history, and techniques involving vocalization and orchestral and band instruments. You'll learn music's fundamental structure and elements in U.S., European, and non-European repertoires. As you progress, you'll focus on a particular aspect of performance—singing, composing, conducting, or playing an instrument. Intensive, supervised training, combined with solo and ensemble work, will provide key skills. Take electives such as choral arranging, jazz improvisation, vocal teaching, and digitial recording and editing. Learn the music of other historic and contemporary cultures.

Trends

Trends in music reflect the rapid changes in contemporary society. The cultural dominance of the Baby Boomer generation, with its continued interest in popular songs of the 1960s and 1970s, affects the demand for live concerts and recording of other stylistic forms. Significant budget cuts in government and private sources involving performance, arranging, and composition will also create financial challenges for audiences and musicians. There will be increased demand for music of ethnic and racial minorities, including immigrant groups. A separate development will be the growing acceptance of music as a therapeutic tool for people with mental and physical impairments, such as developmentally disabled children and the elderly in nursing homes and rehabilitation centers.

What You Need to Succeed

Is music an intense and passionate force in your life? Do you experience great pleasure in singing, playing an instrument, or composing? Is daily existence without music unthinkable for you? And, because competition is merciless in this field, are you unusually talented musically, and are you poised and self-confident when appearing before the public? Such qualities form the basis for a musical career, coupled with the technical knowledge and skills to help you to achieve that goal. To acquire expertise—rather than mere proficiency—in performing, composing, conducting, or arranging, you'll be expected to spend countless daily hours, including weekends and holidays—practicing alone or in ensembles. Patience, strong concentration, self-discipline, and of course, an innate sense of melody and rhythm are likewise essential for success. Because musicians typically perform in ensembles and orchestras, you'll also need a cooperative and collaborative attitude. Willingness to travel is an another asset.

Related Fields

Dance
Music History
Theater and Drama

Typical Basic Courses

Acoustics and Music
Form, Analysis, and Compositional
   Techniques
History and Literature of Music
Introduction to Music Theory
Orchestration
Sightsinging
The Songwriter's Vocabulary
Tonal Harmony

An Array of Electives

Advanced Conducting
Choral Arranging
Diction
Digital Recording and Editing
Jazz Improvisation
Literature of the Piano
Musical Theater Rehearsal and
   Performance
Vocal Pedagogy

On-Campus Opportunities

Campus music ensembles
Campus radio and television stations

Job Opportunities

Surplus / Substantial oversupply

Reading to Explore

But Beautiful: A Book About Jazz, by Geoff Dyer (Northport/Farrar, Straus & Giroux)

Emblems of Mind: The Inner Life of Music and Mathematics, by Edward Rothstein (Times/Random House)

Music, the Brain, and Ecstasy: How Music Captures Our Imagination, by Robert Jourdain (Morrow)

Rock Hardware: Forty Years of Rock Instrumentation, by Paul Trynka (Miller Freeman)

The Symphony: A Visitor's Guide, by Michael Steinberg (Oxford University)

To Learn More

National Association of Schools of Music
11250 Roger Bacon Drive, Suite 21
Reston, VA 22090
(703) 437-0700; fax(703) 437-6312

Music History

Wherever Life is, Music is also; she lives in the earth's seismic heavings, in the mighty motion of the planets, in the hidden conflict of inexorable atoms; she is in all the lights, in all the colors that dazzle or sooth the eyes; she is in the blood of our arteries, in every pain, every passion of ecstasy that shakes our hearts.
—*Jean Paderewski, pianist, composer, and political leader, cited in* Your Need of Music

What to Expect

You'll be expected to master the basics of musical theory, literature, and history through such courses as aural skills, keyboard musicianship, and music in Western and non-Western civilization. Through such classes, you'll start to put the history of music into a cultural and social context. To strengthen your competency, master one or more foreign languages.

As you progress, choose among a wide array of electives. For instance, you can focus on the literature of a particular instrument—such as the violin or piano—through the ages, or else explore musical trends and indulgences in a single historical period, such as the Baroque era, the Age of Enlightenment, or the mid-nineteenth century. You can also gain expertise in a particular genre, such as classical music, gospel, jazz, opera, or contemporary Latino. Courses in finance, business administration, management of nonprofit organizations, fundraising, and marketing will also prove valuable. A class in music therapy methods will provide insights into newly discovered benefits of music in applied settings.

Trends

Trends in music history reflect the growing interest in the role of women as composers, performers, critics, arrangers, teachers, and patrons in various historical periods and cultures. Special attention is being paid to how women's issues helped to influence musical forms, such as lullabies, religious compositions, and folk songs. There is also an increased study of the musical characteristics and achievements of non-European peoples, such as those in Africa, Asia, South America, and the Caribbean. More attention is also being paid to the influence that ethnic, racial, and religious minorities have exerted on musical expression—for example, in jazz, ragtime, gospel, rhythm and blues, early rock and roll, reggae, Tex-Mex, and hip-hop—in U.S. history and popular culture.

What You Need to Succeed

A love for music—coupled with an ability to convey that love by teaching and writing—lies at the heart of this field. Many people active in music history today originally planned to become full-time performers, composers, arrangers, or conductors, but instead became

160

fascinated by music's uncanny, powerful role in world history and cultures. Rather than simply present a jumble of isolated names and dates, astute professionals in music history successfully place music at the forefront of human creativity and passion. Aesthetic, analytic, and conceptual research abilities are vital if you're to understand music's differing forms, styles, and functions around the globe. Ease with foreign languages is a decided asset, as is a multicultural sensitivity. Important, too, is your capacity to connect music—including classical, romantic, jazz, rock, hip-hop, and reggae—to historical trends, conflicts, and changing cultural values. Whether teaching children, teens, or adults in schools or community arts centers, or preparing scholarly materials for colleagues or a wide audience, you'll need good oral and written communication skills.

Related Fields

Dance
History
Medieval and Renaissance Studies
Music
Theater and Drama

Typical Basic Courses

History and Literature of Music
Introduction to Music Theory
Introduction to the Musics of the World
Performance Studies in Early Music
Survey of Piano Literature
Survey of Violin and Viola Literature
The Art of Music
The Symphony

An Array of Electives

African-American Music Innovators
Beethoven to Bernstein
Mozart in His Time
Music in the Baroque Period
Nineteenth-Century Piano Music
Ragtime
Studies in Contemporary Music
Women in Music

On-Campus Opportunities

Campus museum
Campus newspaper, magazine, and radio
   and television stations

Job Opportunities

Surplus / Substantial oversupply

Reading to Explore

Rock and Roll: An Unruly History, by Robert Palmer (Harmony)

Schubert: The Music and the Man, by Brian Newbuld (University of California)

The Classical Style: Haydn, Mozart, Beethoven, by Charles Rosen (Norton)

The Private Lives of the Three Tenors: Behind the Scenes with Placido Domingo, Luciano Pavarotti and Jose Carreras, by Marcia Lewis (Birch Lane/Carol)

Violin Virtuosos: From Paginini to the Twenty-First Century, by Henry Roth (California Classics)

To Learn More

Music Educators National Conference
1800 Robert Fulton Drive
Reston, VA 22091
(703) 860-4000; fax: (703) 860-9027
E-mail: lmullins1@aol.com
Internet site: http://www.menc.org

Sigma Alpha Iota
34 Wall Street, Suite 515
Asheville, NC 28801-2710
(704) 251-0606; fax (704) 251-0644
E-mail: webmaster@sai-national.org
Internet site: http://www.sai-national.org

161

Nursing

It may seem a strange principle to enunciate as the very first requirement in a hospital that it should do the sick no harm.
—*Florence Nightingale, nurse, author and activist, in* Notes on Hospitals

What to Expect

Education in nursing seeks to achieve several goals: conveying scientific and medical knowledge, teaching practical and clinical skills, developing interpersonal communication and documentation skills, and preparing you to deal with the patient as a "whole person" who has physical, emotional, and social needs. You'll be introduced to a systems approach to nursing care within the health care system, learn to assess the health status of patients, and recognize the nursing implications of human growth and development throughout the life cycle. A number of your courses will focus on different types of patients from the nurses' perspective. For instance, you can study parent-child health nursing, including reproductory processes, adult health, mental health, and psychiatric nursing, care of the critically ill, and nursing care of women. Clinical work will bring you into hospitals, nursing homes, mental health clinics, and other community settings for experience with patients and health professionals. The program also offers classes on the legal aspects of professional nursing, nursing management and leadership, sexuality, and nursing-related research.

Trends

The aging of the American population means there will be more older people who need diagnostic procedures, radiation therapy, and surgery. Financial pressure from insurance companies will shift some medical technology services out of hospitals and into less expensive physicians' offices and clinics. Cost considerations may delay some new technological applications, such as promising but extremely expensive nuclear medicine procedures.

What You Need to Succeed

The basis of nursing has always been caring. Today, this process is recognized as nurturing the whole person, not simply treating a bag of symptoms. To succeed in this often physically and emotionally demanding field, you'll need an ample supply of empathy and sensitivity—for those under your direct care, as well as their relatives and friends. The ability to communicate clear, timely information to them—and to your own colleagues—is also essential. Because nurses dispense medication to the critically ill, you'll have life-or-death responsibility in carrying out medical orders precisely and efficiently. Reflecting the accelerating trend in community health care today, you'll need a high regard for multicultural differences in family dynamics and attitudes toward health, illness, and death. Such treatment requires you to collaborate daily with professionals in fields such as occupational therapy, psychology, nutrition, pharmacy, physical therapy, and social work. So the ability to be a team player will be vital.

Related Fields

Family and Child Development
Medical Technology
Occupational Therapy
Optometry
Physical Education and Exercise Science
Physical Therapy

Typical Basic Courses

Clinical Problems in Adaptation
Concepts of Nursing Care of Children
    and Their Families
Concepts of Nursing Care of the Adult
Exploring Professional Nursing
Health of Women
Pharmacology in Nursing
Physiology of Altered Health States
Wellness and Health Assessment

An Array of Electives

Ethical Dilemmas in Clinical Care
Health Care Provider as Patient
    Educator
Health Promotion in the Aging
    Population
Holistic Health Practice
Human Sexuality
Play and the Hospitalized Child
Political Activism and Health Care
    Delivery
Rural Health Care

On-Campus Opportunities

Campus health service

Job Opportunities

Adequate supply / Some oversupply

Reading to Explore

A Woman of Valor: Clara Barton and the Civil War, by Stephen B. Oates (Free Press)

Coyote Medicine: Lessons from Native American Healers, by Lewis Madrona-Mehl (Scribner)

"Just a Nurse?" The Hearts and Minds of Nurses in Their Own Words, by Janet Kraegel and Mary Kachoyeanos (Dutton)

Life Support: Three Nurses on the Front Lines, by Suzanne Gordon (Little, Brown)

Nursing, the Finest Art: An Illustrated History, by Patricia M. Donahue and Patricia Russac (Abrams)

To Learn More

American Nurses Association
600 Maryland Avenue SW, Suite 100
    West
Washington, DC 20024
(800) 274-4ANA; fax (202) 651-7001
E-mail: memberinfo@ana.org
Internet site:
    http://www.nursingworld.org/about.htm

Sigma Theta Tau International
550 West North Street
Indianapolis, IN 46202
(317) 634-8171; fax (317) 634-8188
E-mail: sti@sti-sun.iupui.edu
Internet site:
    http:/www.stti-web.iupui.edu

Nutrition and Food Science

Strange to see how a good dinner and feasting reconciles everybody.
—*Samuel Pepys, diarist and philosopher, cited in* The Crown Treasury of Relevant Quotations

What to Expect

To plan nutrition programs, supervise meal preparation, oversee safe food processing, and encourage public health, you must be grounded in natural sciences, health promotion, and home economics. To build that broad foundation, you'll study basic science and nutrition, with application to medical dietetics and community nutrition, food service management, food technology, and consumer lifestyles. Introductory classes teach about the contemporary food system, properties of food, methods of safeguarding food from contamination and deterioration, and processing. You'll learn the role of nutrition in human health and development, quality evaluation, and food chemistry. Many courses involve laboratory work. As you progress, you can delve deeper into food analysis, commercial development of food products, and quality assurance and processing technologies. If you enjoy research, try food microbiology and food biotechnology. If your interest lies with public health and with advising individuals, consider courses in clinical dietetics, community dietetics, and nutrition education. If industry interests you, look for food processing classes and labs that cover irradiation, fermentation, packaging methods, and related topics.

Trends

Trends in nutrition and food science recognize the essential role foods play in overall health and fitness. That means more public education on healthful eating practices, from young children to the elderly. It means closer relations between nutritionists and other health professionals. Another trend reflects growing concern about the quality of our food supply, whether domestic or imported. That concern will be reflected in tighter governmental oversight and inspections, more scientific research, testing of new products and processing techniques, and policy debates about acceptable levels of health risk and the costs of governmental regulation.

What You Need to Succeed

This is a cooperative field, requiring you to work directly with a variety of other professionals. For example, if you go into scientific research, you could be allied with chemists, microbiologists, agricultural engineers, and marketing experts. If you choose a community-oriented career, your partners will include physicians, nurses, social workers, teachers, and pharmacists. In any scenario, you'll be expected to demonstrate strong verbal and written communication skills.

For scientific work, you should enjoy spending time in the laboratory, paying meticulous attention to details, and creatively exploring ideas. Working with individual clients calls for empathy and the ability to explain clearly your reason for designing a particular diet or eating regimen. In an industrial career, you'll spend time in factories and perhaps on a farm or ranch. Some dietitians spend time in steamy, hot kitchens, and some are on their feet most of the workday. Managerial and supervisory skills may prove increasingly valuable as the health care field undergoes rapid change.

Related Fields

Biochemistry
Micro and Molecular Biology
Pharmacy

Typical Basic Courses

Food Principles
Geriatric Nutrition
Introduction to Food Science
Maternal and Child Nutrition
Nutrition and Health: Concepts and
  Controversies
Nutrition and Physiochemical Aspects of
  Food
Personalized Health and Nutrition
Social Science Perspectives on Food and
  Nutrition

An Array of Electives

Applied Dietetics in Food Service
  Systems
Food Chemistry
Food Engineering Technology
Food Microbiology
Nutrition and Exercise
Nutrition and Service Management
Nutritional Counseling
Public Health Nutrition

On-Campus Opportunities

Campus health service
Lab assistant

Job Opportunities

Surplus / Substantial oversupply

Reading to Explore

America's First Cuisines, by Sophie D. Coe
(University of Texas)

Eat Fat, by Richard Klein (Pantheon)

Food Factor: Why We Are What We Eat, by
Barbara Griggs (Viking)

Jane Brody's Nutrition Book, by Jane Brody
(Bantam)

*Stand Facing the Stove: The Story of the
Women Who Gave America the Joy of
Cooking,* by Anne Mendelson (Henry
Holt)

To Learn More

American Dietetic Association
216 West Jackson Boulevard
Chicago, IL 60606-6995
(312) 899-0040; fax (312) 899-1979
E-mail: webmaster@eatright.org
Internet site: http://www.eatright.org

Occupational Therapy

Of all the cancers of human happiness, none corrodes it . . . as indolence. Body and mind both unemployed, our being becomes a burden. . . . Exercise and application produce order in our affairs, health of body, and cheerfulness of mind.
—*Thomas Jefferson, U.S. president, cited in* The Book of Fathers' Wisdom

What to Expect

Through courses and clinical experience, you'll learn the skills necessary to help clients disabled by injury, illness, aging, substance abuse, birth defects, and emotional disorders. Classes build on fundamentals of biology, chemistry, physics, and psychology. You'll get an overview of growth, development, and aging; master medical terminology and professional interpersonal communication techniques; and study the musculoskeletal, neurological, and neuromuscular systems. In addition, you'll cover essential elements of physiological and psychological assessment, including how to administer and interpret tests. You should learn to use computer programs to help clients improve perceptual skills, memory, coordination, abstract reasoning, and decision making for independent living. The program examines in depth the role of occupational therapists in life skills, helping clients with self-care, work, and leisure activities, and sometimes in orthotics, prosthetics, and adaptive or assistive devices such as microprocessors that help clients walk or communicate. Much of your advanced training will occur in clinical settings in which you apply theory to the treatment process. You may specialize in patients of particular age groups or those with particular disabilities.

Trends

Trends in occupational therapy mirror a rising demand for long-term care and rehabilitation services, including medical advances that help more patients—such as highly premature infants and stroke victims—survive with extensive therapy. Employers, government, and insurance companies will press harder to rehabilitate employees so they return to work quickly rather than continue receiving disability benefits. Therapists will help more children with disabilities prepare for early intervention programs.

What You Need to Succeed

Are you interested in combining medical, physiological, psychological, and recreational knowledge to directly help people with disabilities? If so, then this growing health care field may be for you. Whether you work with developmentally delayed children and toddlers, elderly stroke victims, or clients with chronic mental disorders such as manic depression and schizophrenia, you'll need patience, stamina, and a high tolerance for frustration, because clients' gains are often slow and small. The ability to formulate realistic goals for those you guide is also crucial. You'll also need ingenuity, an ease with hands-on contact, and an ability to adapt activities to your clients' unique needs. Virtually all occupational therapy is team oriented. So you'll be expected to communicate short-term and long-term treatment goals— and your clients' progress—in a lucid manner, both orally and in writing. Reflecting the field's growing interdisciplinary focus, it's helpful to see yourself as a generalist, sensitive to the viewpoints of psychologists, social workers, nurses, nutritionists, physicians, and other professionals. For this reason, good interpersonal skills are decisive in working effectively with clients and health-care colleagues.

Related Fields

Nursing
Optometry
Physical Education and Exercise Science
Physical Therapy

Typical Basic Courses

Clinical Experience in Physical
  Disabilities
Gross Anatomy
Independent Living Skills
Introduction to Occupational Therapy
Medicine and Surgery
Occupational Therapy and Psychiatry
Principles of Occupational Testing and
  Measurement
Therapeutic Activities

An Array of Electives

Adaptive Aquatics
Applied Neuroscience
Evaluation and Treatment of the
  Developmentally Disabled
Orthopedics
Practice in Gerontology
Sign Language
Sports for the Disabled
Teaching Wellness

On-Campus Opportunities

Campus health service

Job Opportunities

Good demand / Possible shortage

Reading to Explore

Awakenings, by Oliver Sacks (Penguin)

Dibs, in Search of Self, by Virginia Axline (Ballantine)

Drugs and Behavior, by Fred Leavitt (Sage)

Is There No Place on Earth for Me? by Susan Sheehan (Vintage)

Mind-Body Deceptions: The Psychosomatics of Everyday Life, by Steven L. Dubovsky (Norton)

The Road Back: Living with a Disability, by Harriet Sirof (Macmillan)

To Learn More

American Occupational Therapy Association
4720 Montgomery Lane
Bethesda, MD 20814
(301) 652-2682; fax (301) 652-7711
E-mail: praota@aota.org
Internet site: http://www.aota.org

Operations Research and Industrial Engineering

It is facts that are needed: Facts, facts, facts. When facts have been supplied, each of us can try to reason from them.
—*James Bryce, author and organizational theorist, cited in* The Reader's Digest Treasury of Modern Quotations

What to Expect

You'll learn how to determine the most effective ways for an organization to use people, machines, information, energy, and materials to make or process products. The goal is to enable you to solve production and organizational problems efficiently by engineering, controlling, and designing complex industrial systems. Introductory classes typically cover applications of fundamental economics to engineering alternatives in planning, development, and management. You'll learn about ergonomic concepts in the workplace, optimization analysis and techniques, human-machine interaction, computer modeling of manufacturing systems, and control of material and projects. Take more advanced courses in quality control for products and services, operations analysis and motion economy, and analysis of industrial processes such as fabrication, welding, assembly, and inspection. You'll also deal with production systems, including demand forecasting, capacity planning, scheduling, work flow, and inventory systems. There will be an emphasis on safety and reliability factors to assure that systems are designed rapidly and operate safely. Expect extensive laboratory work, design projects, and computer-related assignments.

Trends

Trends in operations research and industrial engineering focus on efforts by manufacturers to cut costs and improve productivity through safety engineering and scientific management. That development will necessitate the creation of better management control systems to help with financial planning and cost analysis, as well as designing or enhancing systems to distribute products and services. Professionals will also be called on to design efficient production planning and control systems that can better coordinate an organization's activities and control the quality of its products or services.

What You Need to Succeed

To achieve success in increasing operations efficiency—especially in the manufacturing domain—you'll need several key abilities. If you possess an analytic frame of mind, are comfortable with advanced statistics and probability involving sophisticated computer applications, and want to design new or improved production methods for industry, then your foundation in this field is strong. Because those in operations research and industrial engineering always tackle problems in a team, you'll need familarity with the viewpoints and techniques of those in allied disciplines, such as civil engineering, materials science and engineering, mechanical engineering, statistics, finance, and management.

Related Fields

Civil Engineering
Industrial Technology
Materials Science and Engineering

Typical Basic Courses

Economic Analysis of Engineering Systems
Engineering Application of Operations
    Research Optimization
Engineering Probability and Statistics
Financial and Managerial Accounting
Industrial Systems Analysis
Introduction to Game Theory
Material Handling Systems

An Array of Electives

Applied Financial Engineering
Applied Time-Series Analysis
Design and Analysis of Simulated Systems
Inventory Theory
Quality Control
Queuing Theory and Its Application
Scheduling Theory
Statistical Analysis of Life Data

On-Campus Opportunities

Campus supplies department
Research assistant

Job Opportunities

Adequate supply / Some oversupply

Reading to Explore

Defense Conversion: Transforming the Arsenal of American Democracy, by Jacque S. Gansler (MIT)

Elements of Queuing Theory with Applications, by Thomas L. Saaty (Dover)

The Art of Probability for Scientists and Engineers, by Richard W. Hammis (Addison-Wesley)

The Man Who Discovered Quality, by Andrea Gabor (Random House)

The One Best Way: Frederick Winslow Taylor and the Enigma of Efficiency, by Robert Kanigel (Viking)

To Learn More

Institute for Operations Research and the
    Management Sciences
901 Elkridge Landing, Suite 400
Linthicum, MD 21090
(800) 446-3676; fax (410) 684-2963
E-Mail: informs@mail.informs.org
Internet site: http://www.informs.org

Institute Headquarters/Institute of
    Industrial Engineers
25 Technology Park
Norcross, GA 30092
(770) 449-0461; fax (770) 263-8532
E-mail: webmaster@www.iienet.org
Internet site:
    http://www.iienet.org/iie1.htm

Optometry

To meet at all, one must open one's eyes to another; and there is no true conversation, no matter how many words are spoken, unless the eye, unveiled and listening, opens itself to the other.
—*Jessamyn West, author, cited in* The Crown Treasury of Relevant Quotations

What to Expect

First, you must meet an optometry program's preprofessional requirements in biological sciences, mathematics, physics, and chemistry, including laboratory work. From there, you'll take a survey course covering the development of optometry, the scope of optometric services, and current vision research. A series of courses will familiarize you with geometric and opthalmic optics, including image evaluation, measurement, and inspection of lenses, manufacturing processes, and the theory and practice of fitting and adjusting spectacles. Case histories are part of the teaching process, as is an understanding of how optometry relates to public policy issues of health care. Practical optometry and clinical practice courses will demonstrate the use of instruments, investigative and diagnostic techniques, and dealing with conditions you'll encounter in providing patient care. Other offerings include orthoptics, contact lenses, opthalmic and applied pathology, and perceptual-motor disorders. Try to get as much laboratory and clinical practice as possible. You can also work on special areas of interest, such as occupational-related eye safety, sports vision, pediatric or geriatric optometry, and visual therapy. Be sure to learn the business and managerial aspects of optometric practice.

Trends

Trends in optometry encompass the maturing of the Baby Boom generation with its onset of visual problems in middle age, as well as the rapid growth of an elderly population at higher risk for cataracts, glaucoma, hypertension, and diabetes. There will be greater recognition of the importance of optical care and expanded employee vision-care insurance coverage, but insurers will seek to control costs. Meanwhile, the pharmaceutical industry is developing new topical and oral drugs to treat various eye diseases.

What You Need to Succeed

Interpersonal skills, manual dexterity, and attention to visual detail are essential in working with patients who depend on you for primary visual care. Ask technical and personal questions so lay people can understand them, and clearly explain their test results, diagnosis, treatment plan, follow-up instructions, and long-term prognosis. Professionalism includes a need to deal tactfully with patients, a sensitivity to their emotional concerns, and an awareness of their financial pressures. Because most optometrists are private practitioners who handle both the medical and business aspects of running a practice, you'll need the ability to hire and oversee employees, keep records, oversee billing of patients and insurance companies, and order supplies and equipment. Marketing skills pay off in building a patient base and a reputation in the community. Self-discipline is important, particularly if you're self-employed. Even if you're self-employed, you may work closely with other health professionals including opthalmologists, dispensing opticians, pharmacists, and nurses.

Related Fields

Nursing
Occupational Therapy
Pharmacy
Physical Therapy

Typical Basic Courses

Contact Lenses
Geometrical Optics
Ocular Anatomy and Physiology
Ocular Disease
Ocular Pharmacology
Physical Optics
Principles of Optometry
Visual Optics

An Array of Electives

Computer Applications in Optometric
   Practice
Geriatric Patient Care Delivery
Ocular Pharmacology
Ocular Photography
Optometric Research Methods
Practice Development and
   Administration
Public Health
Sports Vision

On-Campus Opportunities

Campus health service

Job Opportunities

Near balance / Supply equals demand

Reading to Explore

A Vision of the Brain, by Semir Zeki
(Blackwell)

Active Perception, by Yiannis Aloimonous
(Lawrence Erlbaum)

Helen Keller, by Johanna Horwitz
(Random House)

Visual Development, by Nigel W. Daw
(Plenum)

Work and the Eye, by Rachel U. North
(Oxford University)

To Learn More

American Academy of Optometry
6110 Executive Boulevard, Suite 506
Rockville, MD 20852
(301) 984-1441; fax (301) 984-4737
E-mail: aaoptom@aol.com
Internet site: http://www.aaopt.org

American Optometric Association
243 North Lindbergh Boulevard
St. Louis, MO 63141
(314) 991-4100; fax (314) 991-4101
Internet site: http://www.aoanet.org

Parks and Recreation

To share the park's grace and vitality one learns new gestures, perceives in a new way. It is . . . a time of patience and gentleness.
—*Mireille Johnston, author, cited in* Central Park Country: A Tune Within Us

What to Expect

Imagine two overlapping circles within the category of parks and recreation. One circle surrounds natural resource management topics, and the other surrounds topics about recreational use of those resources. That's why course work will encompass both areas. At the outset, classes will familiarize you with the scope and status of lands used for recreation, the roles leisure and recreation play in American culture, and the economics and political influences of recreational activities. An overview of necessary scientific and environmental principles will be included. Management is an important part of the curriculum, both at the lower and upper levels. You'll learn about programming, planning, and leadership principles, problem-solving skills, supervision, budgeting and resource economics, and policy and operation of recreational facilities. You should understand basic legal concepts that govern recreation and park programs and facilities, including risk-management planning and the rights of your clientele. Other courses may cover therapeutic recreation, coaching sports for those with disabilities, and commercial tourism enterprises.

Trends

Trends in parks and recreation include the search for an acceptable balance between preservation and recreational use of public lands. That quest will involve policy determinations about the future of low-impact wildernesses and of high-impact activities such as camping, snowmobiling, and motorboating. A second trend reflects battles between those who believe governments own too much public land and those who advocate more public ownership to head off development and spoilation. Another trend reflects the growing importance of therapeutic recreation services for adults and children with physical or mental disabilities, as well as for the elderly.

What You Need to Succeed

You should obviously enjoy outdoor activities. You'll also need well-developed communication skills, both in writing and orally, because you'll have to interact with colleagues and the public. You might be called upon to deal with crises, such as life-threatening accidents and injuries, and with controversies over land use, budgets, and politics. Patience and problem-solving abilities are crucial. You should be outgoing, able to motivate people, and be sensitive to the needs of others with diverse cultural backgrounds. Whether you emphasize parks or recreation, master the scientific aspects of your specialization, such as natural resource management, human physiology, environmental protection, or athletics. Some positions require professional certification or state licensure. Creativity and resourcefulness play a role in activity planning, and many responsibilities demand good physical fitness. Your work will sometimes call for managerial skills, the exercise of discretion, and a willingness to accept responsibility as you supervise co-workers and make decisions.

Related Fields

Forestry
Occupational Therapy
Physical Education and Exercise Science
Social Work

Typical Basic Courses

Foundation of Recreation and Leisure
  Skills
Human Behavior in Park and Recreation
  Settings
Introductory Forestry
Personal Computers in Health, Physical
  Education, and Recreation
Principles of Outdoor Recreation
Recreation for Special Populations
Recreation Leadership
Safety, First Aid, and Emergency Care

An Array of Electives

Commercial Recreation and Tourism
  Enterprises
Facility and Park Management
Law and Resources
Natural Resources Economics
Organization, Administration,
  Recreation, and Leisure Service
Ornamental Horticulture
Resource Ecology
The Role of Planning in Urban and
  Regional Development

On-Campus Opportunities

Campus grounds department

College athletic programs
Research assistant

Job Opportunities

Surplus / Substantial oversupply

Reading to Explore

American Legacy: Our National Forests, by
Kenneth Browler (National Geographic)

Niagara: A History of the Falls, by Pierre
Berton (Kodansha)

*Places of Quiet Beauty: Parks, Preserves, and
Environmentalism,* by Rebecca Conrad
(University of Iowa)

Reflections on Leisure, Play, and Recreation,
by David L. Jewell (Southern Illinois
University)

Urban Parks and Open Spaces, by Gayle
Berens (Urban Land Institute)

To Learn More

American Recreation and Park
  Association
2775 South Quincy Street #300
Arlington, VA 22006
(703) 820-4940; fax (703) 671-6772
E-mail: nrpanesc@aol.com
Internet site:
  http://www.nrpa.org/about/branches/
  apsr.htm

Petroleum Engineering

Smell that! That's gasoline in there. You can't buy any perfume in the world that smells as sweet.
—*William K. Whiteford, CEO, Gulf Corporation, cited in* The Executive's Book of Quotations

What to Expect

In petroleum engineering studies, you'll learn to combine information from geological sciences and engineering to help explore workable reservoirs of oil and natural gas, then profitably recover those resources. That task includes understanding physical and chemical processes, the earth's materials, and the geological features most likely to hold petroleum resources. Introductory courses cover such topics as rock and fluid properties, petroleum development, and drilling engineering. In addition, you'll see how to determine and develop the most efficient production methods. At a higher level, you'll take classes in chemical engineering and thermodynamics, measuring and transporting of petroleum products, and managing oil-producing properties. You'll be exposed to state-of-the-art technology, such as satellite sensors, geographic information systems, mapping software, and sophisticated computer modeling. Important aspects of the curriculum include ecologically safe practices and government regulation of exploration, production, and transportation of oil and natural gas. Fieldwork is an essential part of the program.

Trends

Trends in petroleum engineering reflect uncertainties about access to foreign oil and gas resources in light of ever-changeable political and military situations. The best exploration opportunities are apt to be abroad, because so many of the petroleum-producing regions on this continent have already been explored. A second trend involves tighter environmental scrutiny of exploration and drilling within the United States, on shore and off. Meanwhile, research will continue to enhance recovery and find new ways to increase the proportion of oil and gas that can be taken from a reservoir.

What You Need to Succeed

To become proficient in this well-established scientific field, you'll need strong analytic skills and a talent for practical problem solving. With a foundation in geology, the other physical sciences, mathematics, and computer applications, you'll gain mastery of conceptual material pertaining to rock and fluid properties, petroleum measurement, well logging and well testing, and, especially, advanced drilling engineering. For offshore drilling, coursework in oceanography and ocean engineering will prove helpful. Petroleum engineers typically work in teams with other scientists, including geologists and mechanical engineers, so you'll find oral and written communication skills to be important. Since petroleum engineers work where oil and gas are found, you probably will work in Texas, Oklahoma, Louisiana, or California (including off-shore sites) or abroad. Some living conditions abroad might be rough. In our era of dwindling resources, environmental safeguards, and competing energy sources, the oil and gas industry increasingly seeks to minimize operating expenses through improved drilling or fracturing techniques. To aid in this effort, also get a solid background in business subjects like finance and management.

Related Fields

Geological and Earth Sciences
Mechanical Engineering
Materials Science and Engineering

Typical Basic Courses

Artificial Methods of Production
Basic Drilling Practices
Drilling Engineering
Natural Gas
Petroleum Development
Rock and Fluid Properties
Technical Presentations
Well Logging

An Array of Electives

Advanced Drilling Engineering
Environmental Aspects of Petroleum
 Production
Petroleum Measurement and
 Transportation
Petroleum Project Evaluation
Petroleum Property Management
Subspace Engineering
Well Completions and Stimulation
Well Testing

On-Campus Opportunities

Lab assistant
Research assistant

Job Opportunities

Good demand / Possible shortage

Reading to Explore

Offshore: A North Sea Journey, by A. Alvarez (Houghton Mifflin)

Oil Notes: A Narrative, by Rick Bass (Houghton Mifflin)

The Introspective Engineer, by Samuel Florman (St. Martin's Griffin)

The Prize: The Epic Quest for Oil, Money and Power, by Daniel Yergin (Simon & Schuster)

The Seven Sisters: The Great Oil Companies and the World They Shared, by Anthony Sampson (Viking)

To Learn More

Society of Petroleum Engineers
POB 833836
Richardson, TX 75083
(214) 952-9393; fax (214) 952-9345
E-Mail: sessarec@cadvision.com
Internet site: http://www.speca.org

Tau Beta Pi
University of Tennessee, POB 2697
Knoxville, TN 37901-2697
(423) 546-4578; fax (423) 546-4579
E-mail: tbp@tbp.org
Internet site: http://www.tbp.org

Pharmacy

The past 50 years have encompassed a profound revolution in our age-old battle against death and disease. As revolutions go, it's been a rather quiet one, especially considering the stakes involved. . . . And yet, the pharmaceutical revolution that began with the discovery of penicillin has saved millions of lives and promises to save millions more. In addition it's changed our view of health and disease, and of doctors and the healing arts.
—*Mark S. Gold, physician and author, in* Wonder Drugs

What to Expect

As health practitioners, pharmacists need a strong foundation in chemistry and the biological sciences, as well as in the laboratory. Courses build this groundwork in the specific context of pharmacy. For example, you'll learn pharmaceutical mathematics and the calculation skills used in formulating, compounding, manufacturing, and dispensing medication. Other introductory courses cover pharmaceutical technology, including specialized dosage forms for pediatric and geriatric patients, physiochemical principles used in drug delivery systems, and bio-pharmaceuticals. Dispensing technology, drug use control, and governmental regulation of the industry are part of the program. So is the growing role played by pharmaceuticals in the U.S. health care system. Topics among advanced courses include biomedical chemistry, research principles, the pathophysiology of diseases, and biostatistics. Since pharmacy is on the cutting edge of disease research, you need to understand the fundamental aspects of bio-technology related to basic and clinical sciences, encompassing an emphasis on monoclonal antibodies and recombinant DNA. Many practitioners work as managers in retail, industry, or hospital settings, so study the economic, administrative, and organizational aspects of pharmacy operations.

Trends

Trends in pharmacy include the increased pharmaceutical needs of a larger and older population, and greater use of medications. The increased availability of health insurance will add to that demand, while insurers struggle to keep a lid on medication costs. Anticipated scientific advances will make more drug products available, new developments in administering medication will occur, and increasingly sophisticated patients will want more information about their medications. Consumers will become more active in monitoring their own treatments and in searching for alternative and holistic therapies.

What You Need to Succeed

You'll need scientific aptitude, manual dexterity, and strong interpersonal skills. Precision and an attention to detail are essential, because seemingly small errors may have fatal repercussions. You should be genuinely interested in the people who will use the products you develop or dispense. It's vital that you communicate clearly with patients so they understand how to use prescription and over-the-counter drugs safely and sometimes monitor their own drug therapies. In drug manufacturing, hospitals, health maintenance organizations, research labs, and clinics, pharmacists are part of teams and interact with other professionals, such as physicians, dietitians, biochemists, and nurses. For instance, you may advise the medical staff on the selection and effects of a new product, evaluate drug use patterns in the hospital, and jointly conduct research. You need computer skills for record keeping and analysis, as well as the ability to deal with insurance companies and governmental regulators. Business management training may pay off, too, in this growing health care field.

Related Fields

Biochemistry
Medical Technology
Micro and Molecular Biology
Nursing

Typical Basic Courses

Drug Information
Immunology for Pharmacy
Introduction to Pharmacy
Pharmaceutical Formulations
Pharmacy Drugs and Health Care
Pharmacy Practice Management
Practical Aspects of Dosage Form Design
Principles of Clinical Pharmacology

An Array of Electives

Clinical Nuclear Pharmacy
Clinical Therapeutics
General Toxicology
Medical Errors
Nuclear Pharmacy Instrumentation
Pharmacy Law and Ethics
Pollution Toxicology
Sociology of Medical Practice

On-Campus Opportunities

Campus health service
Lab assistant

Job Opportunities

Good demand / Possible shortage

Reading to Explore

Impure Science: AIDS, Activism, and the Politics of Knowledge, by Steven Epstein (University of California)

Listening to Prozac, by Peter T. Kramer (Viking Penguin)

Medication of the Mind, by Scott Veggeberg (Henry Holt)

Medicine of the Earth: Legends, Recipes, Remedies and Cultivation of Healing Plants, by Sisanne Fischer-Rizzi (Rudra)

Yellow Fever, Black Goddess, by Christopher Wills (Addison-Wesley)

To Learn More

American Pharmaceutical Association
2215 Constitution Avenue NW
Washington, DC20037-2985
(202) 429-7596; fax (202) 628-0443
E-mail: sysop@alphanet.org
Internet site: http://www.alphanet.org/

American Society of Consultant
  Pharmacists
1321 Duke Street
Alexandria, VA 22314-3563
(703) 739-1300; fax (703) 739-1321
E-mail: info@ascp.com
Internet site: http://www.ascp.com

Philosophy

Philosophy begins in wonder, and at the end, when philosophic thought has done its best, the wonder remains.
—*Alfred North Whitehead, philosopher, cited in* The New International Dictionary of Quotations

What to Expect

History of philosophy, ethics, problems, and logic are the bulwarks for this major. Through course work in these four domains, you'll learn philosophy's broad parameters and its specific application to a host of contemporary issues encompassing biology and medical technology, the fine arts and literature, urban planning, economics, and social work. Historically oriented classes will cover ancient thinkers and movements such as Aristotle, Plato, the Stoics, and Epicureans to modern trends such as existentialism, deconstructionism, and feminist philosophy. Take at least one course in the problems of ethics, as well as in applied ethics. Related classes in political philosophy, the philosophy of technology, social philosophy, and aesthetics will be useful. As you progress, you'll have the opportunity to enroll in "problem" or issue-oriented courses on knowledge, mind, and reality. These will include metaphysics, epistemology (theory of knowledge), and philosophical approaches to mind, language, religion, and science. To become proficient in logic, start with a course in symbolic logic or critical thinking, and advance to mathematical logic or artificial neural networks. Environmental ethics and philosophy of law will prove helpful in the business world.

Trends

Trends in philosophy include a much greater emphasis on applying seemingly abstract concepts about human nature and the environment to specific problems confronting society. Reflecting this development, a growing number of philosophers function in hospitals, biomedical centers, and industrial parks to help scientists and administrators grapple with the ethical implications of their work. Increasingly, philosophers teach at professional schools in business, engineering, law, and medicine rather than in exclusively traditional, liberal arts settings.

What You Need to Succeed

Are you drawn to thinking in the broadest terms about the key questions facing humanity? Do you enjoy playing with ideas that cut across many disciplines, and do you possess top-level skills in reading, writing, and analysis? Do you have a logical mind and a willingness to avoid rushing to judgment in discussions? If so, then you're likely to succeed in the philosophy field—and become part of one of the oldest, most respected branches of human knowledge. In the past, philosophers were generally isolated thinkers focused on lofty questions, such as the meaning of life, ethics, and morality—for all humankind. Today, a growing number are employed in applied settings such as hospitals, health care networks, and large corporations concerned with the specific ethical and philosophical implications of their work and its particular impact on society. That's why the ability to function as part of an organization, and yet offer useful advice in clear, relevant terms is increasingly important. Such interdisciplinary activity requires strong oral and verbal communication skills. You'll also need a creative flair for helping others to see the "broad picture" even in highly technical fields.

Related Fields

Anthropology and Archeology
Cognitive Science
Linguistics
Medieval and Renaissance Studies
Religious Studies and Theology

Typical Basic Courses

Ethics
Introduction to Philosophy
Modern Science and Human Values
Philosophy of Human Nature
Philosophy of Law
Philosophy of Religion
Philosophy, Politics, and Society
Ways of Knowing

An Array of Electives

Artificial Neural Networks
Asian Philosophy
Environmental Ethics
Metaphysics
Philosophy of Biology, and Medicine
Philosophy of Language
Philosophy, Psychology, and Psychiatry
Topics in Postmodernism

On-Campus Opportunities

Research assistant

Job Opportunities

Surplus / Substantial oversupply

Reading to Explore

Edges of Science: Crossing the Boundary from Physics to Metaphysics, by Richard Morris (Prentice Hall)

Man's Search for Meaning, by Viktor Frankl (Simon & Schuster)

Modern Philosophy: An Introduction and Survey, by Roger Scruton (Penguin)

Ring of Truth: An Inquiry into How We Know What We Know, by Philip and Phyllis Morrison (Random House)

The Idea of Decline in Western History, by Arthur Herman (Free Press)

To Learn More

American Philosophical Association
University of Delaware
Newark, DE 19716
(302) 831-1112;fax (302) 831-8690
E-mail: burt@udel.edu
Internet site: http://www.udel.edu/apa

Photography and Cinema

A great photograph is a full expression of what one feels about what is being photographed in the deepest sense, and is, thereby a true expression of what one feels about life in its entirety.
—*Ansel Adams, photographer, cited in* The Crown Treasury of Relevant Quotations

What to Expect

What we "see" is shaped not just by what the lens shows and not just by what the photographer or filmmaker intends to express, but also by each viewer's personal experience and imagination. That's why those studying photography and cinema should recognize the cultural aspects of visual imagery, not merely the techniques for creating and transmitting images. At the entry level, students will learn the role of pictures in journalism and mass media, practice picture taking and darkroom procedures, and become familiar with techniques for editing film and videotape. You'll also encounter computer graphics and develop an understanding of how to use graphics effectively for enhancing a photographic or film message. As you continue, classes will cover the history of photography, photojournalism and film, the ethical and aesthetic issues pertaining to imaging technology, and the application of new technologies to capture, process, edit, alter, display, and transmit images. Specialized courses can help prepare you for a career in print or broadcast journalism, scientific and technical photography, the fine arts, advertising, public relations, documentaries, telecommunications, or portraiture. Your courses should provide extensive opportunities for field work in a variety of settings including the outdoors, the photography studio, and the film-editing room.

Trends

Trends in photography and cinema include the growing importance of computers as tools to take pictures, scan them into digital form, manipulate them in diverse ways, and store them on compact disc. Photographers and filmmakers will see their work used more often as educational and teaching media, as well as methods of persuasion, idea marketing, and art.

What You Need to Succeed

Obviously, you'll need a flair for visual imagery as well as creativity and technical expertise. For instance, you must use your imagination in the use of lighting, lenses, filters, and camera settings to tell stories or capture moods. Technical expertise includes mastery of rapidly changing equipment and computers. Specialists must understand the arenas they work in, such as consumer merchandise, medicine, and engineering.

Patience is a virtue, since it may take repeated efforts to get the "right" shot or scene. Verbal communication skills are mandatory, since most photographers, camera operators, and cinema photographers work closely with other professionals, including photo technicians, publication and broadcast editors, film directors, screenwriters, advertising clients, reporters, models, and performers. This field can be exciting and even glamorous. But you'll be expected to meet deadlines—often with little advance notice. Photographers and camera operators may also work long hours in adverse weather, and may travel to uncomfortable or even dangerous places in covering events such as natural disasters, wars, or crimes. Always be aware that visual images have a unique power to sway public opinion and emotions.

Related Fields

Art
Art History
English
Graphic Design
Journalism
Theater and Cinema

Typical Basic Courses

Color Photography
Computer Graphics
Film Production
Fundamentals of Photography
History of Photography
Introduction to Filmmaking
Screenwriting
The Filmic Tradition

An Array of Electives

Advertising and Illustration Photography
American Film
Documentary Photography
Major Filmmakers
Photojournalism
Studio and the Constructed Image
Video: Art, Theory, Politics
World Film Cultures

On-Campus Opportunities

Academic department newsletters
Campus museum
Campus newspaper, magazine and television station

Job Opportunities

Adequate supply / Some oversupply

Reading to Explore

American Photography: The First Century, by Merry A. Foresta (Smithsonian)

Charlie Chaplin and His Times, by Kenneth S. Lynn (Simon & Schuster)

The Civil Rights Movement: A Photographic History, 1954–1968, by Steven Kasher (Abbeville)

Wildlife Through the Camera, by Peter Bale (Parkwest)

Without Lying Down: Frances Marion and the Powerful Women of Early Hollywood, by Cari Beauchamp (Scribner)

To Learn More

American Society of Media Photographers
14 Washington Road #502
Princeton Junction, NJ 08550-1503
(609) 799-8300; fax (609) 799-2233
E-mail: info@asmp.org
Internet site: http://www.asmp.org

Professional Photographers of America
57 Forsyth Street NW, Suite 1600
Atlanta, GA 30303-2206
(800) 786-6277; fax (404) 614-6400
E-mail: membership@ppa-world.org
Internet site: http://www.ppa-world.org

Physical Education and Exercise Science

Sports are wonderful; they can bring you comfort and pleasure for the rest of your life. Sports can teach you so much about yourself, your emotions and character, how to be resolute in moments of crisis, and how to fight back from the brink of defeat.
—*Arthur Ashe, tennis pro, in* Days of Grace

What to Expect

This field's broad emphasis is on understanding relationships between physical activity and life sciences, and on helping children and adults use physical activity as part of a healthy lifestyle. Introductory courses provide an overview of the discipline, address lifestyle habits and aerobic capacity, and cover first aid and personal safety, including prevention of injuries and trauma. They also teach essential information about human development, anatomy, growth and maturity, and psychology. Learn the fundamentals of as many diverse sports as possible, as well as the principles of coaching, fitness, and conditioning. At an advanced level, you can become skilled in coaching particular sports (such as track and field, basketball, and swimming) and coaching particular groups (such as people with disabilities or elementary-school students). Other options include design and evaluation of physical activity programs, sports administration and marketing, planning and construction of athletic facilities, and rehabilitation of sports injuries.

Trends

Trends in physical education and exercise sciences include the development in children of a lifelong interest in physical activity. Another trend is the generation of greater interest among adults in maintaining fitness through sports such as volleyball, softball, and golf as well as aerobic exercises (at a health club or at home), jogging, and bicycling. Yet another trend is the recognition that physical fitness, nutrition, and preventive health care work together. Finally, expect more emphasis on creating athletic opportunities for the elderly, and for people with physical or mental impairments.

What You Need to Succeed

Certainly, the qualities of patience, empathy, and personal organization are important. Also, you must be able to communicate broad ideas, as well as narrow facts, in a clear, age-appropriate manner. In physical education and exercise science, several additional traits come into play: adequate physical coordination and stamina, awareness of a healthy lifestyle's ingredients, and an ability to manage large groups of children, teens, or adults effectively. You must react quickly to hazardous—even life-threatening—sporting and exercise situations. You'll need to be well grounded conceptually in such subjects as human physiology, stress management, adapted physical activity, prevention and care of athletic injuries, and the effects of exercise and sports on varying types of individuals. Good social skills are a definite plus in teaching those of various cultural, ethnic, and racial backgrounds, and in understanding and accommodating their respective viewpoints about physical exercise, sports, and lifestyles.

Related Fields

Early Childhood Education
Elementary Education
Occupational Therapy
Parks and Recreation
Physical Therapy
Secondary Education

Typical Basic Courses

Aerobic Exercise and Dance
Competitive Softball
Curriculum and Methods in Elementary and Secondary School and Physical Education
Exercise Physiology
Physical Activity for Special Populations
Student Teaching in Physical Education
Tests and Measurement in Physical Education
Weight Training

An Array of Electives

Adaptive Aquatics
Care and Prevention of Athletic Injuries
Coaching Sports for Athletes with Disabilities
Community Health
Development and Evaluation of Health Programs
Organization and Administration of Physical Education Programs
Sociocultural Analysis of Physical Activity
Stress: Its Nature and Management

On-Campus Opportunities

Campus athletic programs and teams
Campus health service

Job Opportunities

Surplus / Substantial oversupply

Reading to Explore

Coach's Guide to Sport Rehabilitation, by Steven R. Tippett (Leisure Press)

Creating the Big Game: John W. Heisman and the Invention of American Football, by Wiley L. Umphlett (Greenwood)

Fit for America: Health, Fitness, Sport and American Society, by Harvey Green (Pantheon)

Never Be Tired Again, by David C. Gardner and Grace J. Beatty (HarperCollins)

Top Spin: Ups and Downs in Big-Time Tennis, by Eliot Perry (Henry Holt)

To Learn More

American Alliance for Health, Physical Education, and Dance
1900 Association Drive
Reston, VA 22091
(703) 476-1340; fax (703) 476-9527
E-mail: webmaster@deepspace9.aahperd.org
Internet site: http://www.perd.org/

National Association for Sport and Physical Education
1900 Association Drive
Reston, VA 20191
(800) 213-7193; fax (703) 476-8316
E-mail: naspe@aahperd.org
Internet site:
http://www.aahperd.org/naspe/naspe.html

Physical Therapy

Today, as never before, one must love the body, must be gently patient with it.
—*Francis Thompson, author, cited in* The Crown Treasury of Relevant Quotations

What to Expect

Course work in physical therapy begins with a detailed examination of life stages and their relationship to patient health conditions, an introduction to patient coordination, and an overview of patient-care skills and techniques, such as problem solving and patient interaction. You'll learn to evaluate medical histories, test and measure patients' strength and range of motion, and develop and implement appropriate treatment plans. There is a strong emphasis on clinical experiences with real patients, coupled with instruction about health care delivery systems, physical therapy practice issues, and biomedical and professional ethics. Through courses and clinical training, you'll become familiar with treatment tools and techniques such as electrical stimulation, ultrasound to relieve pain and improve muscle condition, deep-muscle massage, hot and cold compresses, and prostheses and wheelchairs. You'll learn to document progress and identify problems needing more attention. Look for courses to help you focus on specialties of interest, such as sports medicine, geriatrics, pediatrics, cardio-pulmonary therapy, burns, and neurology.

Trends

Trends in physical therapy revolve around changes in the population, in medical technology, and in health promotion. The expanding elderly segment is vulnerable to chronic and debilitating disorders, while Baby Boomers are reaching the age at which they are at risk for heart attacks and strokes that require cardiac and physical rehabilitation. High-tech advances will lead to more hip and knee replacements, with patients who need help to improve flexibility and strengthen muscles. Physical therapists will become more involved in evaluating worksites, developing exercise programs, and teaching safe work habits.

What You Need to Succeed

To attain your place in this high-demand profession, you'll need a solid background of course work on such topics as human anatomy and kinesiology, normal motor development, applied physiology, orthopedic clinical medicine, and specific forms of therapy—including mobility training, prosthetics, and musculoskeletal intervention—for infants, children, generally healthy adults, and the elderly. In daily work, physical therapists need considerable patience, empathy, warmth, perseverance, and optimism to help often-discouraged clients achieve their maximum goals for well being. It's essential that you enjoy hands-on work with other people.

You'll also be expected to be in good physical condition and have manual dexterity, as such work sometimes involves lifting and sustained movement. Whether you function independently in private practice or on the staff of a medical facility or rehabilitation center, skills in oral and written communication involving clients, families, and professional staff are essential. In today's changing climate of health care, physical therapists must also be aware of the financial realities affecting treatment planning, measurement, billing, and insurance documentation of services.

Related Fields

Nursing
Occupational Therapy
Optometry
Physical Education and Exercise Science

Typical Basic Courses

Anatomy and Kinesiology
Applied Physiology
Exercise, Muscle Physiology, and
    Plasticity
Introduction to Physical Therapy
Mobility Training
Normal Motor Development
Orthopedic Clinical Medicine
Physical Agents for Physical Therapists

An Array of Electives

Basics of Physical Therapy Research
Cardiopulminary Physical Therapy:
    Evaluation and Treatment
Musculoskeletal Physical Therapy:
    Evaluation and Treatment
Neurological Physical Therapy:
    Evaluation and Treatment
Orthotics and Prosthetics
Pediatric Physical Therapy: Evaluation
    and Treatment
Psychosocial Aspects of Patient Care
Rehabilitation for Older Adults

On-Campus Opportunities

Campus athletic departments and teams
Campus health service

Job Opportunities

High demand / Limited supply

Reading to Explore

No Pain, No Strain, by Arnold Roth (St. Martin's Press)

Sports Injuries: Diagnosis and Management, by James G. Garrick and David R. Webb (Saunders)

Sports Medicine: Fitness, Training, and Injuries, by Otto Appenzeller (Urban and Scwarezenberg)

Staying Supple, by John Jerome (Bantam)

The Modern Book of Stretching: Strength and Flexibility at Any Age, by Anne Kent Ruth and Patrick Harbron (Dell)

To Learn More

American Physical Therapy Association
1111 North Fairfax Street
Alexandria, VA 22314
(800) 999-APTA; fax (703) 684-7343
E-mail: education@apta.apta.org
Internet site: http://www.apta.edoc.com

Physics

The universe is to be valued because there is truth in it and beauty in it; and we live to discover the truth and beauty no less than to do what is right. Indeed, we cannot attain to that state of mind in which we shall naturally do what is right unless we are aware of the truth and beauty of the universe.

—*A. Clutton Brock, author, cited in* The Crown Treasury of Relevant Quotations

What to Expect

Education should prepare you to explore and identify basic principles concerning the structure and behavior of matter, including generation and transfer of energy. Education should also prepare you to apply physics theories to practical problems such as electrical and optical devices, medical and industrial equipment, and advanced materials. In the beginning, you'll cover elementary mechanics including kinematics and dynamics of particles, work and energy, linear and angular motion, electric forces and fields, ray optics, and thermodynamics. Other low-level classes focus on waves and particles, mechanics, and electricity, magnetism, and light. From there, options become more specialized as you delve into thermal physics, wave motion, electricity and magnetism, modern optics, and mechanics. If you choose an optics course, for example, you'll deal with reflection and refraction, interference, and holography among other topics. There will be extensive laboratory work that teaches research and experimental techniques, use of electronic and other instrumentation, and the statistical analysis of data. You should also understand how to use science to help solve societal problems such as nuclear and alternative energy systems, environmental contamination, and the arms race.

Trends

Trends in physics include anticipated reductions in military-related research, but growth of research and development in private industry. There will be less emphasis on basic research and more attention paid to applied and manufacturing research and product development. That will include development of instrumentation used in telecommunications and optics medicine. There will be more overlap that combines disciplines such as chemical physics, geophysics, and biophysics.

What You Need to Succeed

To make it in physics calls for computer skills, mathematical ability, and an inquisitive, inventive mind. Analytic and problem-solving techniques are essential as well, whether you do basic or applied research. Frequently, you'll be asked to apply physics principles and laws to develop new devices, processes, and products. The field today is highly research oriented, with much of the work involving computers and laboratory equipment. Precision and an attention to detail count. Although many assignments are tackled by teams of physicists with other scientists and engineers, you're also likely to work independently at times. The teamwork aspect of the field, as well as contact with clients and customers, requires good written and verbal communications. If you're employed in industry, you'll benefit from a broad educational background that includes business and economics, computer technology, engineering, and current events.

Related Fields

Aerospace and Astronautical Engineering
Astronomy and Astrophysics
Mathematics

Typical Basic Courses

Computational Methods of Physics
Electricity and Magnetism
General Physics
Introduction to Classical Physics
Introduction to Special Relativity
Mechanics
Optics, Waves, and Particles
Physics by Inquiry: Matter and Heat

An Array of Electives

Biological Physics
General Relativity
High-Energy Particle Physics
Laser Physics and Quantum Electronics
Methods of Experimental Physics
Modern Experimental Optics
Physics of Black Holes, White Dwarfs,
   and Neutron Stars
Relativistic Quantum Field Theory

On-Campus Opportunities

Lab assistant
Research assistant

Job Opportunities

Surplus / Substantial oversupply

Reading to Explore

Cosmic Code: Quantum Physics as the Language of Nature, by Heinz L. Pagels (Bantam)

Lise Meitner: A Life in Physics, by Ruth Lewin Sime (University of California)

Surely You're Joking, Mr. Feynman: Adventures of a Curious Character, by Richard P. Feynman (Bantam)

The Physics of Star Trek, by Lawrence M. Krauss (Harper Perennial)

The Whole Shebang: A State-of-the-Universe Report, by Timothy Ferris (Simon & Schuster)

To Learn More

American Physical Society
1 Physical Ellipse
College Park, MD 20740-3844
(301) 209-3269; fax (301) 209-0865
E-mail: webmaster@aps.org
Internet site: http://www.aps.org

Society of Physics Students
1 Physical Ellipse
College Park, MD 20740-3844
(301) 209-3007; fax (301) 209-0839
E-mail: sps@aip.org
Internet site: http://www.aip.org/
   education/sps/sps.htm

Political Science

Politics is the science of who gets what, when, and how.
—*Sidney Hillman, labor leader, cited in* The Concise Columbia Dictionary of Quotations

What to Expect

Political science is not merely the study of the structure of governments, but also how political institutions and citizens collectively make decisions. Your program covers the origins of governments, their rise and fall, diverse philosophies of governance, and relations among nations. Introductory courses discuss historical and theoretical concepts, political behavior and citizen participation, and the operation and organization of national, state, and local governments in the United States. At this level, you'll also learn about comparative political systems, public administration, and world politics. As you progress, you can explore specific institutions, such as the U.S. Congress, the activities of lobbyists and special-interest groups, political parties, the governmental bureaucracy, and the judiciary. Specialized courses address the roles of particular groups, such as women, immigrants, and minorities, in American politics and government. If you're interested in foreign affairs, study political ideologies such as communism and fascism, international organizations such as the United Nations, and approaches to government in Eastern Europe, Latin America, the Middle East, or Africa. Other advanced topics, such as the U.S. civil rights movement, urban policies, voting behavior, and law, cross disciplinary lines.

Trends

Trends in political science include a greater focus on governments in technologically developing nations, conflict resolution, and political economics as the world shrinks. Within the study of American government, there's additional examination today of the role of traditionally marginalized or excluded groups, the power of advertising, mass media, and public relations in shaping elections, and practical issues such as voter apathy, downsizing of government, and the shift of power from Washington, D.C., to state and local decision makers.

What You Need to Succeed

Naturally, you will need a strong interest in public affairs and how society develops structures—from local zoning boards to state legislatures to federal regulatory agencies to multinational organizations—in weighing and meeting public needs. Intellectual curiosity and imagination are essential, because you seek new information about people and ideas. Because this is mainly an analytical field, you must be able to address problems and issues logically and systematically, and to assess and compare data. Master the application of computers for research and communication.

Surveying and interviewing skills are crucial. So is the ability to communicate clearly in writing and orally on often complicated and emotional topics of public concern. Develop a high level of self-confidence and emotional maturity, because work can involve you with appointed and elected governmental officials, special-interest lobbyists, public opinion and polling experts, and a cross-section of the public. It may even catapult you into elected office and a career in national politics.

Related Fields

Economics
History
International Relations
Public Policy Studies
Urban Planning

Typical Basic Courses

American Political System
Ancient Political Thought
Comparative Politics
European Political Systems
Modern Political Thought
Public Opinion and Political Behavior
The Presidency
Third World Politics

An Array of Electives

Analysis of U.S. Foreign Policy
Comparative Politics in Developing
  Nations
Professional Sports and the American
  City
Refugees, Displaced Persons, and Exiles
Strategy in Politics
Theory of Institutions
Urban Life and Urban Politics
Women in Politics

On-Campus Opportunities

College policy-making bodies
Research assistant
Student organizations

Job Opportunities

Surplus / Substantial oversupply

Reading to Explore

Dead Right, by David Frum (Simon & Schuster)

The Brethren: Inside the Supreme Court, by Bob Woodward and Scott Armstrong (Simon & Schuster)

The Rise and Fall of the American Left, by John D. Diggins (Norton)

Who Will Tell the People: The Betrayal of American Democracy, by William Greider (Simon & Schuster)

Why Americans Hate Politics, by E. J. Dionne, Jr. (Simon & Schuster)

To Learn More

Academy of Political Science
475 Riverside Drive #1274
New York, NY 10115-1274
(212) 870-2500; fax (212) 870-2202
E-mail: aps321@aol.com
Internet site:
   http://www.epn.org/psq.html

American Political Science Association
1527 New Hampshire Avenue NW
Washington, DC 20036
(202) 483-2512; fax (202) 483-2657
E-mail: aps@apsa.com
Internet site: http://www.aps@net.org

Psychology

Know yourself, and your neighbor will not mistake you.
—Scottish proverb, *cited in* The Crown Treasury of Relevant Quotations

What to Expect

In psychology, your cornerstone will be an understanding of human behavior, cognition and learning, motivation and personality, perception and social relations, as well as abnormalities in these domains. Beginning studies will familiarize you with basic biological concepts to view the human individual as a member of a species sharing specific cognitive, behavioral, and social characteristics with other animal species. If you're drawn to this approach, take additional courses in comparative (animal) psychology, ethology, and experimental design. As you advance, a wide variety of electives is available. Depending on your interest in either research or applied work such as school psychology or psychotherapy, you may choose courses on such subjects as mental retardation and childhood disabilities, the psychology of learning, human sexuality, adulthood and aging, health psychology, survey design and advanced statistics, or the psychology of women. Typically required for a psychology major are courses in statistics and laboratory experimentation.

Trends

Trends in psychology today include the rise of managed health care, which is causing an upheaval in work with clients having cognitive, emotional, or social problems. Increasingly, psychologists are required to subordinate their therapeutic goals, plans, and approaches to financial, cost-cutting considerations. The ability to master different forms of short-term therapy, to document treatment precisely, and to interact with business administrators as well as clinicians will become increasingly important. Another development involves the growth of early-intervention programs serving very young children and their families. Also, reflecting greater societal interest in quality-of-life issues regarding the elderly, psychologists with geriatric training will find a high demand for their services in skilled-nursing care settings.

What You Need to Succeed

Are you fundamentally interested in what makes people "tick"? Strong verbal and analytic skills are vital. In research settings, you'll need to know computer technology, statistics, and experimental design, since you'll often be collaborating with allied disciplines such as sociology and social work, occupational therapy and speech-language therapy, and even management and marketing. The ability to present research findings in a meaningful way to professionals as well as to the wider public is paramount, so you'll need good communication skills. Psychologists who work diagnostically or therapeutically—whether in family homes, schools, clinics, hospitals, or nursing homes—require empathy, emotional openness, and a sensitivity to cultural differences in values, feelings, and perceptions. Yet, you must be able to retain your objectivity in helping others. In such settings, psychologists typically work as part of a team, so openness to the viewpoints of other disciplines is important. Because the field is rapidly changing due to wider changes in American health care today, a capacity for self-starting activity, innovation, and entrepreneurship are desirable qualities for success.

Related Fields

Cognitive Science
Family and Child Development
Human Resources and Personnel
Occupational Therapy
Social Work

Typical Basic Courses

Abnormal Psychology
Developmental Psychology
General Psychology
Introduction to Health Psychology
Personality
Psychology of Motivation
Psychology of Thinking
Social Psychology

An Array of Electives

Adolescence: Biology, Psychology, and
    Gender
Eating Behavior and Disorders
Human Sexuality
Minority Mental Health
Physiological Psychology: Drugs and
    Behavior
Sleep: Its Nature and Function
The Psychology of Women
Theories of Psychotherapy

On-Campus Opportunities

Research assistant
Student counseling service

Job Opportunities

Surplus / Substantial oversupply

Reading to Explore

Alfred Adler and the Founding of Individual Psychology, by Edward Hoffman (Addison-Wesley)

Emotional Intelligence, by Daniel Goleman (Bantam)

The Enchanted World of Sleep, by Peretz Lavie (Yale University)

Touched with Fire: Manic-Depressive Illness and the Artistic Temperament, by Kay Refield Jamison (Simon & Schuster)

Uncommon Genius: How Great Ideas Are Born, by Denise Shekerjian (Viking)

To Learn More

American Psychological Association
750 First Street NE
Washington, DC 20002
(202) 336-5500; fax (202) 336-5568
E-Mail: webmaster@apa.org
Internet site: http://www.apa.org

National Association of School
    Psychologists
4340 East-West Highway
Bethesda, MD 20814
(301) 657-0270; fax (301) 657-0275
E-mail: NASP8455@aol.com
Internet site: http://www.naspweb.org

Public Policy and Administration

The object of government in peace and in war is not the glory of rulers or of races, but the happiness of the common [person].
—*William Beveridge, economist, cited in* The Concise Columbia Dictionary of Quotations

What to Expect

Think of public policy and administration as a blend of political science, management, economics, and sociology, where decisions potentially carry broad implications. Develop a firm understanding of these allied fields, then use that knowledge to recognize how policy is made and carried out. Government doesn't function in a vacuum, so courses place public policy in the perspective of today's issues such as education, crime, taxes, and the environment. Classes in federal, state, and local government finance include the economics of governmental spending and taxation, relations among different units of government, and analysis of governments' fiscal roles. Explore business-government relationships, including how business influences public policy and how government regulates business. On an administrative level, examine and analyze public administration, government organization, and legal and political restraints on what managers and bureaucrats can do. Master the concepts and methods of evaluating taxpayer-financed programs, strategically managing and restructuring agencies, assessing and distributing grants, and making budgeting and spending decisions. Specialized courses focus on public policy in criminal justice, public education, agriculture, health care, and other topics.

Trends

Trends in public policy studies require professionals to address difficult issues concerning the role of government. Should traditionally "public" functions such as running schools, sanitation services, prisons, and even police work be turned over to profit-oriented businesses? Should parks and other public lands be sold? Should voters rather than Congress or state legislatures have the final say on tax hikes? Professionals must better prepared to explain how tax money is spent, and then revamp or eliminate programs that don't meet goals.

What You Need to Succeed

You need a strong interest in how government decisions are made and their ramifications, as well as the capacity to focus on the nuts-and-bolts of the government process. A multidisciplinary outlook is required, as are analytical skills to examine budgets, competing demands for services, and alternative decisions. Be sensitive to the fact that people hold intense feelings—not all favorable—about government, and that their tax dollars will pay your salary. The field calls for patience to work with individuals and groups, a willingness to consider divergent viewpoints in a democratic society, and the ability to explain clearly the role of government amid vocal—and sometimes violent—dissatisfactions. Because computer systems are essential for public welfare, military, transportation, the fire and police departments, and other operations, you should understand government information systems, data analysis, and systems analysis. Also, administrative and managerial skills are needed.

Related Fields

Economics
Environmental Studies
History
International Relations
Urban Planning
Urban Studies

Typical Basic Courses

Economic Analysis for Public Policy
    Making
Geography and Public Affairs
Introduction to Policy Analysis
Political Analysis for Public Policy
    Making
Political Theory and Public Policy
Social Policy in America
Women as Leaders

An Array of Electives

Managing Public Agencies
Politics of Health Care
Public Budgeting and Financial
    Management
Regulation of Vice and Substance Abuse
Resource and Environmental Policy
Schools and Social Policy
Telecommunications Policy and
    Regulation
The Palestine Problem and U.S. Public
    Policy

On-Campus Opportunities

Campus administrative offices
Campus personnel department
Student organizations

Job Opportunities

Surplus / Substantial oversupply

Reading to Explore

A Civil Action, by Jonathan Harr
(Vintage)

Banishing Bureaucracy: The Five Strategies of Reinventing Government, by David Osborne and Peter Plastrik (Addison-Wesley)

George Ball: Behind the Scene in U.S. Foreign Policy, by James A. Bill (Yale University)

One World, Ready or Not: The Manic Logic of Global Capitalism (Simon & Schuster)

The Cigarette Papers, by Stanton A. Glantz, John Slade, Lisa A. Bern, Peter Hanauer, and Deborah E. Barnes (University of California)

To Learn More

American Society for Public
    Administration
1120 G Street NW, Suite 700
Washington, DC 20005
(202) 393-7878; fax (202) 638-4952
E-mail: info@aspanet.org
Internet site: http://www.aspanet.org

Public Relations

Towering over presidents and state governors, over Congress and state legislatures, over conventions and the vast machinery of party, public opinion stands out in the United States as the great source of power, the master of servants who tremble before it.
—*James Bryce, historian and diplomat, in* The American Commonwealth

What to Expect

We often think of public relations practitioners as spin doctors and weavers of illusion, but they also serve important public information functions in our society. Courses lead you through public relations principles and techniques, management and administration, print and broadcast press operations, and writing with an emphasis on news releases, proposals, speeches, scripts, and annual reports. Visual communications are part of the curriculum, including desktop publishing, computer graphics, and use of the Internet to spread a client's message. And because public relations involves more than telling the organization's story, you'll learn social science research techniques—especially how to design and implement opinion polls and surveys, and how to conduct interviews—to keep management aware of public attitudes and concerns.

More advanced courses build on those basics and provide opportunities to develop your own public relations campaigns. You also can take classes that focus on public relations in specific areas such as politics, nonprofit organizations, or corporate communications. Throughout, you'll be exposed to ethical issues that relate to fairness in advocacy.

Trends

Trends in public relations include growing use of new communications technologies such as the Internet, video, and CD-ROM to spread a client's message and to get more comprehensive feedback on individual and community attitudes about products, candidates, ballot issues, political parties, government services, and business operations. Professional public relations will also become more widely used by cultural, scientific, educational, and other charitable groups that formerly relied on staff members or volunteers to handle publicity, media contacts, "damage control," and fund-raising.

What You Need to Succeed

Communication skills top the must-have list. If you can't clearly articulate a position—verbally, graphically, or in writing—you can't sell an idea or credibly advocate a position. A willingness to cooperate is far more effective than a confrontational attitude to win and keep the support of a targeted public—voters, perhaps, or investors—if your organization, business, or government agency hopes to maintain its reputation, financial stability, and even its continued existence. You must be willing to listen to suggestions and criticisms from a variety of sources, enabling you to better advise your clients on strategy and policy.

Aside from professional skills, you'll need an outgoing personality, an understanding of psychology, self-confidence, initiative, and an eagerness to motivate people. You'll have to be competitive yet flexible, and learn how to operate on a team. Finally, you'll have to hone your decision-making, problem-solving, and research abilities.

Related Fields

Advertising
Graphic Design
Journalism
Marketing
Technical Writing
Telecommunications

Typical Basic Courses

Corporate Communication Techniques
Graphic Communication
Intercultural Communication
Persuasive Public Speaking
Presentation Media
Principles of Public Relations
Public Relations and Organizations
Public Relations Writing and Directing

An Array of Electives

Broadcast Sales
International Public Relations
Message Composition
Nonverbal Communication
Political Communication
Psychology of Language
Public Relations Campaigns
Small Format Video Production

On-Campus Opportunities

College fund-raising office
College information and public affairs
    office
Sports information office

Job Opportunities

Near balance / Supply equals demand

Reading to Explore

Call the Briefing! Reagan and Bush, Sam and Helen: A Decade of Presidents and the Press, by Marlin Fitzwater (Times)

Guerrilla PR: How You Can Wage an Effective Publicity Campaign Without Going Broke, by Michael Levine (HarperBusiness)

PR! A Social History of Spin, by Stuart Ewen (Basic Books)

Speaking Out: The Reagan Presidency from Inside the White House, by Larry Speakes (Scribner)

Toxic Sludge Is Good for You: Lies, Damn Lies, and the Public Relations Industry, by John C. Stauber and Sheldon Rampton (Common Courage)

To Learn More

Public Relations Society of America
33 Irving Place
New York, NY 10003
(212) 995-2230; fax (212) 995-0757
E-mail: hdq@prsa.org
Internet site: http://www.prsa.org

Religious Studies and Theology

The fact of the religious vision and its history of persistent expansion, is our one ground for optimism. Apart from it, human life is a flash of occasional enjoyments lighting up a mass of pain and misery, a bagatelle of transient experience.
—*Alfred North Whitehead, philosopher, cited in* The Crown Treasury of Relevant Quotations

What to Expect

Your studies will examine the phenomena that diverse cultures and societies treat as sacred, including rituals, institutional practices, and narratives. This analysis weaves together elements of anthropology, sociology, history, psychology, education, philosophy, and faith. The building blocks are an understanding of the world's major religions—Christianity, Islam, Judaism, Hinduism, and Buddhism—and their texts and practices. Foreign-language courses—ancient and modern—will be of great benefit. Electives cover such varied topics as witchcraft and the occult, Old Testament prophecy, African American religious music (from spirituals to gospel), Jewish mysticism, and Native American shamanism. You can focus on the religions of specific geographic areas, such as India or Southeast Asia, or historical periods, such as the lifetime of Jesus or the Renaissance. Some electives place religious beliefs and observances into a broader context—for example, exploring spirituality in popular culture, spiritual dimensions of death and dying, and the interaction of religion and politics in the United States.

Trends

Trends in religious studies and theology address the role faith and lack of faith play in contemporary issues, ranging from abortion to racial discrimination, from assisted suicide to business ethics. Another focus is on the role of women, who historically have been excluded from equal treatment by some major religions. Yet another concern is finding ways to use religion in bridging cultural differences rather than in creating barriers, whether in the Middle East, Africa, the Balkans, or small-town America.

What You Need to Succeed

In daily life, do you feel a strong sense of spirituality and ethics? Do the great religious writings of world history inspire you? Are you interested in helping to apply this wisdom to global problems today? If so, then you might decide to explore one of civilization's oldest and most respected fields. With training in religious studies and theology, you'll acquire expertise on major traditions such as Buddhism, Christianity, Hinduism, Islam, Judaism, and Sikhism. You'll also be knowledgeable about lesser known religions of Africa and Asia, and such specialized topics as medical ethics, religion and social movements, paganism, New Age belief systems, and especially, the interaction of religion with issues of gender, ethnicity, race, and political and economic power. Whether your career involves activity mainly in the pulpit, religious-sponsored community service, or education, it's vital to have strong communication skills to offer meaningful help. Analytic ability, enthusiasm, empathy, and sociability are also important. For those working chiefly as scholars, adeptness in foreign and classical languages and methodical research skills are critical.

Related Fields

Anthropology and Archaeology
Asian Languages and Cultures
Judaic Studies
Philosophy

Typical Basic Courses

Asian and African Religious Traditions
Buddhism
Hinduism
Islam
Judaism and Christianity
Religion and Psychology
Religion and Society
The Religious Heritage of the West

An Array of Electives

Chinese Philosophy
Hispanic and Latino Theology
Justice, Law, and Commerce in Islam
Medical Ethics
Question of Human Suffering
Religion and Film
Religious Movements
Witchcraft in New England

On-Campus Opportunities

Campus chaplains
Campus counseling center

Job Opportunities

Surplus / Substantial oversupply

Reading to Explore

A Big-Enough God: A Feminist's Search for a Joyful Theology, by Sara Maitland (Riverhead)

God-Talk in America, by Phyllis A. Tickle (Crossroad)

Oxford Annotated Bible (Oxford University)

Siddartha, by Herman Hesse (New Directions)

Visions of Innocence: Spiritual and Inspirational Experiences of Childhood, by Edward Hoffman (Shambhala)

To Learn More

American Academy of Religion
1703 Clifton Road NE, Suite GS
Atlanta, GA 30329-4019
(404) 727-7920; fax (404) 727-7959
E-mail: aar@emory.edu
Internet site:
  http://www.acls.org/aarelig.htm

Society for the Scientific Study of
  Religion
1365 Stone Hall
Purdue University
West Lafayette, IN 47907-1365
(765) 494-6286; fax (765) 496-1476
E-mail: ssrexe@fhss.byu.edu
Internet site:
  http://www.fhss.byu.edu/soc/sssr

Romance Languages

The French and English traditions in this epoch are at opposite poles to each other. French poetry is more radical, more total. In an absolute and exemplary way, it has assumed the heritage of European Romanticism. . . . which culminates in surrealism. It is a poetry where the world becomes writing and language becomes the double of the world.
—*Octavio Paz, novelist, cited in* Twentieth-Century French Poetry with Translations by American and British Poets

What to Expect

Mastery of at least two of these languages—French, Italian, Portuguese, Rumanian, and Spanish—and familiarity with the others is the cornerstone of the study of Romance languages. You should develop fluency in the modern forms and also be able to read and understand older versions to analyze fully and appreciate the literature and culture of the entire region, such as French texts of the eleventh through fifteenth centuries. Elementary and intermediate courses build language skills with drills, lectures, rote memorization, writing and translating exercises, and dialogues. In addition, plan to take classes about the cultures and current social, economic, and political events and issues of these countries. From there, you can explore literature and the arts in depth. You may review literature by period (perhaps Portuguese literature in the twentieth century), by genre (maybe the plays of Molière), or a single work (say, the Cervantes classic, *Don Quixote*). You're not limited to the written word. For instance, you can study French films or Italian Renaissance music.

Trends

Trends in Romance languages include greater attention to how these languages evolved and are used in non-European settings. This development requires recognizing and understanding linguistic and cultural differences, including Portuguese as spoken and written in Brazil, Spanish as transposed to Latin America, and French in Francophone societies such as Haiti and Quebec. Experts in Romance languages will also be concerned about preserving linguistic traditions.

What You Need to Succeed

Do you enjoy reading and writing in foreign languages? Do you have a talent for translating wide-ranging materials, from journalistic pieces to legal documents to evocative contemporary fiction? Are you outgoing, and able to communicate well with people of various backgrounds and viewpoints? Such abilities—coupled with a keen interest in southern European culture and history—are the bulwark for achievement in this interdisciplinary field. If you specialize in education or scholarly research, you'll need solid training in linguistics, medieval and renaissance studies, geography, and history. Equally important, you'll need an ability to weave knowledge from such realms in producing meaningful solutions to academic problems. If your bent is business or government service, you'll benefit from course work in finance, marketing, political science, and international relations. It's essential that you have strong verbal-analytic skills in order to negotiate and reach agreements quickly and accurately with your counterparts in other countries. Ease with extensive international travel is also important.

Related Fields

English
History
Medieval and Renaissance Studies

Typical Basic Courses

Elementary French, Italian, Portuguese,
  or Spanish
French Civilization
Introduction to French Literature
Italian Women Writers
Latin-American Literature in Translation
Portugese for Current Affairs
Spanish-American Short Fiction
The French Enlightenment

An Array of Electives

Contemporary Culture Wars
Film and the Italian Novel
French Cinema
Hispanic Literature and Popular Culture
Italian Theater
Literature of the Hispanic Minorities of
  the United States
Spanish Civil War in History and
  Literature
Topics in Portugese and Brazilian
  Literature and Culture

On-Campus Opportunities

Campus museum
International student center
Translator for foreign visitors

Job Opportunities

Surplus / Substantial oversupply

Reading to Explore

A New History of French Literature, by Denis Hollier (Oxford University)

Europe, by Jon Arrizabalaga (Yale University Press)

Guide to Impressionist Paris: Nine Walking Tours to the Impressionist Painting Sites in Paris, by Patty Lurie and Daryl Evans (Robson)

The Great Pox: The French Disease in Renaissance Voices of the French Revolution, by Richard Cobbs and Colin Jones (Salem House)

To Learn More

Modern Language Association of
  America
10 Astor Place
New York, NY 10003
(212) 475-9500; fax (212) 477-9863
E-mail: info@mla.org
Internet site: http://www.acls.org/mla.htm

Russian and East European Studies

Russia is a riddle wrapped in a mystery inside an enigma.
—*Winston Churchill, British prime minister, cited in* The New International Dictionary of Quotations

What to Expect

No region is undergoing such massive changes as the former Soviet Union and its longtime satellites in eastern Europe. The transformation is shaking up the world's balance of political, military, and economic power. To dive into this multidisciplinary field requires you to become fluent in Russian and at least one eastern European language. Such proficiency will necessitate extensive time in the language laboratory, plus lectures, reading assignments, and writing. Elementary language courses also introduce you to the cultures and current issues of the region. You need a course that surveys the history of the Russian empire, the Soviet Union, and the Commonwealth of Independent States, and another that reviews eastern Europe in the twentieth century. At a more advanced level, pick electives that hone in on areas of interest. If history is your focus, courses could cover imperial Russia until World War I, the Balkans since 1800, or Russian intellectual history. A language-oriented concentration might include Polish drama, modern Serbo-Croatian literature, or Slavonic church texts. A political science focus could include problems in post-Soviet politics, political processes in eastern Europe, or a comparison of capitalism, communism, and socialism.

Trends

Trends in Russian and eastern European studies reflect the continued drama of ethnic and national realignments, the chasm between expectations and reality, and the pressure to "catch up" to the West in material goods and opportunities. The progress and pitfalls of free market economies will draw much attention. So will such problems as the legacy of environmental degradation, high unemployment, demilitarization, and disparities between rich and poor citizens.

What You Need to Succeed

Since the breakup of the former Soviet Union and the end of the Cold War, this region has been undergoing tremendous change. New developments occurring today in business, politics, technology, and social trends—dominating even music and the fine arts, religion, and journalism—would have seemed unthinkable only a decade ago. To succeed in this fast-changing field, you'll need strong verbal and analytical skills for absorbing economics, geography, international relations, and political science, and an ability to integrate and apply knowledge from such realms to contemporary problems. Since you'll be expected to master Russian and often other eastern European tongues, a flair for foreign languages is important. In the past, most students in this interdisciplinary field pursued careers in eduation or government service. However, many global corporations, smaller companies, and entrepreneurs are actively seeking new markets in this region. So a knowledge of finance, international marketing, and telecommunications is a valued asset. You'll also need a capacity for difficult travel, a tolerance for economic uncertainties, and an openness to the viewpoints of those in highly divergent cultures.

Related Fields

Asian Languages and Cultures
Geography
History
International Relations
Middle Eastern and Near Eastern
  Studies
South and Southeast Asian Studies

Typical Basic Courses

Comparative Economic Systems
Culture Area Analysis: Eastern Europe
Early Russian History
Imperial Russia
Introduction to Russian Literature
Marxist Economics
Russia and Central Eurasia in World
  Affairs
Russia: Past and Present

An Array of Electives

Capitalism, Socialism, Communism
Comparative Change in Eastern Europe
Modern Russian Social History
Political Institutions and Processes in
  Eastern Europe
Political Institutions and Processes in the
  Former Soviet Union
Russia and the United States
Russian Drama
Writers in Revolutions

On-Campus Opportunities

International student center
Research assistant
Translator for foreign visitors

Job Opportunities

Surplus / Substantial oversupply

Reading to Explore

Cafe Europe: Life After Communism, by Slavenka Drakulic (Norton)

Resurrection: The Struggle for a New Russia, by David Remnick (Random House)

St. Petersburg: Architecture of the Tsars, by Alexander Orloff and Dmitri Shivdkovsky (Abbeville)

The Patriot's Revolution: How Eastern Europe Toppled Communism and Won Its Freedom, by Mark Frankland (Ivan Dee)

The Russian Revolution, by Richard Pipes (Knopf)

To Learn More

American Council of Teachers of Russian
1776 Massachussetts Avenue NW, Suite
  300
Washington, DC 20036
(202) 833-7522; fax (202) 833-7523
E-mail: general@actr.org
Internet site: http://www.actr.org

Secondary Education

Human history becomes more and more a race between education and catastrophe.
—*H. G. Wells, novelist, cited in* Bartlett's Familiar Quotations

What to Expect

Training in secondary education involves a blend of courses designed to prepare you for a rapidly changing teaching career. At the introductory level, you'll get a solid grounding in general education courses pertaining to children's development, cognitive and academic functioning, classroom methods and curricula, and educational philosophy. Reflecting the limited-English background of many secondary students in the United States today, you'll find course work in bilingual and bicultural education highly useful. Also take classes in developmental psychology, reading instruction, and learning disabilities. At the advanced level, supervised student teaching is mandatory. You'll have the opportunity to choose electives on such subjects as educational media and computer technology, multiculturalism in the practice of schooling, literature for children and youth, and the education of American women and minorities in historical and cultural perspective. Secondary education is becoming more oriented to the emotional and social needs of its students. Courses in adolescent psychology, conflict resolution in classroom settings, and contemporary issues in school counseling will therefore prove valuable.

Trends

Trends in secondary education involve a greater emphasis on objective, standardized tests to assess more accurately what students actually learn in their middle-school and high-school classrooms. Educators are increasingly expected to be familiar with statewide or national measures, and to orient their lesson plans, goals, and even teaching methods accordingly. Meanwhile, secondary educators will experience greater accountability in their dealings with supervisors, administrators, school board officials, and parents. Because more secondary students are being raised in immigrant and limited-English-speaking families, a proficiency in at least one foreign language, such as Chinese, Haitian-Creole, Russian, or Spanish, will gain increased worth.

What You Need to Succeed

Like those who guide younger pupils in learning, high-school teachers require strong communication skills to explain concepts, terms, and facts clearly and succinctly. You might prefer a lecture format, structured class discussion, or out-of-school projects for helping students to learn. But whatever method you find most effective in presenting language arts, mathematics, social studies, science, or any other subject, you'll be expected to teach a state-mandated curriculum in an organized and disciplined manner. For this reason, you must maintain mastery of your educational specialty through continuing education. Secondary students today are extremely sensitive to the issue of teacher fairness—in ethnic, gender, and racial terms as well as in treating each class member respectfully and without favoritism.

Related Fields

Early Childhood Education
Elementary Education
Family and Child Development
Special Education

Typical Basic Courses

Adolescent Psychology
Foundations of Secondary Education
Methods and Materials in Secondary
  Education
Motivation in Education
Secondary Assessment and Curriculum
Small Group Dynamics
Student Teaching: Secondary
The Student in the Secondary Classroom

An Array of Electives

Conflict Resolution in Classroom Settings
Creativity in the Classroom
Foxfire: A Student-Centered,
  Experiential, Community-Based
  Approach to Instruction
Literature for Children and Youth
Multiculturalism and the Practice of
  Schooling
The Education of American Women: A
  Social and Cultural History

On-Campus Opportunities

On-campus school
Student counseling services

Job Opportunities

Surplus / Substantial oversupply

Reading to Explore

Brave New Schools: Challenging Cultural Illiteracy Through Global Learning Networks, by Jim Cummins and Dennis Sayers (St. Martin's)

Reading, Writing, and the Hickory Stick: The Appalling Story of Physical and Psychological Abuse in American Schools, by Irwin Atayman (Lexington)

Reviving Ophelia: Saving the Selves of Adolescent Girls, by Mary Pipher (Ballantine)

Teacher Education in America: Reform Agendas for the Twenty-First Century, by Christopher J. Lucas (St. Martin's)

Teachers Talk, by John Goodar (Glenridge Publications)

To Learn More

American Federation of Teachers
555 New Jersey Avenue NW
Washington, DC 20001
(202) 879-4400; fax (202) 879-4556
E-mail: afteditor@aol.com
Internet site: http://www.aft.org

National Education Association
1201 16th Avenue NW
Washington, DC 20036
(202) 833-4000; fax (202) 467-6783
E-mail: neaworks@aol.com
Internet site: http://www.nea.org

Social Work

'Tis not enough to help the feeble up, but to support him after.
—*William Shakespeare, playwright, in* Timon of Athens

What to Expect

In recent decades, social work has increased dramatically in scope and function. Your course work, therefore, will provide skills relevant to traditional social service in public schools, child and family guidance centers, and mental health agencies, as well as skills relevant to such new realms as home-based intervention for families with disabled young children and group living centers for the elderly. Basic courses will provide overviews of such topics as human behavior and social environment, ethnic minority families in the United States, psychopathology and the family, and modern social problems. Advanced course work offers a wide gamut of electives, encompassing health issues such as AIDS and other epidemics and pediatric programs in African American and Latino communities, as well as more psychologically oriented subjects such as group counseling, women's mental health, and therapeutic strategies for working with immigrants. Expect considerable fieldwork in a wide range of settings. Training in fiscal management, program evaluation, and business administration will prove helpful in a social climate marked by an increasing emphasis on cost cutting and efficiency in delivery of services.

Trends

Trends in social work encompass broad changes occurring in contemporary American society. There is a higher demand for services to immigrants, especially from South America, the Caribbean, Asia, and the former Soviet Union, whose cultural and familial values are often very different from those of people born in this country. More social workers, therefore, will need to be proficient in at least one foreign language. There is also a greater demand for expertise in the geriatric field, where clients experience physical, emotional, and social problems related to aging. Also, the advent of managed health care, causing shifts and reductions in individual treatment planning and therapy, will force social workers to pay greater attention to financial issues and alternative services.

What You Need to Succeed

Do you have a strong sense of empathy, compassion, and sensitivity to the moods of others? Are you able to gauge accurately when people around you are feeling angry, depressed, "stressed out," pained, or just plain confused? And, perhaps even more importantly, do you have a talent for helping individuals or groups deal with such emotions constructively? Can you resolve social conflicts well? Such qualities—along with an ability to respect ethnic, racial, and religious differences—are vital for success in this challenging and emotionally demanding field. To be effective as a social worker, you'll also need good conceptual skills and an ability to see your clients' problems—such as poverty, unemployment, physical illness, and emotional distress—within a larger societal, and increasingly global, context. The ability to cope with crises, which may arise on nights, weekends, or holidays, is crucial. Because so much day-to-day social work involves interacting as a team member with other professionals (such as teachers, counselors, psychologists, occupational and physical therapists, nurses and physicians), the capacity for communicating your viewpoint articulately—both orally and in writing—is paramount.

Related Fields

Family and Child Development
Occupational Therapy
Psychology
Sociology

Typical Basic Courses

Contemporary Moral Issues
Ethnic Minority Families in the United States
Foundations of Social Work Practice
Human Behavior and Social Environment
Introduction to Social Work
Psychopathology and the Family
Research Methods in Social Work
Sex and Gender

An Array of Electives

Epidemics and AIDS
Fiscal Management and Evaluation in Social Work
Health Psychology
Immigration and Ethnic Identity
Latinos in the United States
Social Welfare Policy and Services: Aging
Social Work Planning, Evaluation, and Administration
Theories of Groups, Organizations, and Communities in Social Work

On-Campus Opportunities

Campus counseling services
Chaplain's office

Job Opportunities

Near balance / Supply equals demand

Reading to Explore

Elephants in the Volkswagen: Facing the Tough Questions About Our Overcrowded Country, by Lindsey Grant (Freeman)

Life Without Father, by David Popenoe (Free Press)

Somebody Else's Children: The Courts, the Kids, and the Struggle to Save America's Troubled Families, by John Huber and Jill Anderson (Crown)

Turning Stones: My Days and Nights with Children at Risk, by Marc Parent (Harcourt Brace)

Women and Welfare: Ten Victorian Women in Public Social Service, by Julia Parker (St. Martin's Press)

To Learn More

National Association of Social Workers
750 First Street NE, Suite 700
Washington, DC 20002-4241
(800) 638-8799; fax (202) 336-8312
E-mail: website@naswdc.org
Internet site: www.naswdc.org/main.htm

National Federation of Societies for Clinical Social Work
POB 3740
Arlington, VA 22203
(703) 522-3866; fax (703) 522-9441
E-mail: nfscsw@nfscsw.org
Internet site: www.nfscsw.org

Sociology

The vast growth of the social life, steadily encroaching on both private and public life, has produced the eerie phenomenon of mass society, which rules everybody anonymously, just as bureaucracy—the rule of no one—has become the modern form of despotism.
—*Mary McCarthy, novelist and critic, in* The New Yorker, *October 18, 1958*

What to Expect

Here you'll study human groups, societies, and institutions, focusing on the behavior of people in groups and how they influence each other. One introductory course will emphasize contemporary U.S. society, assessing such issues as inequality, changing rural and urban communities, family relationships, and gender roles. Other basic classes cover social organizations, courtship and marriage, youth and crime, and group dynamics. You'll learn techniques for research, data analysis, and field observation. As you progress, you can tackle an array of topics in depth, among them population and food resources, environmental sociology and the environmental quality movement, and deviant and criminal behavior. A course on urban sociology lets you explore city lifestyles and dilemmas that include homelessness and poverty, while a course about agriculture in transition examines changes among farm families and rural communities. Look for options on international sociology, perhaps one that examines social changes in industrially developing countries.

Trends

Trends in sociology include the challenge of applying academic theories and findings to real-world problems. For example, such challenges could involve preparing welfare recipients for steady jobs, developing juvenile delinquency prevention programs, and reducing the high-school dropout rate. In the area of science and technology, sociologists will be called upon to deal with the impact of industrialization on developing nations and of escalating technology in the United States. There will be increased attention paid as well to immigrants and non-English-speaking citizens, and their participation in U.S. culture, business, and politics.

What You Need to Succeed

Reflecting the rapid transformation that sociology is undergoing, you'll need solid skills in computer use, research design, and statistical analysis to achieve success. Of course, a keen interest in people's attitudes, values, prejudices, and social perceptions remains central to this field. Sociologists are increasingly finding employment in business rather than teaching and research, so you'll need familiarity with consumer marketing, organization development and training, public relations, polling, and management consulting. Especially prized will be your abilities to accurately define elusive problems, initiate appropriate social research, tabulate and interpret data, and provide concise and meaningful reports to clients. Consistent with the high-pressure pace of corporate life, sociologists in such settings must work well under deadline pressures, always present their research proposals with a careful eye to financial costs, and clearly communicate their goals, findings, and recommendations. The capacity to function as part of team is also important.

Related Fields

American Studies and Culture
Family and Child Development
Social Work
Psychology
Women's Studies

Typical Basic Courses

Changing American Family
Introduction to Sociology
Methods of Social Research
Race and Ethnicity
Sex and Gender
Social Issues and Change in
    Contemporary Society
Social Psychology
Social Stratification

An Array of Electives

Advertising and Society
Comparative Health Care Systems
Economics of Development
Media in Comparative Perspective
Modern Nationalist Movements
Social Basis of Politics
Sociology of Entrepreneurship
Work: Sociological Perspectives

On-Campus Opportunities

Campus counseling centeer
Research assistant

Job Opportunities

Surplus / Substantial oversupply

Reading to Explore

A Piece of the Action: How the Middle Class Joined the Money Class, by Joseph Nocera (Touchstone/Simon & Schuster)

Driving the Amish, by John Butterfield (Herald)

Sociobiology: The New Synthesis, by Edward O. Wilson (Harvard University)

The Divorce Culture: How Divorce Became an Entitlement and How It Is Blighting the Lives of Our Children, by Barbara Defoe Whitehead (Knopf)

When Work Disappears: The World of the New Urban Poor, by William J. Wilson (Knopf)

To Learn More

American Sociological Association
1722 North Street NW
Washington, DC 20030
(202) 833-3410; fax (202) 785-0146
E-mail: executive.office@asanet.org
Internet site: http://www.asanet.org

Rural Sociological Society
Department of Sociology
Western Washington University
Bellingham, WA 98225-9081
(360) 650-7571; fax (360) 650-7295
E-mail: ctolbert@lapop.lsu.edu
Internet site: http://www.lapop.lsu.edu/rss

South and Southeast Asian Studies

Southeast Asia is perhaps the most intriguing part of the world: nations of beautiful people who warmly welcome a visitor, of ancient cultural traditions, of great religious monuments and works of art. But Southeast Asia is also a place of tyranny and repression, where governments view the most severe environmental degradation as a small price to pay for economic growth.
—*Stan Sesser, author, in* The Lands of Charm and Cruelty: Travels in Southeast Asia

What to Expect

Fast growing, rapidly changing, and diverse in languages and cultures, South and Southeast Asia are playing a greater role in the world economy. In this multidisciplinary field, you'll immerse yourself in diverse languages, fine arts, literary traditions, history, economics, religions, geography, and political systems spanning vast areas and time periods. Overview courses familiarize you with the region's civilizations, from ancient to the present. Courses are available in commonly spoken tongues such as Hindi-Urdu, Vietnamese, Tagalog, Burmese, and Vietnamese, although India alone has more than 1,000 languages and dialects. In the arts, you'll be introduced to sculpture, paintings, tapestries, music, and theater. Political science-oriented classes will review the sharply divergent government systems found in the region, including democracy, communism, and monarchy. In advanced courses, you can explore countries in depth. If history fascinates you, for instance, there are specialized classes in the history of Malaysia and Singapore, Thailand, Indonesia, or Burma. If comparative religions appeal to you, try courses in Buddhism, Hinduism, or Sikhism. Of course, a major goal is to better understand the roles South and Southeast Asia are now playing in the international economy and balance of power. Definitely plan to study abroad.

Trends

Trends in South and Southeast Asian studies reflect the growing number of immigrants from the region and their part in U.S culture and the economy. In addition, U.S. businesses and industries are expanding sales and operations in the area, viewing it as an important export, tourism, and investment market, as well as a significant source of imports and natural resources.

What You Need to Succeed

The cornerstone is a deep interest in this region of the world and the wealth of cultures and traditions it's home to. Naturally, mastery of written and spoken languages, fluency, and communication skills are vital. Enjoyment of foreign travel, of meeting people from diverse backgrounds, and of living in unfamiliar—even exotic—settings are valuable. Dealing with a multidisciplinary field of study means you need to integrate and analyze information and problems in a wide-open process. This could involve such matters as business practices, theological disagreements, gender and caste systems, national and ethnic rivalries, educational opportunities, population controls, environmental practices, and economic development patterns.

Related Fields

Asian Languages and Cultures
Geography
History
International Relations

Typical Basic Courses

Art of Southeast Asia
Languages (Vietnamese, Burmese, Thai, Hindi-Urdu, Indonesian)
Monsoon Asia
Music of Southeast Asia
Politics of Developing Areas
Religion in the Indian Tradition
South Asian Civilization
The Vietnam War

An Array of Electives

Classical India and the Coming of Islam: 320–1526
Hinduism
History of Malaysia and Singapore
History of Southeast Asia Since 1800
Indian Art
Introduction to Indonesian Literature
Public Administration in Southeast Asia
Sikhism

On-Campus Opportunities

Campus museum
International student center
Translator for foreign visitors

Job Opportunities

Surplus / Substantial oversupply

Reading to Explore

Dragon Ascending: Vietnam and the Vietnamese, by Henry Kamm (Arcade)

The Angkor: The Hidden Glories, by Michael Freeman and Roger Warner (Houghton Mifflin)

The Pacific Century: America and Asia in a Changing World, by Frank Gibney (Macmillan)

The Tragedy of Cambodian History, by David P. Chandler (Yale University)

Travels in Southeast Asia: The Lands of Charm and Cruelty, by Stan Sesser (Knopf)

To Learn More

The Asia Society
725 Park Avenue
New York, NY 10021
(212) 288-6400; fax (212) 517-8315
E-mail: robertas@asiasoc.org
Internet site: http://www.askasia.org

Association for Asian Studies
University of Michigan
One Lane Hall
Ann Arbor, MI 48109
(313) 665-2490; fax (313) 665-3801
E-mail: postmaster@aasianst.org
Internet site:
   http://www.acls.org/aasianst.htm

Special Education

Right education is the method of developing individuals, with all their inherited abilities and disabilities. By courage and training, disabilities may be so compensated that they even become great abilities.
—*Alfred Adler, medical psychologist and author, in* Problems of Neurosis

What to Expect

The focus of special education is to provide the training—involving both theory and technique—necessary to teach children with learning problems. Introductory courses will familiarize you with the basic aspects of children's cognitive, emotional, and academic abilities and needs. You'll also take survey classes on specific disabilities, such as mental retardation, emotional disturbance, and learning disorders. Courses on both classroom management and curricula for special students are generally required. You'll do supervised student teaching in a special educational setting. As you gain a solid foundation with basic courses, you'll have the opportunity to choose from a variety of electives. Consider advanced classes on topics such as educating young children with developmental disabilities, visual impairments, or health problems. Try classroom-oriented subjects such as microcomputers for special educators, the arts in special education, and screening and diagnosis. Also useful are courses covering developmental psychology, adolescent psychology, and the families of exceptional children. For administrative preparation, take classes in educational supervision, the philosophy of education, and curricular change for school-age exceptional children.

Trends

Trends in special education include a greater emphasis on early intervention, involving home-based services to infants and toddlers and including their parents or other adult caretakers. Special education teachers will be required to communicate educational assessment results, goals, and progress to family members. Reflecting the broader demographic changes occurring in American society today, many more students in special education are being raised in immigrant and limited-English-speaking homes. Therefore, a proficiency in at least one foreign language will be in demand. Another trend involves a greater integration of disabled students into regular educational programs at all levels, from preschool through college.

What You Need to Succeed

The career of teaching children and adolescents effectively requires several key traits, including an outgoing personality and empathy, a commitment to long-term professional learning, and patience and perseverance. In working daily with youngsters who have a broad range of mental and physical disabilities, you'll additionally need a strong sense of flexibility, emotional spontaneity, warmth, and personal openness. In this growing educational field, you'll find that the traditional boundaries marking curriculum, "acceptable" classroom behavior, and the student-teacher relationship itself are often fluid and challenging. Be innovative, creative, and constantly willing to try new methods of learning until you discover success with a particular class, or even with a single, educationally unique pupil. Equally important is a capacity to handle and resolve tensions among students before they escalate.

Related Fields

Early Childhood Education
Elementary Education
Family and Child Development
Secondary Education

Typical Basic Courses

Behavior Management: Theory and
    Applications
Curriculum and Methods for Special
    Education
Emotional Disturbance: Concepts and
    Theories
Learning Disabilities: Concepts and
    Theories
Psychology and Education of Exceptional
    Children
Student Teaching of Exceptional
    Children
Teaching Students with Physical
    Disabilities

An Array of Electives

Arts in Special Education
Atypical Development of the Young Child
Classroom Procedures for the
    Emotionally Disturbed
Curriculum Change for School-Age
    Exceptional Children
Measurement Theory and Techniques for
    Classroom Teachers
Microcomputers for Special Educators
Screening and Diagnosis

On-Campus Opportunities

Campus day-care center
Campus school

Job Opportunities

Good demand / Possible shortage

Reading to Explore

Attention Deficit Disorder from Childhood to Adulthood, by Edward M. Hallowell and John J. Ratey (Simon & Schuster)

Autism: Explaining the Enigma, by Uta Frith (Basil Blackwell)

Carla, Growing with a Retarded Child, by Martha A. Jablow (Temple University)

Driven to Distraction: Recognizing and Coping with ADD Success Stories: A Guide to Fulfillment for Families with Attention Deficit Disorder, by Thom Hartmann (Underwood Books)

Some Just Clap Their Hands: Raising a Handicapped Child, by Margaret Mantle (Adams)

To Learn More

Council of Administrators of Special
    Education
615 Sixteenth Street NW
Albuquerque, NM 87104
(505) 243-7622; fax (505) 247-4822
E-mail: casecec@aol.com
Internet site:
    http://www.tera-sys-inc.com/case.html

Council for Exceptional Children
1920 Association Drive
Reston, VA 22091-1589
(703) 620-3660; fax (703) 264-9494
E-mail: cec@cec.spd.org
Internet site: http://www.cec.sped.org

Speech Science and Audiology

The ears of the deaf shall be unstopped . . . and the tongue of the dumb sing.
—*The Bible (Isaiah 35:5)*

What to Expect

The ability of humans to communicate with one another may be the most complex and vital aspect of human behavior. Your studies in speech science and audiology will prepare you to help others overcome impairments in communications, once you learn how to evaluate, treat, and research human communication disorders. The foundation is course work on how we hear and speak and how those functions can break down or fail to ripen. That includes study of the anatomical and physiological elements of speech and hearing, acoustics, the International Phonetic Alphabet, and clinical laboratory work. Through these courses, you'll learn how language skills develop and how to assess gaps in that development. In addition, you'll come away with a better understanding of the role of language in contemporary society.

Advanced courses focus more on specific types of disorders among adults and children, such as aphasia, stuttering, developmental language disorders, and voice disorders. You'll practice diagnostic and rehabilitation techniques. An essential part of your training will be clinical work and college-approved practicums at medical facilities, preschool centers, schools, work activity centers, voice and hearing clinics, nursing homes, and otolaryngologists' offices.

Trends

Trends in speech science and audiology reflect a growth in demand for professional services, coupled with research advances. That demand reflects the aging of our population, legal mandates that all disabled children receive free and appropriate public education, earlier detection of hearing and speech disorders, and more effective means to evaluate and treat those disorders. Technology is providing improved diagnostic tools and more rehabilitation options.

What You Need to Succeed

Enter this field with a genuine commitment to help people with special needs. Then combine classroom knowledge of speech-language pathology, audiology, and linguistics with clinical experiences and strong oral and written communications skills. That includes the ability to write scientific and clinical discipline-specific reports and to evaluate literature in the field critically. The profession involves close contact with clients who, by definition, have communication problems and often frustrations, so you should understand psychology and human development as well. You'll need patience and empathy, because improvements in a client's speech or hearing often comes in incremental steps. Familiarity with scientific methods used to evaluate and investigate disorders is necessary. That requires keeping up with technological advances in hardware, peripheral devices, software, and adaptive equipment. You also must feel comfortable working in teams and in consultation with other professionals, including physicians, teachers, psychologists, social workers, and therapists.

Related Fields

Early Childhood Education
Elementary Education and Teaching
Linguistics
Psychology
Secondary Education
Special Education

Typical Basic Courses

Anatomy and Physiology
Audiology Evaluation Procedures
Descriptive Phonetics
Introduction to Communication
  Disorders
Oral Communication Skills
Oral Language Development
Speech and Hearing Science
Speech-Language Pathology Evaluation

An Array of Electives

Acquired Language Disorders
American Sign Language
Assessment of Childhood Language
  Disorders
Auditory Psychophysics
Augmentative Communication
Clinical Practice Guidelines
Language Intervention
Voice and Fluency Disorders

On-Campus Opportunities

Speech, hearing, and language clinic

Job Opportunities

Near balance / Supply equals demand

Reading to Explore

Deaf Culture, Our Way: Anecdotes from the Deaf Community, by Roy K. Holcomb (Dawn Sign)

Knotted Tongues: Stuttering in History and the Quest for a Cure, by Benson Bobrick and Deborah Baker (Kodansha America)

No Walls of Stone: An Anthology of Literature by Deaf and Hard of Hearing Writers, by Jill Jepson (Gallaudet University)

Speechless: Facilitating Communication for People Without Voices, by Rosemary Crossley

The Conscious Ear: My Life of Transformation Through Listening, by Alfred A. Tomatis, Marilyn Ferguson, and Don Campbell (Station Hill)

To Learn More

American Speech-Language-Hearing
  Association
10801 Rockville Pike
Rockville, MD 20852
(800) 638-8255; fax (301) 571-0457
E-mail: irc@asha.org
Internet site: http://www.asha.org

Statistics and Probability

Numerical precision is the very soul of science.
—*Sir D'Arcy Wentworth Thompson, philosopher, cited in* Bartlett's Familiar Quotations

What to Expect

In statistics and probability, you'll learn how to collect, analyze, and present numerical data, how to design surveys and experiments, and how to apply your knowledge of statistical methods to fields ranging from biology and engineering to economics and medicine. You'll be introduced to descriptive statistics, elementary probability, sampling distributions, statistical inference, graphical display of data, and regression. Also from the start, you'll become familiar with use of computers (both personal and mainframe) and software packages for statistical work, including exploratory and confirmatory statistical analysis. Statisticians in all industries rely on computers to process data for modeling and graphical analysis. Higher-level courses deal in depth with statistics in research, methods of multivariate analysis, survey sampling techniques, and applied time series. There are a number of specialized courses as well. For example, you can study statistics, probability, and statistical inference for engineers, with a focus on the design and analysis of engineering-related experiments. Similar offerings are available for applied business statistics, the social sciences, and genetics.

Trends

Trends in statistics include a rising demand to monitor and improve quality and productivity in manufacturing in the automotive, pharmaceutical, chemical, and food industries, among others. Motor vehicle manufacturers will increasingly call on statisticians to develop tests for new and existing motor vehicle and component designs, for example, while drug companies will depend on them to measure the safety and effectiveness of new medications. On the business front, statisticians will be counted on to analyze business conditions, forecast sales, and solve management problems.

What You Need to Succeed

Is mathematics your strong suit? Are you comfortable in using such aptitude to tackle specific and highly varied puzzles in the "real world" of consumer products, health care management, social policy, science and engineering, and many other domains? Can you subordinate your views and allow decision makers to act, according to their own goals but based on your work? If so, this field is likely to bring you a strong sense of personal satisfaction and practical influence. You'll need to demonstrate mastery in state-of-the art computer technology and the latest developments in its applied use. Whether employed in education, government, or the corporate world, you'll use mathematics deftly in gaining answers to research questions. Additionally, be prepared for an important—and sometimes highly visible—role in advising executives, policy chiefs, and public relations experts how to interpret and present your findings. So good communication skills—especially the ability to articulate statistical concepts and results in clear, nontechnical language—are instrumental to success.

Related Fields

Computer Science
Mathematics

Typical Basic Courses

Actuarial Mathematics
Applied Statistics for the Biological
  Sciences
Basic Statistics
Business and Economic Statistics
Introduction to Probability
Introduction to Statistical Software
Linear Programming and the Theory of
  Games
Ordinary Differential Equations

An Array of Electives

Design and Analysis of Experiments
Multivariate Analysis
Nonparametric Statistics
Regression Analysis
Sampling Techniques
Statistics in Quality and Productivity
Stochastic Studies in Operations
  Research
Time-Series Analysis

On-Campus Opportunities

Lab assistant
Research assistant

Job Opportunities

Adequate supply / Some oversupply

Reading to Explore

Against the Odds: The Remarkable Story of Risk, by Peter L. Bernstein (Wiley)

Science and Judgment in Risk Assessment, written and published by the National Research Council

Searching for Certainty, by John L. Castri (Morrow)

Statistical Concepts for the Behavioral Sciences, by Harold O. Kiess (Allyn and Bacon)

Two Hundred Percent of Nothing, by A. K. Dewdney (Wiley)

To Learn More

American Statistical Association
1429 Duke Street
Alexandria, VA 22314-3402
(703) 684-1221; fax (703) 684-2037
E-mail: asainfo@amstat.org
Internet site: http://www.amstat.org

Institute of Mathematical Statistics
3401 Investment Boulevard, Suite 7
Hayward, CA 94545-3819
(510) 783-8141; fax (510) 783-4131
E-mail: deleeuw@stat.ucla.edu
Internet site:
  http://www.stat.ucla.edu/~abraverm/ims

Technical Writing

A good style must, first of all, be clear. It must be appropriate.
—*Aristotle, philosopher, cited in* The New International Dictionary of Quotations

What to Expect

Technical writers and editors communicate through words, making industrial and scientific concepts comprehensible to readers who have varying levels of pertinent knowledge. Yet, in this developing field, words won't be your only tools; you also will work with diagrams, charts, photos, and drawings. So you should have a solid grounding in writing, science, medicine, or engineering—and, increasingly, graphic design. A key foundation course will cover scientific writing, demonstrating how to gather and write news about medicine, the physical and life sciences, and technology—and how to make that news understandable to lay and professional audiences. Editing of technical materials and combining written material with illustrations are part of the curriculum, too. At an advanced level, you can hone your skills in graphic design and video production, including development of commercial productions for the Internet, cable and network television, and radio. Additional courses in technical writing, journalism, and other fields will build expertise in one or more specialized topics, such as the environment, health, business and finance, high technology, agriculture, and engineering. In these courses, you can work with computers, computer-assisted design hardware and software, and video and audio laboratory and studio equipment.

Trends

Trends in technical writing include the escalating demand to adapt increasingly technical information for mass audiences. For example, as computers and other electronic products reach more homes, professionals will be called upon to prepare clear instructional and operational manuals. Mushrooming use of the Internet will mean opportunities to present information in appropriate and easy-to-use forms. The proliferation of VCRs and CD-ROMs creates the need for people to master multimedia technology.

What You Need to Succeed

Think of the technical writer as a translator. That image makes clear how communication skills form the most essential attribute for success. No matter how well you understand a technical or scientific concept or event, that information remains inaccessible to the broader public—unless you're capable of translating it into written, oral, or visual formats. Get comfortable with doing interviews, because you'll gain much of your technical knowledge by asking questions of experts. Attention to detail and precision in self-expression is required, because even a small error can exert a harmful impact when a user needs to follow directions or master an industrial or medical process. You must feel at ease with technology and computers, both as working tools for conveying information and as topics you may write about. Master advanced video and telecommunications equipment, as well as graphic design and desktop publishing software. Learn to work under deadline pressure.

Related Fields

English
Journalism

Typical Basic Courses

Business and Technical Publications
Effective Business Communication
Environmental Communications
Scientific Writing
Technical and Scientific Editing
Visual Communication in Agriculture and
    Natural Resources
World of Graphic Design
Writing for the Professions

An Array of Electives

Agricultural and Natural Resources
    Communications Campaigns
Case Studies in Environmental
    Journalism
Commercial Video Production
Communication Research Design
Communications Strategies in the
    Sciences
Investigative Reporting
Persuasion
Writing as a Critic

On-Campus Opportunities

Campus museum
Campus newspaper, magazine, and radio
    and television stations
Departmental newsletters

Job Opportunities

Good demand / Possible shortage

Reading to Explore

Plain Language: Principles and Practice, by Edwin R. Steinberg (Wayne State University Press)

Science and Technical Writing: A Manual of Style, by Philip Rubens (Henry Holt)

The Liter of Science: Perspectives on Popular Scientific Writing, by Murdo W. McRae (University of Georgia Press)

Writing About Business and Industry, by Beverly E. Schneller (Oxford University Press)

Writing Well for the Technical Professions, by Anne Eisenberg (HarperCollins)

To Learn More

Society for Technical Communications,
    Inc.
901 North Stuart Street, Suite 904
Arlington, VA 22203
(703) 522-4114; fax (703) 522-2075
E-mail: stc@stc-va.org
Internet site: http://www.stc-va.org

Telecommunications

In the struggle for freedom of information, technology not politics will be the ultimate decider.
—*Arthur C. Clarke, science fiction writer, cited in* The Executive's Book of Quotations

What to Expect

We live in an information-based society, in which social policy and economics blend with the sharing of information. The rapidly evolving field of telecommunications will help prepare you for this society, for you'll gain a better understanding of technology and its cultural ramifications. For example, on a scientific level, you'll learn the operational principles of audio, data, image, and video telecommunications. On a societal level, you'll learn about the major effects of mass media on audience behavior, political consciousness, and consumer decisions. Other classes cover public policy, evaluation and selection of programming, and basic production skills. You'll delve deeper into telecommunications management, organization, economics, business planning, law, and financial analysis. Classes go into detail on current and future applications, such as teleconferencing, electronic information services, and multichannel television. There's also advanced training available in design and production of hypermedia, audio, and video, in engineering techniques, and in graphics. This array of courses allows you the chance to work in audio and video production studies, and in integrated telecommunication systems laboratories. To acquire a global perspective, study international telecommunications problems, policies, and regulations.

Trends

Trends in telecommunications reflect the increasingly "wired" world in which we live—and our power to use technology and computer networks for nearly instantaneous communications, education, and business—even in geographically remote areas. There will be a push to make this technology more affordable, especially in economically developing regions. At the same time, telecommunication systems hold the potential to become powerful political tools, and thus run the risk of becoming pawns in national and international power struggles.

What You Need to Succeed

This innovative field combines technology, business, economics, and public policy—so you must think and analyze issues across disciplinary lines. You're therefore required to keep up with the latest technological—hardware and software—developments, as well as with the financial aspects of an industry in rapid transition with constantly new ventures, mergers, and international expansion. The degree of government regulation, both in the United States and abroad, and the quick, social-ripple effects of telecommunications require an interest in public affairs and policy decision making. Because this is a communications arena, strong writing, verbal, and computer abilities are expected—even if you focus on the hardware aspects of the profession. Also essential are creativity and planning skills, the ability to look ahead and imagine how much different the field will be tomorrow. Finally, teamwork is crucial, because you'll be working with an array of colleagues in business, technology, on-air talent, and sales.

Related Fields

Computer science
Electrical engineering
Industrial technology
Journalism

Typical Basic Courses

Basic Telecommunication Policy
History and Economics of
   Telecommunication
Human Communication in Organizations
Introduction to Telecommunications
   Technology
Media Campaigns and Formative
   Evaluation
Telecommunication Media Arts
Telecommunication Technologies
The Information Society

An Array of Electives

Audience Research
Data Communications and Networking
Financial Aspects of Telecommunication
Hypermedia Design
Multichannel Television
Online Systems Analysis and Design
Telecommunication Management
Theory and Research in Information
   Technologies and Services

On-Campus Opportunities

Campus radio and television station
Research assistant

Job Opportunities

Good demand / Possible shortage

Readings to Explore

Broadcasting and Cable (magazine)

Deeper: My Two-Year Odyssey in Cyberspace, by John Seabrock (Simon & Schuster)

Defining Vision: The Battle for the Future of Television, by Joel Binkley (Harcourt Brace)

What Will Be: How the New World of Information Will Change Our Lives, by Michael Dertouzos (Harper Edge)

To Learn More

Industrial Telecommunications
   Association
1110 North Glebe Road, Suite 500
Arlington, VA 22201
(703) 528-5115; fax (703) 524-1074
E-mail: info@ita-relay.com
Internet site: http://www.ita-relay.com

Tele-Communications Association
74 New Montgomery Street, Suite 230
San Francisco, CA 94105
(415) 777-4647; fax (415) 777-5295
Internet site: http://www.tca.org

Textiles and Apparel

Gave thee clothing of delight . . .
—*William Blake, poet, in "The Lamb"*

What to Expect

Your classes will provide a broad understanding of textile and apparel products, merchandising, and marketing strategies, as well as production processes, science, and business. Basic courses in design, apparel manufacturing, and textile science will give you a grounding in technology, applications, and cultural aspects of the field. You'll learn how to analyze the clothed body as a basis for developing new products, how to work in a laboratory with colors, finishes, and natural and artificial fibers, and how to appreciate the ways clothing shapes and reflects societal values. As you advance, the mix of scientific, technical, and commercial elements continues with classes that cover such topics as textile engineering, visual marketing, experimental design, quality assurance, fashion illustration, production operations, and fiber, dye, and detergency chemistry. You may choose a focus on design, production, product development, historic costume and textiles studies, merchandising, or the relationship between apparel and human behavior.

Trends

Trends in textiles and apparel will lead to new alliances with professionals in interdisciplinary fields, including apparel and accessory designers, biomechanical engineers, textile chemists and physicists, and medical scientists. Fashions will continue to change, of course, and computer-aided design technology will be used to create innovate solutions to functional and aesthetic design projects. You'll also see a practical evolution as designers develop new clothing specially tailored to different components of our population, such as older women, whose body changes can include a forward head and neck angle, forward shoulder roll, back curvature, increased girth, and decreased height. Retailing strategies and planning will change as well.

What You Need to Succeed

Creativity is one keystone to success. That involves not just the ability to design textiles, clothing, accessories, and carpeting but also the ability to evaluate those designs and how they will interact with people who wear or use them. You must assess the interdependency of needs, values, goals, and resources as you propose design solutions and develop products that promote comfort, performance, and aesthetic satisfaction. A sense of aesthetics—what pleases the eye—and an ability to adapt to stylistic changes are critical for careers in fashion. Teamwork skills pay off because the textile, design, and fashion industries are heavily collaborative. On the technical and scientific side, laboratory and chemical research techniques are essential for working with fibers and dyes, as are a commitment to product safety, and an understanding of manufacturing and production processes. State-of-the-art computer skills are important in design, pattern making, illustration, and merchandising.

Related Fields

Art
Graphic Design
Marketing
Theater and Drama

Typical Required Courses

Apparel Assembly Processes
Apparel Manufacturing
Appearance in Society
Fashion Retailing
Introduction to Product Development
Merchandise Planning
Textile Fundamentals
Textile Science

An Array of Electives

Aesthetic Analysis and Product
  Development
Apparel Engineering
Fashion Illustration
History of Costume
Quality Assurance
Socio-Psychological Aspects of Clothing
Textile and Apparel Industries
Visual Merchandising

On-Campus Opportunities

Costuming for theatrical and musical
  productions
Research assistant

Job Opportunities

Adequate supply / Some oversupply

Reading to Explore

20,000 Years of Fashion: The History of Costume and Personal Adornment, by Francois Boucher (Harry N. Abrams)

Christian Dior: The Man Who Made the World Look New, by Marie-France Pochna (Arcade)

Costumes by Karinska, by Toni Bentley (Harry N. Abrams)

Labors of Love: America's Textiles and Needlework, by Judith R. Weissman, Wendy Lovitt, and Lee Schecter (Random House Value)

Yves St. Laurent: A Biography, by Alice Rawsthorn (Nan A. Talese/Doubleday)

To Learn More

American Fiber Manufacturers
  Association
1150 17th St. NW, Suite 310
Washington, DC 22036
(202) 296-6508; fax (202) 296-3052
E-mail: afma@aol.com
Internet site: http://www.apparel.net/afma

Fashion Group International
597 Fifth Ave.
New York, NY 10017
(212) 593-1715; fax (212) 593-1925
E-mail: info@fgi.org
Internet site: http://www.fgi.org

Theater and Drama

The play's the thing / Wherein I'll catch the conscience of the king.
—*William Shakespeare, playwright, in* Hamlet

What to Expect

Training in theater and drama involves both onstage and backstage activities, with a curriculum that ranges from acting through design, makeup, stage direction, stage management, and theater history. Introductory courses will familiarize you with acting fundamentals, voice and music for the stage, script analysis, and stage makeup. You also should gain an overview of the impact of theater on ancient and contemporary societies around the globe. An important part of your training is implementation of classroom theories and principles through performances for "real" audiences. You'll also have opportunities to assess how others implement these theories through field trips to off-campus professional and amateur productions. Higher-level courses will provide experience in a variety of design areas including lighting, sets, costumes, sound, and props. You can take classes in directing, theater management, theater history, and creative dramatics, such as storytelling and improvisation. Look for advanced courses on specialized topics such as African American theater production styles, mime, stage combat, musical theater, theater graphics, and play writing.

Trends

Trends in theater and drama encompass the encouragement of new writers, including youth, minorities, and women, and the production of their works by professional and community-based troupes. There is a growing emphasis on regionally oriented plays, in which the playwrights, directors, and casts focus on local and regional themes and issues. Expect more integration of new media and technology in lighting, sound, and set design. Finally, non-commercial performing groups will increasingly confront funding problems, including cuts in government grants, as they strive to offer cultural opportunities in their communities.

What You Need to Succeed

You'll undoubtedly enjoy the opportunity to use your talents, on stage or back stage, to entertain and move the public. However, this field requires patience and commitment, with long and often irregular hours, evening and weekend work, and mundane travel. For performers, there's the tedious memorization of lines and stage movements, with repetitive and energy-draining rehearsals, coupled with the uncertainty of how audiences and critics will respond. Designers, playwrights, and directors need an ample supply of creativity, the ability to react to crises, and the stamina to deal with performers, musicians, and dancers with strong egos. There's also the ego-bruising prospect of rejection for auditioning performers and playwrights. Whether you're on stage, behind the stage, or in the business office, you must understand what's involved in everybody else's job. Teamwork is essential, since performances involve the blending of diverse talents. Deadline pressures can be enormous, regardless of your position. But if the glitter of the stage excites you, it's worth it.

Related Fields

Dance
English
Medieval and Renaissance Studies
Photography and Cinema

Typical Basic Courses

Drafting for the Theater
Introduction to Acting
Introduction to Modern Dance
Introduction to Western Theater
Scene Study
Stagecraft
Theatrical Makeup
Voice and Movement for the Stage

An Array of Electives

American Drama and Theater
Costume History: From Fig Leaf to
   Vanity
Directing
Female Dramatic Tradition
Stage Lighting
Styles of Acting
Theater Arts Management
Theater Sound Production

On-Campus Opportunities

Campus theater
Campus radio and television stations

Job Opportunities

Surplus / Substantial oversupply

Reading to Explore

Making It Big: The Diary of a Broadway Musical, by Barbara Isenberg (Limelight Editions)

Making Movies, by Sidney Lumet (St. Martin's)

Orson Welles: The Road to Xanadu, by Simon Callow (Penguin)

The Agency: William Morris and the Hidden History of Show Business, by Frank Rose (HarperBusiness)

Voices and Silences, by James Earl Jones (Scribner)

To Learn More

Association for Theater in Higher
   Education
c/o Theater Service
200 North Michigan Avenue, Suite 300
Chicago, IL 60601
(312) 541-2066; fax (312) 541-1271
E-mail: athe@smtp.bmai.com
Internet site: http://www.hawaii.edu/athe

Educational Theatre Association
3368 Central Parkway
Cincinnati, OH 45225-2392
(513) 559-1996; fax (513) 359-0012
E-mail: eta-its@one.net
Internet site: http://www.etassoc.org

Travel and Tourism

For my part, I travel not to go anywhere, but to go. I travel for travel's sake. The great affair is to move.
—*Robert Louis Stevenson, novelist, in* Travels with a Donkey

What to Expect

The world is on the move, for pleasure and for business. Tourism professionals need education to provide travel-related services, improve the quality and scope of those services, and conduct research into planning, development, and marketing of tourism products. Your courses will discuss the types of services available, consumer expectations, and the financial importance of tourism to local, regional, and national economies. You'll become familiar with the tools, concepts, and techniques of tourism management and encouragement. You'll explore the economic, social, and environmental impacts of tourism development, as well as related political and public policy implications. Higher-level courses delve more deeply into marketing, economic analysis, finance, and legal issues. Research projects will teach you how to survey and assess traveler expectations and requirements, then to apply those findings in advertising, promotion, and creation of additional facilities and services. You'll also address ethical issues such as the implications of tourism and tourist-related technologies on less developed societies and the potential for adverse environmental effects from tourism projects.

Trends

Trends in travel and tourism include mushrooming interest in environmentally conscious tourism ("ecotourism"), in adventure tourism, in ethnically oriented tourism, and in visits to formerly off-limits countries. Ecotourism could encompass vacations at rain forest lodges, canoeing and horseback treks, and bird-watching tours. Adventure tourism may take travelers white-water rafting on remote rivers, scuba diving on shipwrecks and coral reefs, and on mountain biking expeditions. Ethnically oriented tourism leads to sites of ethnic and ancestral importance, sometimes in the United States but more often abroad. And tours of formerly off-limits areas may take travelers to the former Soviet republics, Eastern Europe, Tibet, or Vietnam, for example.

What You Need to Succeed

You'll need an outgoing personality, enjoyment of travel, and a yearning for new places and experiences to succeed as a tourism professional. You'll also need strong interpersonal, communication, and sales skills because you'll be involved in customer relations, marketing and promotion, and possibly presentations to social, business, and special interest groups. A foundation in economics is important for work on tourism development projects and policy issues. It's also essential to keep up with current events, including rapidly changing political situations, international economic crises, terrorism, and disasters such as earthquakes and volcanic eruptions. Travel experience is an asset because personal knowledge about a city or country may influence clients' travel plans. You must be thorough, detail oriented, and well prepared because businesses and individuals make important decisions based on your advice. Patience and self-confidence are essential when you're called on to field complaints and deal with government bureaucracies in the United States and overseas, frequently under time pressure.

Related Fields

Hotel and Restaurant Management
Marketing
Parks and Recreation
Public Relations

Typical Basic Courses

Advertising and Promotion Management
Introduction to the Hospitality Industry
Leisure and Society
Marketing Research
Our National Parks and Recreation
  Lands
Tourism and Tour Operations
Tourism Destination Development
Tourism Management

An Array of Electives

Carrier Quality and Performance
Commercial Recreation and Tourism
  Enterprises
Community and Natural Resource-Based
  Tourism
International Tourism
Interpretive Services and Visitor
  Information Systems
Law and Leisure Services
Policy Issues in Hospitality Management
Services Marketing Strategy

On-Campus Opportunities

Campus tour guide service
Campus travel office

Job Opportunities

Adequate supply / Some oversupply

Reading to Explore

Heritage, Tourism and Society, by David T. Herbert (Books International)

Judson's Island, by Mark J. Okrant and Stephen L. Smith, (Wayfarer)

Monet on the Normandy Coast: Tourism and Painting, by Robert L. Herbert (Yale University)

The Tourist Image, by Tom Selwyn (John Wiley and Sons)

Wildlife Tourism, by Myra L. Shackey (Routledge)

To Learn More

American Hotel and Motel Association
1201 New York Ave. NW
Washington, DC 20005
(202) 289-3100; fax (202) 289-3199
E-mail: comments@ahma.com
Internet site: http://www.ahma.com

Travel and Tourism Research Association
546 E. Main St.
Lexington, KY 40508
(606) 226-4344; fax (606) 226-4355
E-mail: ttra@mgtserv.com
Internet site: http://www.ttra.com

Urban Planning

The plain fact is that most cities are not organized to cope with their problems. Their haphazard growth has brought such rampant administrative disorder that good government is scarcely possible.

—*John W. Gardner, city planner, cited in* The Crown Treasury of Relevant Quotations

What to Expect

Urban planning is not limited to city settings. Indeed, planners use their training to confront issues affecting suburbs and even rural communities. Whatever the setting, they help develop long-term and short-term land use plans to provide for growth and revitalization. Introductory classes explore the role and history of planning in urban and regional development, site design for development projects, and data-gathering and analytic methods. You'll learn graphic, photographic, video, and computer techniques to make presentations to community groups, government agencies, and clients. Computers will be an important tool throughout your education. At an advanced level, courses in land and environmental planning will illustrate environmentally sensitive management of growth and change, as well as ethical and political issues. Try specialized courses, such as real estate project design, geography of transportation or housing, reclamation of former mining sites, golf-course planning, and use of geographic information systems. To combine theory with applications, study local economic development, comparative planning, or urban design.

Trends

Trends in urban planning encompass an emphasis on making cities more livable, including the renovation and restoration of historic buildings, the so-called "gentrification" of former slum neighborhoods, and attracting shopping and jobs back from the suburbs. Urban planners will also seek economical ways to clean up and reuse abandoned industrial sites. Increasingly, rural communities will call on planners to draft revitalization proposals, ward off overdevelopment, and improve recreational housing, pollution prevention, and transportation facilities. Planners will help shape government policies on social issues such as housing for the elderly, prison planning, and landfill locations.

What You Need to Succeed

Urban and regional planners need to think about spatial relationships and visualize the ramifications of their designs and plans. They must be flexible, reconcile divergent opinions, and make reasonable policy recommendations. They often spend time communicating and meeting with citizen groups, government officials, and developers, so they must be able to express themselves clearly in writing and aloud. In some instances, they help mediate community disputes and negotiate compromises. Problem-solving and long-term vision skills are required. Computer mastery is necessary to record and analyze information, prepare reports, determine program costs, develop maps, manipulate geographic information, and forecast trends in housing, employment, transportation, and population. Some positions require time spent in the field and at development sites, and planners frequently attend night and week-end meetings. It's important to cope with deadlines, tight work schedules, and political pressure from interest groups with a stake in land-use decisions.

Related Fields

Architecture
Political Science
Public Policy Studies
Sociology
Urban Studies

Typical Basic Courses

Geographic Information Systems
Introduction to Computers in Planning
Introduction to Urban and Regional
    Theory
Planning, Power, and Decision Making
The American City
The Global City: People, Production, and
    Planning in the Third World
Urban Economics
Urban Land Management

An Array of Electives

Environmental Law
Housing and Real Estate Development
Issues in African Development
Principles of Spatial Design and
    Aesthetics
Real Estate Marketing and Management
Social Policy and Social Welfare
Urban Design and Project Development
Urban Transportation Planning

On-Campus Opportunities

Campus housing office
Campus planning department

Job Opportunities

Surplus / Substantial oversupply

Reading to Explore

City Life: Urban Expectations in a New World, by Witold Rybozynski (Scribner)

Dual City: Restructuring New York, by John H. Mollenkopf (Russell Sage)

Sustainable Communities: A New Design Synthesis for Cities, Suburbs, and Towns, by Sim Van der Ryan and Peter Calthorpe (Sierra Club)

The Consequence of the Eye: The Design and Social Life of Cities, by Richard Sennett (Knopf)

The Power Broker: Robert Moses and the Fall of New York, by Robert A. Caro (Vintage)

To Learn More

Association of Collegiate Schools of
    Planning
Office of the Provost
Hunter College/CUNY
695 Park Avenue
New York, NY 10021
(212) 772-4150; fax (212) 650-3655
E-mail:
    genie.birch@+zayid.hunter.cuny.edu
Internet site:
    http://gis2.arch.gatech.edu/acsp

Urban Studies

What is the city but the people?
—*William Shakespeare, playwright, in* Coriolanus

What to Expect

Urban America is undergoing considerable change, with shifting populations, an influx of immigrants, and the overcrowding of suburbs. You will have to navigate a wide-ranging educational gamut that combines aspects of sociology, political science, economics, education, business, public policy studies, criminal justice, and other fields. You'll learn the concepts of urban government and politics, including municipal administration and policy making. You'll get an overview of the diversity of urban populations and shifting residential and employment patterns. You'll also look at historical and contemporary issues, including housing, transportation, education, employment, crime, poverty, and the environment. You'll explore urban issues in depth. Perhaps you'll take a class on urban political economy covering the fiscal crisis and financial resources of the cities. Perhaps it will be an in-depth examination of the role of police or public school teachers or political party organizations. You can study changing economic, social, and political relationships among cities, suburbs, and rural areas, or among urban ethnic, racial, and religious groups. If you're interested in government services, electives in public administration and urban planning will prove helpful.

Trends

Trends in urban studies include the declining political clout of "older" cities that lose legislative and congressional seats as suburban population booms. That development, coupled with a sometimes-declining property tax base, will help spur the movement toward regional projects and programs, whether in mass transit, public safety, education, or recreational services. At the same time, abandoned urban industrial sites will become in greater demand for new commercial and business projects, if cost-effective ways to clean up their environmental contamination are found.

What You Need to Succeed

By concentrating in urban studies, you can examine urban problems more comprehensively than within a single discipline. This approach requires you to master the research, analytical, and technical methods and tools of various fields of study. Solid communication skills, written and oral, are vital so you can share information and discuss issues with community residents and your colleagues as well. Learn how to interview people and to use computers. You'll be expected to collaborate with a variety of people, including school and city agency administrators, elected officials, regional planners, business and nonprofit group leaders, and civic activists. Learn to assess problems and weigh a variety of potential solutions, conventional and creative, rather than rushing to judgment. Keep your mind open to ideas from other communities. For example, a job-training program in one city may teach you a lesson about what could—or could not—work in your city.

Related Fields

American Studies and Culture
Economics
History
Public Policy and Administration
Sociology
Urban Planning

Typical Basic Courses

Politics and Poverty
Population and History
Pre-Industrial Cities and Towns of North
    America
The Progressive City
The Urbanization of American Society:
    1600–1860
The Urbanization of American Society:
    1860–2000
Urban Archaeology
Urban Geography

An Array of Electives

African American Women
Child Welfare
Community Development and Local
    Control
Geography of Transportation
Social Demography
Stereotypes, Prejudice, and
    Discrimination
The Regional Question: The Case of Italy
The Worker in American Life

On-Campus Opportunities

Campus newspaper, magazine, and radio
    and television stations
Research assistant

Job Opportunities

Surplus / Substantial oversupply

Reading to Explore

Amazing Grace: The Lives of Children and the Conscience of a Nation, by Jonathan Kozol (Crown)

Crabgrass Frontier: The Suburbanization of the United States, by Kenneth T. Jackson (Oxford University)

Remaking Our Everyday World for the Twenty-First Century, by James Howard Kunstler (Simon & Schuster)

The Life and Death of American Cities, by Jane Jacobs (Vintage)

The New American Ghetto, by Camilio J. Vergara (Rutgers University)

To Learn More

Urban Affairs Association
University of Delaware
Newark, DE 19716
(301) 831-1681; fax (301) 831-3587
E-mail: uaa@mvs.udel.edu
Internet site: http://www.udel.edu/uaa/

Women's Studies

Woman has her work to do, and no one can accomplish it for her. She is bound to rise, to try her strength, to break her bonds. . . .
—*Elizabeth Blackwell, nineteenth-century feminist, in* Feminist Quotations

What to Expect

Women's studies is a relatively new, interdisciplinary field focusing on women's status and achievements in various cultures and historical periods. With course work in the humanities and especially the social sciences, you'll gain a solid foundation for careers ranging from social work and psychology to education, law, or public policy and administration. Introductory classes will orient you to fundamental concepts such as gender and sexuality, socialization, class and race, identity, roles, and power. You'll become familiar with broad forces—including economic, social, and political—affecting women's situations today and in the past. As you progress, you can specialize. For example, try courses on women and politics, male-female communication, the history of women in science and medicine, the psychology of lesbianism, and the literature of women in African American, Latina, and other minority cultures in the United States and abroad. Allied classes in economics, psychology, sociology, social work, communication, and political science may help you apply your knowledge in practical settings.

Trends

Trends in women's studies include an increasing interest in the way that women's health issues throughout life are viewed, defined, treated, or neglected in American society. The advent of managed health care is especially likely to bring economic, as well as social and political aspects, to the fore. Sexual harassment will continue to generate attention, as concerns will broaden beyond the workplace to encompass such domains such as public schooling and institutional religion. The relatively unexplored influence of women in science, the fine arts, and politics—both historically and at present—will be the focus of greater study. So, too, will be the interplay between biology and culture in affecting women's sexuality, including lesbianism and bisexuality, and the role of women in non-Western societies.

What You Need to Succeed

Is the role of women in the United States and other countries—both today and historically—of keen interest to you? Do you view women's ongoing struggle for equality at home and the workplace, in government, religious, and cultural institutions—of major importance? And, do you feel that your own experiences and views can advance this cross-disciplinary field? If you enjoy reading, research, and tackling controversial issues with political, cultural, and economic ramifications, then you certainly have traits desirable for women's studies. Whether women's studies brings you into business, education, health care, law, or science, you'll need solid analytic and conceptual skills, a flair for multidisciplinary thinking, and a receptivity to other cultures. It's also important to see seemingly inviolate cultural norms—for example, with regard to sex, gender, and family relations—as relative and changeable. To articulate your positions, good communication skills, both oral and written, are also keys to success.

Related Fields

American Studies and Culture
History
Public Policy Studies
Sociology

Typical Basic Courses

Issues in Women's Health
Literature by Women
Sex Roles in Economic Life
Sex, Gender, and Culture
Sexuality and Culture in America
The Social Reality of Women
Women and Work
Women in Modern America

An Array of Electives

African American Women's Literature
History of Feminism in the United States
History of Women in Science and
  Medicine
Latina Women Writers
Pattern of Women's Religious Experience
Politics of Sexuality
Women and Islam
Women and Mental Health

On-Campus Opportunities

Campus counseling center
Campus newspaper, magazine, and radio
  and television stations

Job Opportunities

Adequate supply / Some oversupply

Reading to Explore

Profiles of Female Genius: Thirteen Creative Women Who Changed the World, by Gene Landrum (Prometheus)

Swim with the Dolphins: How Women Can Succeed in Corporate America on Their Own Terms, by Connie Glaser and Barbara Steinberg Smalley (Warner Books)

Where the Girls Are: Growing up Female with the Mass Media, by Jeanine Basinger (Times/Random House)

Woman as Healer, by Jeanne Achtenberg (Shambhala)

Women on the Margins: Three Seventeenth-Century Lives, by Natalie Zemon Davis (Harvard University)

To Learn More

National Women's Studies Association
University of Maryland
7100 Baltimore Road, Suite 301
College Park, MD 20740
(301) 403-0524; fax (301) 403-4137,
  ext. 0525
E-mail: nwwsa@umailumd.edu
Internet site:
  http://www.usml.edu/divisions/
  artscience/iwgs

Zoology

I think I could turn and live with animals, they are so placid and self-contained, I stand and look at them long and long.
—*Walt Whitman, poet, cited in* The New International Dictionary of Quotations

What to Expect

As a branch of the biological sciences, zoology involves all aspects of animal life—ranging from the structure and function of cells to how animals and animal populations behave. You'll survey vertebrate and invertebrate biology and comparative anatomy as you study the origin, behavior, life processes, and diseases of animals. You'll learn about ethological and sociobiological approaches to animal behavior, the host-parasite relationship among major animal groups, and cell biology. Expect considerable laboratory work, field trips, and hands-on work with animals in both natural and controlled settings. At an advanced level, you can take courses in vertebrate histology, embryology, physiology, and biological evolution. To better understand how zoology is related to other natural sciences, try courses in ecology and particular habitats such as oceans, streams, the tropics, or deserts. Other options include genetics, cytochemistry, cancer biology, and hormones. Also, you can take specialized electives in the biology of birds, amphibians and reptiles, mammals, insects, and fish, where you'll merge laboratory and classroom work.

Trends

Trends in zoology reflect a growing concern with overall environmental protection and biodiversity, scientific and political tactics for species preservation, and applying ecological principles to problems facing government, private property owners, and businesses. On the technological front, zoologists are developing better breeding and genetic techniques and researching new pharmaceuticals to prevent and control disease among wild and domesticated species. There will be more efforts to create and expand preserves and wilderness areas, often in cooperation—rather than confrontation—with businesses and landowners.

What You Need to Succeed

Strong scientific skills, from the computer terminal to the laboratory to field instrumentation, are vital for success in zoology. That requires having an analytical mind, including the ability to identify a problem, assess it, and plan scientifically sound strategies to find a solution. Be able to explain those issues, strategies, and potential answers to lay and scientific audiences, both orally and in writing. Be able to work independently and also as part of a team. Patience is definitely a virtue, because your work—whether it involves cancer research, a breeding program for an endangered species, or reintroduction of a wild species to a former habitat—can take years or even decades to reach fruition. Some of your work may take place in remote areas with relatively primitive living facilities, and there's the risk of exposure to dangerous organisms and toxic substances in the lab and the field. Strenuous physical activity may be required, too. But zoology can be a true scientific adventure for those drawn to biological, particularly animal, research.

Related Fields

Animal Science
Biology
Entomology
Fisheries and Wildlife
Marine Biology and Oceanography

Typical Basic Courses

Animal Behavior
Comparative Anatomy and Biology of
　Vertebrates
Developmental Biology
Ecology
Evolution
Fundamental Genetics
General Parasitology
Invertebrate Biology

An Array of Electives

Biology of Amphibians and Reptiles
Cancer Biology
Cytochemistry
Ecological Aspects of Animal Behavior
Ecology, Evolution, and Organismic
　Biology
Environmental Physiology
Hormones and Development
Tropical Biology

On-Campus Opportunities

Campus museum
Lab assistant
Research assistant

Job Opportunities

Adequate supply / Some oversupply

Reading to Explore

Altered Fates: Gene Therapy and the Retooling of Human Life, by Jeff Lyon and Peter Garner (Norton)

Into the Wild, by Jon Karakauer (Anchor/Doubleday)

The Modern Ark: The Story of Zoos: Past, Present, and Future, by Vicki Croke (Scribner)

The Rarest of the Rare: Vanishing Animals, Timeless Worlds, by Diane Ackerman (Vintage)

Woman in the Mists: The Story of Dian Fossey and the Mountain Gorillas of Africa, by Farley Mowat (Warner)

To Learn More

Animal Behavior Society
Department of Biology
Clark University
950 Main Street
Worcester, MA 01610-1477
(508) 793-7204; fax (508) 793-8861
E-mail: sfoster@black.clarku.edu
Internet site:
　http://www.cisab.indiana.edu/abs/
　index.html

Society for Integrative and Comparative
　Biology
401 North Michigan Avenue
Chicago, IL 60611-4267
(312) 527-6697; fax (312) 245-1085
E-mail: sicb@sba.com
Internet site: http://www.sicb.org

Want more information about our services, products, or the nearest Kaplan educational center?

HERE

Call our nationwide toll-free numbers:

1-800-KAP-TEST
(for information on our live courses, private tutoring and admissions consulting)

1-800-KAP-ITEM
(for information on our products)

1-888-KAP-LOAN*
(for information on student loans)

Connect with us in cyberspace:
On **AOL**, keyword **"Kaplan"**
On the Internet's World Wide Web, open **"http://www.kaplan.com"**
Via E-mail, **"info@kaplan.com"**

Write to:
Kaplan Educational Centers
888 Seventh Avenue
New York, NY 10106